The Citizen's Presidency

The Citizen's Presidency
Standards of Choice and Judgment

Bruce Buchanan
University of Texas at Austin

A division of Congressional Quarterly Inc.
1414 22nd Street N.W., Washington, D.C. 20037

Library of Congress Cataloging in Publication Data

Buchanan, Bruce.
　The citizen's presidency.

　Bibliography: p.
　Includes index.
　1. Presidents—United States—Evaluation. I. Title.
JK518.B82 1987　　　　　353.03'1　　　　　86-19669
ISBN 0-87187-398-2

For my family

PREFACE

This book is for those who want to do better the two things citizens must do well if the presidency is to work: choose and judge presidents. My aim is to offer useful answers to the question, "Where should I look and what should I look for to better choose and judge?" The concepts and information identified as worthy of attention are often discussed elsewhere, but with one important difference. Here they are explicitly and consciously subordinated to the citizen's-eye view of the presidency and are assessed by their relevance to the evaluation of candidates and presidents.

"How has the president done?" and "How would someone else do?" are no doubt the most frequently posed questions during a campaign season. Few citizens, whatever their level of political sophistication, are reluctant to answer such questions. Indeed, most do so confidently and assertively. But when pressed for the reasons behind their judgments, they answer more haltingly, in tones less assured. Their conclusions about promise and performance are clear in their minds and are often felt with special force. But the process by which conclusions are reached and the reasoning that explains and justifies them seem difficult for many people to articulate.

Interestingly, the same appears to be true about presidency specialists. Virtually everything written about the presidency contains direct appraisals of presidents or information relevant to making such appraisals. The grounds for these evaluations and the relative importance of the criteria used in judging can be inferred from context, but they are rarely the focus of systematic, conscious inquiry. Room exists, then, for a book that does explicitly address the grounds for choice and judgment.

This book is written primarily for undergraduates taking courses on the presidency, which may pay some systematic attention to the evaluation of candidates and presidents—the central responsibility of what could be called presidential citizenship. But I am also hoping to reach those whose business is to teach as well as learn about the presidency— journalists and academics. I can think of few more important subjects for their research and teaching than the problem of leadership appraisal, with dimensions at once theoretical and urgently practical, normative and objective, partisan and significantly nonpartisan.

The first three chapters of the book are devoted to describing and illustrating certain influences on choice and judgment that usually operate instinctively, outside conscious awareness. For example, Chapter 2 examines how the American political culture uses the presidency and argues that the culture implants expectations that affect choice and judgment. Chapter 3 considers how certain innate characteristics of people in general interact with the media to create opportunities for unnoticed, unintended errors in the acquisition and interpretation of information about candidates and presidents. These strands of cultural and psychological analysis are pulled together and illustrated in Chapter 4, which compares public reactions to Presidents Jimmy Carter and Ronald Reagan.

Chapters 5 and 6 deal, respectively, with the traditional grounds for judgment and choice. An important purpose of both chapters is to assess the logical, conceptual, and operational status of the grounds themselves. Primary concerns are with the intrinsic sense the grounds make as evaluative criteria and with their actual and potential uses and abuses in practice. But each chapter also offers something new, derived from my analysis of the strengths and weaknesses of the existing grounds and aimed at supplementing and improving upon current evaluative practice.

The book concludes with an assessment of the single-term presidency. This kind of reform proposal emerges when elite opinion finds the use of citizen power to be irresponsible and unacceptable, and can thus be seen as an alternative to the sort of improvement advocated in this book. In offering a review of the pros and cons of the six-year term, I have two purposes in mind: to reconsider, in a different light, certain dimensions of presidential functioning discussed elsewhere in the book and to convey my urgent belief that the stakes are high—that failure to improve the quality of evaluation could ultimately result in a diminution of citizen power.

I owe thanks to the hundreds of graduate and undergraduate students who listened patiently and responded critically as ideas took shape during my decade and one-half of presidency lectures and seminar discussions. I also appreciate the comments from many of my colleagues in political science on the series of American Political Science Association conference papers that formed the groundwork leading to this book. A semester's leave, financed by the University Research Institute at the University of Texas, gave me the opportunity to launch the project. The critical reviews of the various drafts of the manuscript offered by Benjamin I. Page, Erwin Hargrove, Harold W. Stanley, and Paul Quirk are gratefully acknowledged. These exacting critics saved me from many errors of omission and commission but cannot be blamed for the ones that remain. The hard-working professionals at CQ Press, Joanne D. Daniels and Colleen McGuiness, deserve special thanks for helping me to produce the best book I could. It is a pleasure to work with sensitive people who know their business. Finally, the Buchanans—Stephanie, Douglas, and Kate—get credit for making me feel good enough to show up for work every day.

CONTENTS

Contents

The Citizen's Presidency

CHAPTER 1

The President and the Public:
A Troubled Alliance

*Public opinion sets bounds to every government, and is the real sovereign in
every free one.*

—James Madison
National Gazette, December 19, 1791

*Democratic institutions are never done—they are, like the living tissue, always
a-making. It is a strenuous thing this of living the life of a free people; and we
cannot escape the burden of our inheritance.*

—Woodrow Wilson
Address at Middletown, Conn., April 30, 1889

*The constant danger to democracy lies in the tendency of the individual to
hide himself in the crowd—to defend his own failure to act forthrightly
according to conviction under the false excuse that the effort of one in one
hundred forty million has no significance.*

—Dwight D. Eisenhower
Speech at Northfield, Vt., June 9, 1946

The words of Madison, Wilson, and Eisenhower, men who eventually would serve as presidents of the United States, have the familiar
sound of political rhetoric. Platitudes or not, these statements ring true.
They convey three important messages, as timely today as when they
were uttered: (1) in a democracy, the citizenry exercises real power; (2)
to use this power wisely and well requires effort; and (3) not everyone is
willing to make this effort, which can threaten the democratic enterprise.

Citizens of the United States are entitled to decide who will govern them and to take measure of how their leaders perform. Members of nations such as the Soviet Union, Nicaragua, Cuba, and Poland have no such right. That this contrast represents a significant difference in actual power as well as symbolic privilege cannot be seriously questioned. When aroused and focused, American public opinion can determine national policy and drive public servants from office. Such power is collective rather than individual, is subject to a variety of potentially unsavory manipulations and influence, and is often passive and undisciplined. It is, however, quite real.[1]

The citizenry's power of concern here is the power to choose among presidential candidates and to evaluate the performance of an incumbent president. Responsible exercise of this power is surely part of the "burden" of living in a democracy described by Wilson. To make informed choices and rational judgments are not easy tasks; nonetheless, a goodly number of Americans must be willing to do the necessary work if the presidency is to remain a viable institution. Fortunately, many have been, despite the "constant danger to democracy" Eisenhower described—the "false excuse" that participation is not worthwhile because no single individual's input will determine election outcomes or government policies.

The major reason for citizens to invest time and effort in upgrading their ability to evaluate candidates and presidents is *obligation:* an internalized commitment citizens have to participate effectively in the affairs of a political system of which they are members and with which they identify. The obligation stems from the theory of democracy, which requires that ordinary citizens exert a relatively high degree of control over leaders (Dahl 1956).[2] The electoral process is the primary mechanism by which this control is exerted. Citizens control leaders by choosing them in the first place and by deciding whether to keep them after evaluating their performance (Fiorina 1981). To neglect this responsibility or to discharge it thoughtlessly is to invite the "danger to democracy" Eisenhower warned against.

A Contribution to Improving Choice and Judgment

Those who write about the presidency rarely offer guidance on how to choose or judge presidents, do not attempt to define or clarify the standards used by the general public or more specialized observers of the office, and generally sidestep the issue by stressing the subjectivity inherent in all such attempts. Because what one thinks of presidential acts and purposes "depends ultimately on what one expects of the office" and because these expectations "flow and ebb with personalities and events," evaluation "boils down to an ideological judgment" and, thus, is, by implication, not worthy of extended analysis (Hoekstra 1981).

This diffidence in the face of value questions is characteristic of modern political science (Ricci 1985). In studying the presidency-public relationship, however, such a posture has not been useful. Instead, it has inhibited consideration of a question of practical importance: What criteria for choosing presidents and judging their performance can yield adequate levels of public support, while simultaneously holding presidents to account for their effectiveness in office? This book attempts to answer that question. Room exists for improving the grounds people use to choose and judge presidents, and an effort to identify and define both existing and potential standards for choice and judgment could contribute to that improvement. But even without such a pragmatic incentive, the search for an answer to this question would be worthwhile, for the citizen's-eye view of the presidency that it evokes is intrinsically fascinating and potentially illuminating.[3] The question invites a new look at some old material. It forces a confrontation with the most fundamental of questions: What is the presidency for? How does it work? How can good, fair, and poor presidential performance be meaningfully distinguished? What kind of person makes a good president?

The brand of scholarship displayed in these pages is called normative theory. A theory is a coherent group of general propositions used as principles of explanation for a class of phenomena. Here, it is a theory in the broad sense of distinguishing the important from the unimportant, with importance defined by relevance to the evaluation of candidates and presidents. It is a theory of attention, however, not a deductive or formal theory. The aim is to suggest where to look and what to look for to better choose and judge. It is a citizen's theory because I seek to do all this from the vantage point of those who stand "at a distance and out of sight," those who, for various personal reasons, wish to take seriously the responsibilities of choice and judgment (Young 1966, 13).[4] Agreement with the stands I take and the conclusions I reach is not necessary; benefit can be derived from reflecting on the questions I raise. For this reason, I feel safe in claiming that anyone who reads this book seriously and carefully will be better equipped to choose and judge presidents. The importance of the questions, not the quality of the answers, ensures this result.

How can this book influence the behavior of ordinary citizens, as most of them will never read it? The same way any academic writing ever reaches average citizens: by means of a diffusion process mediated by attentive citizens (university students, community leaders, and other members of the well-informed public), opinion makers (media figures, columnists, public officials), and intellectuals (university professors and others who traffic in ideas). Although slow and uncertain, this is a time-honored method, as the popular impact of such diverse academic authors as John Maynard Keynes and Benjamin Spock will attest. Of course academics must have something to say worth hearing. But if they do, their messages will eventually get through.

The State of the Presidency

Left by itself, the presidency is weak, its constitutional powers inadequate to carry out its responsibility for giving energy and direction to government. To be sure, presidents have awesome prerogative powers and, like Abraham Lincoln or Franklin D. Roosevelt (FDR), can become virtual dictators in times of genuine national emergency (Fisher 1985). Moreover, they can act with or without public and congressional support (Pious 1979). But these powers are used as a last resort and are not workable foundations for stable, orderly government under normal circumstances. Indeed, their use is actually a confession of weakness instead of evidence of strength. The country, in effect, admits that its normal political procedures are inadequate to contend with some pressing problem and that it is forced into a kind of crisis receivership, ultimately enforced by military power. As Pious (1979) notes, such assertions usually are followed by a period of presidential weakness and decline.

Theodore C. Sorensen, who served as an aide to President John F. Kennedy, aptly describes the president's normal constitutional position as being in a political "gridlock" (1984, 23). The term was originally coined to describe an urban traffic tangle in which lines of waiting vehicles blocking intersections in all directions become so long and unyielding that none can move forward or backward. The constitutional system of checks and balances amounts to an invitation for president and Congress to struggle for control of government, with stalemate a frequent result (Corwin 1957). Most of the president's powers are shared with Congress, and that institution is only occasionally responsive to presidential efforts to exert leadership, notably during crises and the postelection "honeymoon" period.

Further complicating the presidential task of course charting is the presence of a skeptical, probing media and a host of well-financed, well-organized special interests. Both are capable of thwarting leadership initiatives of the executive. Add to this the fact that, unlike leaders of other Western democracies, the president lacks the assistance of a disciplined political party in the legislature to deliver votes for administration proposals, and a good picture of the presidency's problem emerges: institutional impotence.

This is why Richard Neustadt (1980), in the most influential book yet written on the power position of the presidency, gives center stage to the power of persuasion as the solution to the presidential impotence dilemma. This is why journalists and political scientists have written books with themes such as the deadlock of American democracy (Burns 1963) and how difficult it is to make the presidency work (Johnson 1980). This is why the most frequently proposed reform of the executive is a parliamentary system with a party tradition (Hardin 1974; Shogan 1982; Burns 1984) of implementing the leader's policies. And this is why presidency watchers in the late 1970s, noting that presidents had to put together coalitions from the ground up on each issue, posed the question: Is the presidency possible (Barger 1984)?

In 1979, many feared the answer to be no, just as others had in 1828 after a string of failed presidencies. Early in the nation's history it was discovered that a system of separate institutions sharing powers was fundamentally flawed, not a workable design for the stable functioning of the central government. Means had to be found to generate consensus between and within the executive and legislative branches. If the constitutional plan was to function effectively in the real world, extraconstitutional support mechanisms needed to be created.

The first such invention was the cabinet, a body composed of executive branch department heads that serves to advise the chief executive. Unmentioned in the Constitution, the cabinet met regularly during the administrations of George Washington and John Adams and emerged as the "only institution in the executive community which brought spokesmen for different sections, political factions and bureaucratic interests together in a work group affording the President a leadership role" (Young 1966, 230). While Presidents Washington and, particularly, Thomas Jefferson, through a combination of personal skill and favorable circumstances, were able to forge a measure of policy agreement within the cabinet and Congress and thus to exert leadership, the cabinet was not enough for James Madison, James Monroe, and John and John Quincy Adams. They watched consensus break down, factions emerge within their cabinets and in Congress, and paralysis ensue. The cabinet itself could not compensate for the weaknesses of the constitutional framework for the presidency.

The basic problem was the president's lack of power over the executive branch and, especially, over Congress. The president had too

5

few resources upon which to draw to convince others to support administration policies. Congress controlled departmental operations, governmental purse strings, and the legislative agenda. In addition, being the setting for presidential nominating caucuses, Congress controlled access to the presidency itself (selection of presidential candidates by national party conventions did not begin until 1832). To be autonomous and to prevent Congress from exerting undue influence over the executive branch, the president needed to exercise authority over Congress. Apart from a brief period during Washington's term in office and a more sustained period during Jefferson's, presidents before Andrew Jackson failed to do this. The result was the institutional failure of the presidency. For its part, Congress was fractured into sociopolitical blocs and thus was unable to develop sufficient internal cohesion to provide national direction. With Congress unable to take the place of the presidency, the necessary leadership functions of government simply went unperformed.

If the constitutional system was to be preserved, a capacity for leadership had to be produced within a framework that had been deliberately designed to make leadership difficult. Strong pressure to accept this leadership apparently had to come from without, since the system proved unable to create and sustain it from within. The historical solution was the Jacksonian Revolution, which ushered in the second and most important invention needed to overcome the limitations of the formal constitutional structures: mass public support for the presidency.

For the 40 years between the inaugurations of Washington and Jackson, most people felt little stake in national public affairs. For a century prior to 1789, they had established ways of living and organizing their public business that centered around local communities. This would be little changed by the swearing-in of the first president. Besides the delivery of mail, daily life was untouched by the government. Indifference would reign until well into the nineteenth century. The presidency had not yet become the people's office.

Andrew Jackson, for a time at least, changed all that. Aided by the growing enfranchisement of an emerging middle class and its perception that the federal government was lining the pockets of privileged eastern mercantile interests at the expense of southern and western farmers and workers, Jackson used his charismatic personality to arouse the consciousness of this class and focus its attention on the presidency as the instrument for protecting and furthering its interests. In the process, he showed that a president backed strongly by the mass public had the leverage to impose his leadership and make the constitutional system work. James S. Young explains:

> An aroused and demanding citizenry would nudge the officeholders at Washington to develop the political skills and the political organization necessary to satisfy popular demands—and necessary also for a viable government. A disposition to negotiate differences, a willingness of disparate groups to collaborate, and a craft of consensus-building would ultimately ensue from the need to win the confidence and the votes of a politically-attentive populace. Serving the needs of an aroused and demanding citizenry would ... provide incontestable justification for leadership initiatives in a governmental community committed to the representative principle. Above all, Jacksonian democracy would retrieve a chance for leadership for the Presidency. Moving the nominating function from Washington to a popular forum would release incoming presidents from bondage to kingmakers in Congress.... Nomination and election by popular acclaim would give the Presidency the stature of popular spokesmanship and an independent electoral strength which was convertible, on occasion, to bargaining advantages over Congress. Party organization outside Washington, dependent in part upon presidential patronage, would begin to gird the Presidency for pressure politics.... A major lesson of the [pre-Jacksonian] experience seems to be that a viable governmental establishment could not be maintained as long as the governmental community confronted a remote and indifferent citizenry. (1966, 252-253)

The Jackson presidency was the first great historical demonstration of the contribution made by public support to presidential effectiveness. But it would not be the last. Similar examples can be found in the twentieth century, in the administrations of Theodore Roosevelt (TR), Woodrow Wilson, Franklin D. Roosevelt, Dwight D. Eisenhower, and Ronald Reagan. Conversely, the costs associated with lack of public support are painfully illustrated in the presidencies of Herbert Hoover and Jimmy Carter.

Public Support: The Core Resource

Public support empowers the contemporary presidency and is extraordinarily important to its viability. Following are five propositions, largely drawn from recent history (FDR to the present), concerning different dimensions of presidential effectiveness. Collectively they make the case that without substantial public support no modern president can expect to succeed in office.

First, *public support increases the support a president's programs receive in Congress.* This is taken as conventional wisdom by presidents, their advisers, and political pundits, and has recently been demonstrated statistically by political scientists (Edwards 1980, 86-100). A popular president has no ironclad assurance of winning passage of every legislative measure proposed. But public support greatly enhances the prospects for success, and its absence, as Neustadt observes, puts the president on the defensive:

> The weaker his apparent popular support, the more his cause in Congress may depend on negatives at his disposal, like the veto, or "impounding." He may not be left helpless, but his options are reduced, his opportunities diminished, his freedom for maneuver checked in the degree that Washington conceives him to be unimpressive to the public. (1980, 67)

Neustadt (1980) and Edwards (1980) argue plausibly that individual members of Congress listen and respond to a popular president because they believe that, as formal representatives of their constituents, they are obligated to support the president if their constituents do, or that failure to support the president could reduce their prospects for reelection, or both.

Unsurprisingly, the ebbs and flows in the historical struggle for dominance between Congress and president have corresponded closely to changes in the mass popular support for the incumbent president (Sundquist 1981). Congressional resurgence has occurred during the terms of weakly supported presidents. For example, Andrew Johnson lost control of the government mainly because he failed to counter the well-organized public influence of the Radical Republicans in Congress after the Civil War (Jacobs 1968). And more recently, Richard Nixon, whose popular support was undermined by the Watergate scandal, saw Congress override his veto of a measure imposing tough new constraints on presidential warmaking authority (War Powers Resolution of 1973) and witnessed the establishment of a law to reduce presidential influence in budgetary matters (Congressional Budget and Impoundment Control Act of 1974). Conversely, the most impressive legislative successes of the twentieth century have been achieved by presidents enjoying popular acclaim: Wilson, FDR, Lyndon B. Johnson (LBJ), and Reagan.

Second, *public support can decisively influence a president's ability to conduct foreign policy.* Ordinarily, the role of mass public opinion in foreign policy is permissive and supportive of presidential discretion (Spanier and Uslaner 1974). Most Americans are poorly informed about and not especially interested in foreign policy and they are content to leave matters to the president and the experts. But certain issues and events can rouse the public and rivet its attention. When American prestige is threatened (as in the Iranian hostage crisis of 1980), when the prospect of military involvement looms (as in Central America in 1986), or when the costs of foreign entanglements intrude upon the lives of average citizens (as in the Vietnam War), public opinion is stirred. In such circumstances, a president's ability to contend successfully with foreign policy matters may be directly proportional to the public support mustered.

The Vietnam War, the most significant foreign policy problem to confront this nation since the Second World War, dramatically illustrates this point. Real or anticipated public attitudes had a decisive impact on presidential decision making at every stage of U.S. participation in that conflict. In every instance, the presidential motive was, at least in part, either to sustain approval or to avoid disapproval. Some frequently argue, for example, that Kennedy's decision to increase U.S. involvement and Johnson's to intensify the U.S. combat role were based on a desire to avoid the appearance of weakness—in the eyes of the world and, especially, the American public (Kattenburg 1980; Valenti 1973; Halberstam 1972). Johnson, plagued by a lack of credibility with the American people, would decide not to run for reelection because of a shortage of public support. The memoirs of Nixon and former secretary of state Henry A. Kissinger are filled with references to the crucial importance of public support to their efforts to extricate the country from the war. Nixon explains the influence public opinion had on two key policy decisions, Vietnamization—the gradual transference of responsibility for the staffing and the conduct of the war against North Vietnam from the United States to South Vietnam—and the secret bombing of North Vietnamese sanctuaries inside the Cambodian border:

> Early in the administration we had decided that withdrawing a number of American combat troops from Vietnam would demonstrate to Hanoi that we were serious in seeking a diplomatic settlement; it might also calm domestic opinion by graphically demonstrating that we were beginning to wind down the war. (1978, 392)

> Another reason for [the secret bombing] was the problem of domestic antiwar protest. My administration was only two months old, and I wanted to provoke as little public outcry as possible at the outset. (1978, 382)

As the war dragged on and the Paris peace talks stalemated, it became increasingly clear that the U.S. and North Vietnamese leadership were engaged in a struggle for the support of American public opinion. In a speech that an outraged Nixon described as a "blatant intervention in our domestic affairs," North Vietnamese premier Pham Van Dong openly appealed for American support in opposition to Nixon's policies:

> This fall large sectors of the U.S. people, encouraged and supported by
> many peace-and-justice loving American personages, are launching a
> broad and powerful offensive ... to demand that the Nixon administra-
> tion put an end to the Vietnam aggressive war and immediately bring
> all American troops home.... May your fall offensive succeed splen-
> didly. (Nixon 1978, 402)

This provoked Nixon to issue an ultimatum to the North Vietnamese to
either negotiate seriously or face severe military reprisals. But when the
impact of his ultimatum was undercut by the massive antiwar Morato-
rium of October 15, 1969 (highly publicized, nationally organized demonstrations aimed at forcing the end of U.S. involvement in the war),
Nixon concluded that he had to either generate public support or fail in
Vietnam. He admitted as much in his now famous "silent majority"
speech of November 3, 1969, which brought on a demonstration of
support.

> The more support I have from the American people, the sooner we can
> [end the war,] for the more divided we are at home, the less likely the
> enemy is to negotiate at Paris.... Let us understand: North Vietnam
> cannot defeat or humiliate the United States. Only Americans can do
> that. (1978, 409)

Nixon's speech gave him the boost in support he needed in the short
term. But the continuing presence of vocal domestic antiwar sentiment
encouraged North Vietnamese intransigence at the bargaining table.
The effect of this, in conjunction with Nixon's stubborn determination
to hold out for "honorable" terms for disengagement, was to prolong the
war through January 1973. Nixon claims that a breakthrough finally
came only because he and Kissinger managed to convince North Vietnamese negotiator Le Duc Tho that the American president "would not
be affected by either Congressional or public pressures" and might thus
resume bombing in the absence of concessions. Apparently believing
this, the North Vietnamese finally signed an agreement (1978, 747).

Despite this tactical denial that he would be constrained by public
pressure, Nixon concludes his assessment of the war by underlining the
importance of public support. To him, it was the key to both the failure
of Johnson's policy and the success of his own:

> It was when my November 3 [silent majority] speech came along that
> we really ginned up some public support for winning a peace with
> honor. LBJ gave away this ground, and that was why he really failed in
> the end and was driven out of public office. (1978, 754)

Third, *a strongly supported president receives more favorable
media treatment*. The mass media—newspapers and, particularly, tele-

vision—are the major link between the presidency and the people. The public learns about the presidency through the media, and the media provide the president with direct and immediate access to the public. These facts invest the media with extraordinary power and importance. Because space and time limitations make it impossible to cover and report everything, the media are forced to be selective; they must decide what to report and how to report it. The selection of presidential news for coverage and the tone of its presentation cannot help but influence how the audience perceives and judges the president. Therefore, selection and tone will have some impact on the level of public support. This familiar observation has only recently found empirical support in political science research. Presidents have always assumed, and studies are beginning to show, that the more favorable the media coverage of the president, the stronger the audience support for the president (Smoller 1986; Iyengar, Peters, and Kinder 1982). As a result, presidents go to great lengths to secure favorable coverage and are unhappy when they do not get it (Edwards 1983, 106-107).

But if the content and tone of media coverage influence the level of support for the president, is the reverse also true? Does a strongly supported president receive more favorable press than a weakly supported one because of strong support? Does support have an impact of its own on media decisions about what to cover and how to cover it?

Hard evidence is scarce, but inferential evidence suggests that the answer is yes. Decisions concerning media coverage are guided by three discernible motives: (1) the adversarial or "democratic watchdog" motive, which emphasizes critical coverage of presidential mistakes and abuses of power; (2) the "professional neutrality" motive, which encourages objective journalistic coverage of important presidential words and actions; and (3) the profit motive, which encourages coverage of events that interest consumers and presentation in a manner that will sell newspapers and increase ratings. All three usually are at work, but the predominant characteristics of media treatment of the presidency reveal that the third motive has the largest and most decisive impact. The content and tone of news stories are influenced more by what the public wants to know than by journalistic or academic judgments of what they should know. Research has shown (and presidents have complained) that news coverage of the presidency is superficial, distorted, and incomplete, emphasizing the personal and trivial at the expense of substantive principles and policies (Edwards 1983, 146-163). In addition to consumer demand, factors such as the limitations on line space and broadcast time and the education and background of reporters contribute to the makeup of news coverage (Edwards 1983, 153-154).

The significance of sales and ratings, however, commands priority, for they determine the profits and, ultimately, the viability of news organizations. Despite watchdog and professional motives, the media operate in a market and must respond to its demands. Most people want extensive coverage of the presidency, full of short, easily understood personality and political horse-race stories, and they get it. They also want their perceptions of individual presidents confirmed—their heroes praised and their villains blamed. They are likely to get this, too.

A recent case of the press's responsiveness to public preferences is the comparatively gentle treatment given to Reagan, a popular and well-liked president. It became an article of faith among journalists on the presidency beat that the public simply would not stand for harsh treatment of this president (Greenstein 1983). Consequently, Reagan's press has been noticeably less critical than Carter's was.

Of course the watchdog and professional motives also have an impact on the content and tone of news coverage. They produce short-term departures from the dictates of consumer preference. Media organizations are sensitive to their reputations for professional integrity and seek to avoid the appearance of blatant commercialism. But the long-term primacy of the profit motive cannot be denied. It ensures that a president's standing with the public will strongly affect the media treatment of that president.

Perhaps the best example of the public's influence on the media and of the significance this influence has for presidential credibility and effectiveness is the emergence of presidential stereotypes: "tricky" Dick Nixon, "bumbling" Gerry Ford, "incompetent" Jimmy Carter, and "Teflon-coated" Ronald Reagan. What are stereotypes? They are standardized conceptions or images of a person, group, or idea, for example, invested with special meaning and held in common by a number of people. Why do stereotypes develop? Because people want simple and fixed ways of understanding and judging important social phenomena. Where do presidential stereotypes come from? Initially, from presidential actions or words or both. But what determines which actions or words will be perceived as typical or characteristic of a president and come to define the stereotype? Some say the media,[5] but my answer is the public. For like presidential policies, media stereotypes must be accepted by average Americans to survive.

Media organizations respond to their audience's desire for a short-hand, descriptive label that captures a president's distinguishing personal qualities and style. In the early months of a new administration, the media experiment with various characterizations of the chief executive that are based on real or presumed public responses to presidential words and deeds. The media collectively decide which alternatives to test, but they do so in anticipation of public response. Ultimately, the public determines which stereotype catches on, gets repeated, and becomes entrenched. The media cannot force a stereotype on an unresponsive market, and they rarely try.

Once established, a stereotype can exert decisive influence on subsequent news coverage of a president. News that is consistent with the stereotype is emphasized and receives more prominent attention than news that conflicts with it (Edwards 1983, 159). This activates a cycle of reinforcement in which a stereotype initially selected by public response is imbedded ever more deeply in the public consciousness by news coverage that repeatedly plays it back.

Because stereotypes resist inconsistent or disconfirming evidence, they take on lives of their own and increasingly diverge from reality. The relationship between actual presidential performance and press coverage of that performance is mediated by the stereotype, and this affects a president's ability to get whatever public credit the real performance may warrant. Negative stereotypes thus can create "can't win" situations and positive stereotypes "can't lose" situations for presidents. Media treatment of "ineffective" Carter and "Teflon-coated" Reagan strikingly illustrates this point. On balance, Carter received more negative and Reagan more positive press than either man's actual performance deserved on its merits, a difference largely attributable to stereotypes (Greenstein 1983).

The crucial question is, how can a president get a desirable stereotype, one that affords favorable media treatment? The answer is, cultivate the affection and support of the American people. The public will compel the media to portray a well-liked and supported president in the most generous light that circumstances will permit. And as a result, the president's chances of being effective in all arenas will be greatly increased.

Fourth, *strong public support increases the president's credibility inside the executive branch of government and among issue networks, interest groups, lobbyists, think tanks, and other segments of the Washington community.* Put another way, support enhances the president's reputation among government and policy professionals in the nation's capital. Congress, although part of the Washington community, is not the focus here. This proposition deals with a president's prospects for effectiveness during the stages that precede and follow enactment of legislation.

During the first stage, policy legitimation, the president seeks to establish credibility among policy experts for the administration's solutions to national problems; this happens prior to the formal submission of legislative proposals to Congress. For reasons having to do with the psychology of mass influence, if public support is strong enough, policy experts, and even issue experts outside the president's partisan circle, will tend toward backing the administration, lending the weight of their intelligence, expertise, and prestige to the push to implement the president's program. By expressing such sentiments in their writings, in testimony before congressional committees, and in interviews, they supplement and reinforce the impact of public support on both the media and Congress. This sort of momentum psychology was particularly apparent in Washington during the prelegislative public discussion of the controversial Reagan supply-side economic program in the winter of 1981.

The second stage, postlegislative policy implementation, is accomplished by career civil servants in the executive branch who are responsible for converting law into practice. A president's ability to shape the policy direction of government is crucially affected by the performance of these bureaucrats. They determine whether the actual execution of policy reflects the intent and spirit of the law. So great is this bureaucratic power that some recent presidents who were unable to persuade Congress to endorse their policies turned to "administrative implementation" strategies as alternatives to legislation (Nathan 1983; Pfiffner 1982). But carrying out policies administratively is no easy thing to do. Bureaucrats have ample resources for resisting presidential efforts to control their policy behavior (Heclo 1977). They only rarely wish to do so, however, contrary to the assumption of many presidents who suspiciously view them as determined obstructionists. Indeed, civil servants are often anxious to respond to presidential leadership (Heclo 1977; Cole and Caputo 1979), particularly when that leadership enjoys strong public support. "Senior bureaucrats," argues Francis E. Rourke (1981, 137), "like Supreme Court justices, follow the election returns." They are no less susceptible to the momentum psychology of mass public support than other denizens of the Washington community.

The proposition that popular support increases the president's professional credibility can be traced to Neustadt's analysis of presidential power (1980). In his original 1960 study, Neustadt argued that "public prestige" and "professional reputation" were not related. He was influenced by the fact that President Eisenhower, who enjoyed extraordinary public support, was held in low professional regard by Washington insiders. By 1980, however, Neustadt had changed his tune. What turned him around? He had observed an increasing tendency among Washington elites to measure a president's professional competence by the ability to sway the masses on television. Neustadt writes:

> At the same time that prestige seems likelier than formerly to reflect reputation, it may come to matter more in reputation. A president's capacity to draw and stir a television audience seems every bit as interesting to current Washingtonians as his ability to wield his formal powers. Their interest is his opportunity. While national party organizations fall away, while congressional party discipline relaxes, while interest groups proliferate and issue networks rise, a president who wishes to compete for leadership in framing policy and shaping coalitions has to make the most he can out of his popular connection. Anticipating home reactions, Washingtonians who sway before a breeze from tax revolt in California are vulnerable to any breeze from home that presidential words and sights can stir. If he is deemed effective on the tube they will anticipate. That is the essence of professional reputation. (1980, 238)

Fifth, and finally, *presidents' faith in themselves and their works, and thus their effectiveness, are influenced by the strength and enthusiasm of public support.* Professional and scholarly political analysis often shies away from such an unprovable psychological proposition as this. In the U.S. political system, however, the executive function is vested in the hands of a single human being, and accession to the presidency does not relieve the president of human susceptibilities and vulnerabilities.

Democratic political leaders are creatures of public sentiment. Those who reach the presidency are expert at discerning it and skilled at shaping and responding to it. Such leadership involves a personal relationship between leader and followers in which each invests significant emotional, physical, and mental energy (Burns 1978). The forging of such ties cannot help but have personal, as well as political or instrumental, meaning to leaders and followers.

Political psychologists from Plato to James David Barber have argued that people drawn into politics are uniquely sensitive to the opinions others hold of them. They are drawn to the public arena in part by an inner craving for the personal affirmation of favorable public response. But a president, with needs of this sort or not, will appreciate the emotional reinforcement of public approval and realize its pragmatic value as a leadership resource. And the pain of rejection implicit in disapproval will be felt. From this perspective, public support is strength and approbation for the president, a nurturing cradle for one so continually and visibly at risk of failure. Though difficult to prove scientifically, no more than a practical familiarity with human nature is required to conclude that presidents in general are touched, in important personal ways, by the sentiments of the mass public. No performer is truly indifferent to the audience's response, if only because it is a crucial measure of performance.

The emotional responses of presidents to public opinion can influence their behavior, and thus the quality of their performance in office. This dictum stems from the truism that the approval of others makes people feel good, while disapproval makes them feel bad. And people who feel good perform better than those who do not. Individual presidents have varied in the extent to which their performances suffered because of lack of public support. The only example that comes to mind of a president whose performance did not seem adversely affected during long periods of significant public disapproval is Abraham Lincoln.

Lincoln's towering historical reputation is due in no small measure to his ability to do what most presidents could not do: sustain courage, faith, and sense of direction in the face of not only mass public disapproval but outright hatred and vindictiveness (Oates 1977). More typical reactions to public disapproval and rejection are the rigid stubbornness of a Hoover confronting outrage at the Great Depression or a Nixon refusing to own up to his part in Watergate, the second-guessing of a Carter as support began to evaporate, and the personal abuse a Johnson heaped on his staff, thereby driving away the very people whose talents he needed most.

Conversely, many of the most impressive presidential achievements have been preceded or accompanied by strong public approval: Jackson's conversion of the presidency into the people's office, TR's assertion of American power in the world, FDR's construction of the welfare state, and Reagan's attempt to dismantle it.

The argument here is that the living president and the institutional presidency function more effectively with mass public approval, and that disapproval invites human malfunction and paralysis of the institutional machinery. Public approval and disapproval, besides simply being political resources and barriers, are two sides of a very powerful single psychological force. As human beings, presidents can hardly be indifferent to approval ratings, whether they admit it or not.

In no fewer than five vital arenas, then—Congress, foreign relations, the media, professional Washington, and within the person—a president is elevated, empowered, and enlarged or diluted, drained, and reduced, according to the magnitude of public support mustered. As a result, public support is justly considered the enabling energy of the presidency, the only consistently reliable force available to the president for transcending constitutional weakness and even personal limitations.

One scholar has described a new style of presidential leadership based on the importance of public opinion and support:

> A proposition of this book is that the degree to which a president goes public determines the kind of leader he will be. With it I have argued that the style of leadership from the White House is changing. Modern presidents rely on public opinion for their leadership in Washington to an extent unknown when [Robert A.] Dahl and [Charles E.] Lindbloom in the early 1950s described the president as "an embodiment of a bargaining society," or later when Neustadt predicated presidential power on bargaining. (Kernell 1986, 105)

Strongly supported presidents find Congress and professional Washington responsive, foreign allies and adversaries respectful, the media generous, and themselves resourceful and vital. Weakly supported presidents, on the other hand, face an uphill struggle. They are thwarted and rebuffed, able to do little more than watch helplessly as events and problems overtake and engulf them.

Diminished Support

Because the federal government cannot function effectively without a viable presidency, and because the presidency is not workable without strong public support, the obvious conclusion is that citizens must support presidents if at all possible. But support cannot be purchased or commanded, it must be earned. Presidents must be worthy of approval, for they cannot presume to receive it automatically. In theory, support is won by meeting public expectations for "competent" or "good" or "great" presidential performance. The presidency-public relationship is thus based on an implicit agreement that imposes obligations of reciprocity on the two parties: support in return for services rendered, services rendered in return for support.

In practice, however, recent evidence indicates the president, the public, or both have reneged:

> Since monthly opinion surveys on the president's performance began in the 1930s, every president except Eisenhower has left office less popular than when he entered.

> No president has served two full terms since Eisenhower.

> Presidents since Kennedy have experienced substantial disapproval in the public opinion polls, often falling below 50 percent support after two years in office.

> Voter turnout in the 1980 presidential election hit its lowest point in almost 40 years, improving only slightly in 1984.

Reagan, by consensus the most effective public relations president since FDR, received lower marks from the public halfway through his first term than any of the four preceding presidents (50 percent disapproval, 41 percent approval in January 1983).

Even though Reagan was able to rebound strongly in the polls and win reelection, the long-term trends of diminished support are disturbing. They continue to imply a structural problem in the presidency-public relationship, one that leaves uncertain whether future presidents will be able to duplicate Reagan's feat. The lengthy list of recent presidents with support problems—Johnson, Nixon, Ford, Carter, and, at times, Reagan—reveals the difficulty modern presidents have had maintaining adequate public support. Approval ratings are down overall. For example, Reagan's highest approval rating in the period from 1981 to 1984 barely exceeded Kennedy's lowest. But Reagan's rating was more impressive than Kennedy's because it contrasted so favorably with that of his predecessors. Kennedy's support scores seemed rather typical after Eisenhower.

Different Explanations, Divergent Remedies

Why has the public recently been so reluctant to give its support? Why does it no longer instinctively and generously back the incumbent for better or for worse, as it seemed to do during the presidencies of FDR, Eisenhower, and Kennedy (Greenstein 1974)? The reduced level of support reflects on the state of the presidency-public relationship, but disagreement exists over just what it means and what should be done about it.

One view shared by some academics, most journalists who cover the presidency, and the general public is that diminished support stems from the succession of flawed, incompetent, and otherwise inadequate presidents who deserved neither support nor reelection. The implicit support-for-performance agreement was violated by presidents, not the public. Such events as Vietnam and Watergate not only led to the rejection of the chief executive but also spawned public skepticism and cynicism toward the presidency itself. This explains why support trends are down. The solution, according to holders of this view, is better presidential candidates, those whose performance in office would be more likely to earn support and restore confidence.

While acknowledging that recent presidential performance has rarely been exemplary, adherents of a second view, including the current generation of academic presidency specialists and certain journalists, place primary responsibility for diminished support on the public.

Authors of a host of textbooks, trade books, and interpretive articles blame declining support on unrealistic public expectations for presidential performance.[6] Citizens want what no president has the power or expertise to deliver, such as the reduction of inflation and unemployment simultaneously or congressional approval for all or almost all of the administration's legislative proposals. In addition, expectations are often vague, ill-defined, and of questionable relevance, for example, expecting someone who looks and sounds "presidential." Expectations are unstable, not fixed or lasting—witness cries against the imperial presidency of the Johnson and Nixon years and compare with cries for decisive presidential leadership during the Carter years. Expectations are becoming increasingly narrow and self-serving, with pressure for action coming from all factions of society, including women, Hispanics, farmers, environmentalists, and industrialists. And expectations often are contradictory in nature, for instance, requiring that presidents be flexible, but also steadfast.

Weak support—adherents of this second view say—is a consequence not of flawed leaders, but of inadequate followers, a disinterested, uninformed electorate. In pressing unrealistic demands on the presidency, citizens fail to acknowledge the powerful constraints undermining presidential potency: the increase in congressional assertiveness and strength, the collapse of economic theory, the rise of special interest groups, the growth in independence of nations allied to the United States, and the increase in number of intractable problems confronting society. The solution, according to Thomas E. Cronin, is for citizens to refine their expectations of the president and raise their expectations of themselves (1980). The appropriate standards, argues Godfrey Hodgson, should enable honorable, average citizens to meet the more important demands that society makes on them (1980).

Holders of a third view also blame the public for diminished support but suggest, as a solution to the problem, restructuring the system. They propose the passage of a constitutional amendment to limit the president to a single six-year term. Citizens would be free to exercise their right to choose the president, but they would be stripped of the power to judge presidential performance where it counts most: at the polls.

Because "the election is the critical technique for insuring that governmental leaders will be relatively responsive to non-leaders" (Dahl 1956, 125), and because incumbents are most responsive when they intend to seek reelection on their records, such a reform would significantly reduce presidential accountability to the electorate. This is precisely what advocates of the six-year single-term presidency want to accomplish, for they believe that presidential failure results more often from attempts to live up to unwise and ill-founded public expectations than from the inadequacies of presidents. Convinced that the people's influence leads presidents astray and that public support is too fickle and unreliable to propel the presidential system, proponents contend that their proposed solution would give presidents a chance to lead—to free them from the need to do what is popular and to enable them to do what is right.

Endorsed by a large body of elite political professionals, including former presidents, cabinet officers, members of Congress, and journalists, the six-year presidency is an old idea that has resurfaced because of the support problems of recent presidents. Although no real prospect exists at this writing that the six-year presidency would soon be adopted, its reemergence as a serious proposal, with the enthusiastic support of a bipartisan group of national leaders, conveys a significant message: the ancient debate over the capacity of ordinary citizens to responsibly exercise political power is not dead. Should elite opinion continue to attribute political failure to followers instead of to leaders, the possibility for this or any other essentially antidemocratic reform to be adopted can only increase.

Implications

The recent downward trends in public support for presidents thus not only reduce the potential effectiveness of the presidency, they also mobilize an influential segment of elite political professionals to seek ways to reduce the importance of public support to presidential functioning. Holders of the first view above and admirers of Ronald Reagan and other popular presidents believe that support problems and antidemocratic reform proposals disappear when the "right" president is put into place. Unfortunately, as history attests, "great" leadership is a scarce commodity. Most of the time the nation makes do with adequate or marginal presidents. The Washingtons and Lincolns are welcomed, of course, but they will not routinely appear. To function reliably in the long run, the presidency must be able to generate majority support even for the lesser lights who will usually be at the helm.

Support for presidents in general must be increased. If significant improvement—short of major reform—is to take place, attention will have to focus not so exclusively on the leaders but also on the followers, as suggested by those academics and journalists who call for standards of judgment that are less simplistic, vague, contradictory, and self-serving and more sophisticated, informed, stable, equitable, and sensitive to the realities of presidential functioning. They argue convincingly that flagging support can be attributed in large part to unrealistic performance expectations. Refined expectations might well result in increased average levels of presidential support, and the charge of inadequate followers would lose credibility. Presidents still unable to generate support presumably would not deserve it. But how is all this to be accomplished? How might expectations be refined? On these questions the academics and journalists are silent. Those who would preserve the power of the citizenry cannot afford to ignore this issue.

How Much Improvement Is Possible?

The aim here is improvement of the ability to choose and judge. Improvement will come with the redefining of expectations. But ideal or perfect choice and judgment are impossible within human limits, simply beyond attainment. The future cannot be foretold (as perfect choice requires), and the past cannot be completely understood (as perfect judgment demands). Even if relevant information could be discerned with certainty, assembly and absorption of even a portion of it would be beyond capability. In addition, citizens must choose and judge in the "here and now," which rules out any extended study or reflection and does not grant the historical perspective of time. Imperfect choice and judgment thus are inevitable.

To improve, therefore, cannot mean to perfect. Instead, it can only mean to ask (and attempt to answer) the question, What is the best that can be done, within human limits, to meet the requirements of good citizenship for responsible here and now choice among candidates and for informed judgment of presidential performance in office?

At a minimum, choice and judgment, and the things that are likely to influence them, should rest on *examined grounds*. Admittedly, appraisal of candidates and presidents engages values, about which people may disagree. But value judgments may issue from mere whim, habit, or tradition, or they may result from a process of deliberation and reflect knowledge of the object of evaluation. The latter can be termed *grounded* value judgments. The ground of a value judgment, argues Abraham Kaplan, is the justification for making that judgment or having that value (1964, 387).

The value judgments of presidents and their performance made by citizens have been labeled unrealistic by influential groups of academic presidency specialists and political professionals. The implicit indictment is that these judgments are not well grounded in (justified by) familiarity with certain realities of presidential functioning, and that whatever grounds do exist are employed haphazardly or unconsciously from habit or impulse more often than from reflection or inquiry.

If these things are true, then one useful step toward improvement is simply to identify and examine both conscious and unconscious evaluative grounds: to make them explicit, categorize them, and assess their reasonableness in light of what is known of how the presidency works. Examined grounds will not eliminate principled disagreement over specific choices or judgments, but the more carefully evaluation is grounded, the more realistic it is likely to be and the better are the prospects for a governing consensus of support for a president who deserves it.

Notes

1. Some analysts of American politics contend that citizen power has been preempted by the pervasive role of money in politics, which makes it possible for the rich and well-organized to determine candidates and to further their interests by barraging the public with misleading information. Big-money concerns have on occasion controlled candidate choices and selfishly influenced public opinion, but the formal powers of presidential choice and judgment reside with the citizenry, who may reject such unsavory influences at any time. A number of recent presidential candidates have achieved political influence and viability without benefit of big-money backing or endorsement, including Adlai E. Stevenson, George McGovern, John B. Anderson, George Wallace, and Jimmy Carter. And having strong financial backing is no guarantee of electoral victory; for example, John B. Connally, who ran an expensive primary campaign for the 1980 Republican presidential nomination, managed to garner only one delegate, largely because thousands of ordinary citizens did not regard him as trustworthy.
2. The personal satisfaction or return on this civic investment is the enhanced self-regard that comes from having fulfilled a responsibility. Modern social choice theorists and classic political philosophers such as Hobbes and Locke conceive the dominant motive for participation to be self-interest rather than civic duty (Rohr 1984) and argue that it is not rational from the standpoint of self-interest to bother to vote or to invest time and effort in upgrading one's ability to evaluate the presidency (Tullock 1967; Downs 1957). But others contend that the rational choice model underpredicts voter turnout and does not adequately explain voting behavior. The most influential study of the electorate yet conducted (Campbell et al. 1960) discovered that even those citizens at the low end of the socioeconomic and educational spectrums, people who reported minimal concern about the election and low political efficacy, still voted in respectable numbers. The authors attributed this to a sense of citizen duty, instilled through socialization by civics courses, media appeals, family traditions, and the like (Asher 1984, 46). The public choice position in the face of such evidence is acknowledgement that voting is not merely instrumental, it is also a consumption good, a source of direct satisfaction in its own right (Riker and Ordeshook 1968).

3. A large number of Americans find the presidency simply fascinating, a wholly unique combination of power, science, mythology, personality, morality, and drama that rivals soap operas or sports as a source of exciting spectacles. This is another important incentive, along with civic responsibility, for investing effort in upgrading evaluative skills. The fact that the presidency is deemed important in ways other entertainment is not adds to its intrinsic appeal. Books about the presidency routinely outsell those dealing with other political topics. Although amusements do not necessarily require study, greater knowledge often enhances interest in a subject and the pleasure derived from attention to it. Just as the fun in following a sport is augmented by understanding its strategic nuances, so is the enjoyment of presidency-watching increased by greater familiarity with the intricacies of government and politics.

4. Another reason that a significant portion of the citizenry elects to devote time and attention to the presidency comes from individual needs for the cognitive and emotional services the institution and its incumbent can provide. These are not the usual services of policies aimed at increasing economic well-being or reducing the size of big government. Instead, they involve the president's potential for helping citizens at all levels of political sophistication make sense of government and feel good about the country and their own prospects. The president gives the government a face to which people can relate and serves as a symbol of national unity and as a source of reassurance, inspiration, and confidence in times of crisis. The president provides an additional psychological service in the role of lightning rod— someone to blame when things go wrong (Greenstein 1974, 146).

5. For example, Richard Neustadt implies that the media created Gerald R. Ford's "bumbling" stereotype. Ford, argues Neustadt, dropped in the polls from "the high forties" to "his low point" following "an outburst of derision in the columns and by anchormen (and comics), making much of moments when Ford physically had stumbled in the sight of mini-cams, the dread invention of the age" (1980, 279). I do not contend that the media have no effect, only that the chains of influence are reciprocal and that ultimately public reaction, not insulated editorial fiat, determines the long-term pattern of media coverage and the contours of the presidential stereotypes that take root. For example, the media tested various equally negative themes from the Reagan administration, including Reagan's frequent press-conference misstatements and his unprecedented disengagement from the operational and policy details of the presidency. Failure of these themes, which reflected on the quality of Reagan's performance in office, to catch on as symbols of the Reagan presidency cannot be attributed to lack of media attention. They did not emerge as stereotypes because the public did not reinforce them by its response to media coverage. No drop in the polls comparable to that experienced by Ford happened to Reagan. The media eventually turned to the "Teflon" label, which stuck.

6. Whether demanding expectations are beneficial or not is open to debate. One view holds that they are desirable because they maximize the incentive for presidents to perform well, while minimizing presidents' access to easy excuses should they fail to do so. Benjamin I. Page (personal communication, November 27, 1984) argues that presidents and events, not the public, deserve the blame for diminished support.

CHAPTER 2

Presidential Culture:
The "Deep Background" of
Choice and Judgment

Evaluation of presidential candidates and the incumbent president takes place not in a vacuum but in the context of a specific political culture, which has evolved certain shared meanings of the presidency. Evaluation is done not by value-neutral information-processing machines but by human beings, who are products of the culture and who bring opinion, emotion, and cognition to bear on choice and judgment. If evaluation is to rest on examined grounds, then the forces of culture and human nature, which influence evaluation, must be taken into account.

Culture is the first subject of concern—the part of American political culture that addresses values and beliefs about the presidency. Culture as a concept is imprecise and does not lend itself readily to exact measurement. The purpose here, however, is neither comprehensive definition nor strict usage (see Shweder and Levine 1985 or Goldschmidt 1959 for elaboration). Instead, culture will stand for the widely held meanings of the presidency, derived from selected episodes in the history of the institution and transmitted from one generation to the next by political socialization. This definition will vary according to an individual's values and political ideology. The focus here, however, is on the broadest and most common understanding of the presidency.

A nation's political culture burrows deeply into the collective psyche of its citizenry. Although most Americans lack detailed knowledge of individual presidents and their performance in office, citizens need not exert themselves much to absorb the cultural meaning of the presidency. An impression of the presidency is imbedded in the public mind by families, schoolteachers, media, social interactions, and other elements of the socialization process. Such cultural imprinting is often invisible to those who share it. Furthermore, its effect on human perception, cognition, and behavior often goes unnoticed by those who are influenced.

The presidency has three interrelated meanings for American culture: efficacy, deliverance, and greatness. These meanings become clearest in times of national crisis, such as when George Washington saved the nation (as commander in chief of the Continental army, then as first president), when Andrew Jackson reshaped the presidency into an instrument of mass democracy, when Abraham Lincoln preserved the Union, when Theodore Roosevelt insinuated the United States onto the world stage, and when Franklin D. Roosevelt overcame both the Great Depression and Adolf Hitler. To be effective, the presidency must contend successfully with any significant national problem that arises. As a result of a favorable outcome, the country is delivered from threats to its well-being. And if the presidency is to be equal to the task of handling such forbidding problems as war, economic collapse, or the threat of nuclear annihilation, it must be great—great enough to stand on equal terms with such larger-than-life challenges.

The problem-solving services performed by the presidency indicate that it is an important pragmatic tool. But the cultural meaning of the presidency also extends into the realm of emotion, where the president and the office function as a psychosocial coping mechanism. American culture has nurtured the concept of presidential greatness to represent the nation's ability to deal successfully with an endless succession of system-threatening trials. Only powerful symbols, like greatness, can quell widespread fears. Failure to respond assertively invites sentiments of hopelessness, impotence, and debilitating anxiety. In the long run, such sentiments are culturally and psychologically intolerable and can result in social disintegration.

A certain preconscious perceptual set is implanted in the minds of most Americans by the cultural influences at work. The set frames and subliminally encodes citizens' approach to the assessment of candidates and presidents. Culture helps to account for the sorts of impressions candidates and presidents must usually create to be regarded favorably and for the kinds of cues that must be evident to support these impressions.

Cognitive psychologists argue that much, if not most, consequential mental activity goes on outside conscious awareness (Goleman 1985). The thesis is illustrated by the enculturation of concepts that define what it means to be presidential and the application of these concepts to the evaluation of candidates and presidents. Focus group research, a methodology developed by market researchers, involves intensive group discussions guided by questions and comments offered by a group leader who has an agenda to fulfill. In a study of voters in which focus group research was applied, people were asked to give their reasons for approving or disapproving of the performance of particular presidents. The research did not elicit anything resembling a theory of cultural influence (Smoller and Moore-Fitzgerald 1981). In fact, interviewees rarely addressed the question of why they judged as they did, which suggests at least indifference to, and perhaps lack of awareness of, the origins of their evaluative stances. But the citizens' remarks did center on styles of performance suggestive of presidential greatness. As an anonymous participant in a randomly selected focus group discussion said:

> I think it is amazing how much style counts. The difference between walking into a hospital after being shot and beating off a killer-rabbit with an oar somehow seems to typify the difference between [Presidents Reagan and Carter] in my feeling. I know that it is drawing an absurd parallel but Reagan seems to have a style that even if I don't agree with him about El Salvador for example on several issues I have to admire that . . . he is doing now what he said he was going to do back in 1964 if he was elected. Or what he said he was going to do in 1968. And he continues to make these statements and he is forcefully sticking to it and I'm willing to give the man a chance. (Smoller and Moore-Fitzgerald 1981, 25)

Why does style count so much to this person and other Americans? Where does the importance of style come from? Such criteria are culturally inspired. Americans have a vision of the presidency, but they seem unaware of why it emerged and took root and of how it affects their approach to the evaluation of candidates and presidents. To begin an examination of the grounds for choice and judgment an effort will be made to step outside the culture to find out how it uses the presidency—as a coping mechanism and security blanket in bad times—and how this use can influence standards of evaluation.

Culture as Inspiration:
The Concept of Presidential Greatness

Concepts similar to presidential greatness have been put forth in recent presidential literature under a variety of names, including the "textbook presidency" (Cronin 1980), the "heroic model" (Hargrove 1974a), and the "savior model" (Nelson 1984). The term "greatness" is employed here because it better connotes two beliefs held by most Americans: (1) that the institution of the presidency, with its galvanic history and tradition, has the potential to make extraordinary events happen; and (2) that the institution's central figure, the incumbent president, should be able to realize that potential. To see the presidency as a great institution is to believe that in worthy hands it can do momentous, exceptional, outstanding things. For most Americans, the presidency is larger than life, transcending normal human limitations.

The idea of presidential greatness may be temporarily suppressed, but it has not been permanently altered by periods of presidential failure and abuse of power, such as Vietnam and Watergate. Those events surely did plant some doubts and provoke some rethinking. Scholars, who during the 1950s and 1960s had described the presidency as omnipotent and benevolent, for a time asserted that the office had exceeded its bounds and needed to be brought to heel (Polsby 1977; Schlesinger 1973; Cunliffe 1968). Journalists covering the presidency developed an attitude of cynical skepticism (Grossman and Kumar 1981). And citizens, in response to pollsters' questions, reported until recently a declining trust in national institutions. They continue to judge an incumbent president more stringently than before Vietnam and Watergate.[1] One scholar, however, concludes that contemporary attitudes toward the presidency reflect an admiration and celebration of presidential strength: Scholars, journalists, citizens, members of Congress, career federal bureaucrats, and others still want and appreciate executive potency (Nelson 1984, 24). Despite a national tendency to periodically reassess the presidency because of the perceived inadequacies of individual presidents, the greatness concept lives.

Americans have not abandoned support for a strong presidency for good reason—the need for a source of authoritative direction for the vast political, economic, and social order that is the United States. The failure of the Articles of Confederation compelled the framers of the Constitution to create an executive capable of imposing order on the newly formed nation, regardless of the threat of tyranny such an executive evoked. The need for executive strength has not lessened by the late twentieth century, as government had increased greatly in size and scope and as complex national and international issues demand attention.

Presidential greatness assumes that considerable talent and expertise, not possessed by everyone, are required for effective service. In addition, the concept of greatness recognizes that whoever fills the role of president comes to personify the government and thus serves as a living symbol of the values and procedures that constitute the political estate. The president's position is described in a constitution that was freely accepted as binding, and the legitimacy of that position is revalidated by the electoral process. Having a human instead of some impersonal institution represent the government makes it easier for ordinary citizens to identify with and feel membership in the political system. A human symbol enhances the vitality of the government in the face of such powerful centrifugal forces as a huge population, geographical dispersion, single-issue interests, and alienation from big government. The office of the presidency should be occupied by an exceptional person who strikes others as worthy of the station.

The presidential concept exists in part because of the need for a powerful central authority to direct this country. A competent president is capable of symbolizing the legitimacy and potency of the political system. Such a leader commands a good measure of respect and deference. But something is missing from this explanation. It does not address why presidents and the presidency are not merely respected but are held in awe and treated with reverence by citizens. Greatness would be a misnomer if the concept reflected no more than simple, straightforward respect, which presidents would rationally deserve for important services rendered. But the presidency has emotional as well as practical meaning for Americans. To fully grasp the concept of greatness and to clearly understand citizens' evaluations of presidential leadership, the emotional, nonrational dimensions of the presidency must be considered.

The Emotional Impact of the Presidency

A variety of evidence supports the notion that the institution of the presidency reaches the psyches of Americans and touches their emotions. For example, strong emotional and physical reactions are displayed when a president dies in office. Such responses were measured in the aftermath of the Kennedy assassination (Sheatsley and Feldman 1964) and were alleged to have occurred following the deaths of Presidents William Henry Harrison, Abraham Lincoln, and James A. Garfield. Another indicator is the sharp jump in public approval a president-elect receives when inaugurated. The rise in the ratings can only be attributed to the psychological impact of ceremonial investiture, as the new president has had no chance to do anything except appoint some officials and give a speech. An additional bit of proof is the "rally-round-the-flag" effect that occurs during crises or important symbolic episodes like summit meetings. Also illustrative are feelings people say they experience when they hear strains of "Hail to the Chief" (Carter 1984) and reports that experienced politicians and other adults find themselves tongue-tied when they come face-to-face with the president in the Oval Office (Carter 1982).

The evidence suggests that for many Americans the presidency has *charisma,* a quality that is usually attributed to human beings and not to impersonal institutions (Willner 1984). For most citizens, however, the institution is *not* impersonal. That charismatic is not too farfetched a word to describe the presidency is suggested by Daniel Katz (1973), who identified two signs of charisma: (1) that the person (or, in this case, institution) elicits some degree of emotional arousal, ranging from wild enthusiasm to passionate hatred; and (2) that followers perceive that the person possesses wide scope and great efficacy. Katz also notes that followers tend to play down or ignore weaknesses in the charismatic personality. Citizens' reactions to the presidency, and on occasion to particular presidents, certainly meet the criteria for charisma set up by Katz.

Why Greatness?

The presidency has gained the stature of greatness primarily because it has been effective in resolving large national problems that engaged the emotions of citizens. Emotion is the key, for without it leadership remains little more than management and does not inspire awe or become enshrouded in mystique.

The presidency has been presented with problems that seemed insoluble and thus threatening and overwhelming, problems that engendered feelings of helplessness and hopelessness. Specifically, such problems have included aggressive actions by hostile foreign powers, social and racial unrest, and severe economic hardship. When drastic circumstances have arisen, the nation has turned to the presidency in desperation. The presidents who traditionally top historians' greatness polls—Washington, Jefferson, Jackson, Lincoln, Wilson, FDR—are credited with knowing what to do in trying times and doing it. Although Reagan faced less portentous concerns than the greatest presidents, his first-term popularity was due in part to the fact that he assuaged widespread anxieties about the workability of the presidency.

The most successful presidents managed to convert negative feelings of fear and despair among the citizenry into positive feelings of optimism and self-confidence by providing various forms of reassurance, inspiration, and relief. In the process of doing what others could not, these presidents won esteem and respect for themselves and their office. Because their attainments were seen as extraordinary, and because in most cases this perception arose during heightened emotional states, "mere" esteem and respect began to assume the proportions of awe.

How did the emotion attached to the presidency become so strong, when the office has been occupied by only a few leaders with any real claims to greatness? The impressions endured beyond isolated events and personalities through cultural socialization. Citizens' need for deliverance from an unending stream of problems continues to trigger great uneasiness. Citizens also want a regular supply of great leadership able to consistently solve those problems. The world is surely not getting less threatening, less dangerous; the possibility of global nuclear war that has emerged is testimony to that. And an individual's ability to understand, control, and cope with such ominous situations is diminishing. A source of reassurance, inspiration, power, and hope—a great presidency—is required.

History's Special Role

The role of the past in sustaining the greatness concept is crucial, for history supplies the proof that serious national problems can be confronted and overcome. If they were successfully dealt with before, they can be again. History thus becomes a cultural coping resource of continuing value. The presidency must be great, not just competent, because it must be perceived as equal to the larger-than-life problems with which it may have to contend.

The proof of presidential greatness supplied by history is sometimes embellished and exaggerated; as a result, the presidency assumes mythological proportions. But strict factual accuracy and thoroughness can be inconvenient, if not potentially damaging. The fact, for example, that substantially more presidents are considered average than great, and that every great president made political blunders is beside the point. Exact faithfulness to what actually happened is much less important than that the stature of the presidency be kept on equal terms, in the public mind, with the problems it is expected to resolve. Murray Edelman makes a related point:

> Leadership symbols may well be a more powerful factor in historical recreation than in contemporary behavior. . . . The leader as an historical figure is not the same symbol as he was to his contemporaries. Always, however, he is made to be what will serve the interests of those who follow him or write about him or remember him. (1964, 94)

The relevance of the greatness concept and its firm anchor in the national consciousness are suggested by the frequent use of evocative and poetic language to describe the presidency: Clinton Rossiter's (1960) "breeding ground for indestructible myth," Emmet John Hughes' (1972) descriptions of the "mystery" and the "destiny" of the presidency, Hugh Sidey's (1983) discussion of "majesty in a democracy" in connection with the presidency, and Hedley Donovan's (1982) references to the "heroic presidency." Despite disillusionment during times of presidential failure and abuses of power, like Vietnam and Watergate, and accompanying feelings that the heroic presidency belongs to some bygone age of innocence, the greatness concept endures. It does so because it serves a purpose.

Three Tests of Presidential Greatness

Ideas of who should be president and of what it means to be a successful president must come from somewhere. When citizens measure presidential candidates and the incumbent, they are likely to do so against a yardstick that makes some use of widely shared conceptions of what it is to be presidential. These conceptions originate from images, however vague and imprecise they may be, created by outstanding past presidents. Citizens' notions of exemplary presidents and presidential performances, and thus their choices and judgments, may be imperceptibly influenced by a highly selective, emotionally inspired vision of the presidency. For standards of evaluation to lie on examined grounds, such potential or actual influences must be scrutinized.

Following is a series of illustrative definitions of three tests that are implicit in the cultural concept of presidential greatness—the character test, the power test, and the success test. The identification of these tests derives from my understanding of published writings on the presidency and from content analysis of interviews with ordinary citizens (Smoller and Moore-Fitzgerald 1981) and of published editorial commentary on the Carter and Reagan administrations.[2] In describing the tests, which represent primordial underpinnings for the consciously rationalized grounds for choice and judgment, two purposes are served: (1) to show how shared understandings and subliminal definitions of the presidency were forged in emotionally significant national experience; and (2) to suggest how a concept forged to bolster national resolve in the crunch—presidential greatness—influences present-day choice and judgment.

The Character Test

The greatness mystique creates the expectation that presidents be presidential, which involves an elusive combination of personal appearance and demeanor, certain modes of self-presentation, and particular mental and moral characteristics. The expectation is often evinced in paired comparisons of presidential qualities: "Buchanan lacked Lincoln's decisiveness," "Nixon lacked Eisenhower's integrity," or "Carter lacked Kennedy's charisma." Americans' collective sense of what it is to be presidential is strongly affected by history's lessons about the great presidents—Washington, Jefferson, Jackson, Lincoln, Wilson, and FDR—and by personal experience with recent presidents. Kennedy and Reagan, for example, seemed presidential, while LBJ and Carter did not.

To begin this nonclinical survey of what most Americans have in mind when they look for "the right stuff" (which amounts to presidential character), no better place exists than with the president who impressed his contemporaries as much as he would later generations and who came closest in reality to having been what legend imagines him—George Washington.

Integrity. Washington's contribution to the character test is integrity, which Hedley Donovan calls the "presidential bedrock" (1982). A person with integrity adheres to moral and ethical principles, is of sound moral character, and is honest. But even more importantly, integrity as defined here prevails in the face of great provocation, temptation, pressure, or tribulation—circumstances under which most people would feel a strong urge to yield, run, or come unglued. The term is also used to imply a certain guilelessness, a distaste for craftiness or cunning, which are usually hallmarks of astute political operators.

Washington's reputation for integrity has endured throughout the nation's history. Hugh Sidey (1983, 24), in a *Time* magazine article commemorating Washington's birthday entitled "Above All, the Man Had Character," marvels at the fact that even the most painstaking scholarship, which so often debunks and dismantles heroes, has "failed to dim the aura of greatness that clings to Washington." British journalist Henry Fairlie, who considers Washington "the greatest man who ever lived," cites Washington biographer James Thomas Flexner: "the gentlest of history's great captains, one of the heroes of the human race." Fairlie also notes the words of Abigail Adams, Washington's contemporary: "Take his character together, and we shall not look upon his like again" (1982, 7).

What accounts for Washington's extraordinary reputation? It was certainly not brilliance or intelligence, for many of his contemporaries— most notably Alexander Hamilton and Thomas Jefferson—were far brighter. Neither was it eloquence; Washington was an average public speaker. And it was not personal magnetism. He was a rather stolid, unexciting personality of a sort unlikely to quicken the pulse in his or any other age. It was not even his great success as general and president, although without these achievements he probably would have gone unnoticed. What seems most impressive about Washington was how he conducted himself under pressure.

Washington had an imposing physical presence. Tall and erect, he projected an air of reserve, gravity, and dignity, without seeming arrogant. By his deportment he conveyed the impression that he was someone special: a leader. He obviously respected himself but was not suffused with a sense of self-importance.

He demonstrated an unswerving dedication to an ideal—the nationhood of the United States—in whose service he compiled an impressive record of great personal risk and sacrifice. His performance as a revolutionary general and later as president indicated that he would not be easily pushed off course by danger or adversity. And Washington did not change his colors under pressure. He was steadfast of purpose, always remaining the same man no matter what.

Those who knew him were impressed with his personal authenticity. He had no hidden agendas or disguised motives. Except for the conscious decision to comport himself with a formal gravity befitting his concept of how a head of state should behave, Washington was without artificial facades or blustery self-promotion.

Genuineness and a seeming lack of personal ambition or egotism combined to project an aura of uncompromising fairness and trustworthiness, which was enhanced by a cautious habit of reviewing all known options before making major decisions. Washington's qualities led even his political opponents, such as Thomas Jefferson, to trust and respect him.

But Washington's reputation for integrity inspired awe, not just respect, because of the emotion-laden circumstances in which his qualities were displayed. The terrors of revolutionary war, the anxious beginnings of a new nation after a failed first start, and the threat of invasion by a host of aggressive, militarily superior foreign powers excited the passions of ordinary citizens. By never despairing, by holding steady on his deliberate course, by sustaining poise in the face of incipient chaos, by showing constancy and integrity, Washington supplied a psychological safe harbor that sustained a nation. Doing this, he converted respect into awe. To a greater extent than usual, his character alone made his accomplishments possible.

Charisma. A second component of the character test is variously called magnetism, electricity, vibrations, or charisma. One scholar complains that charisma is so overworked as to be unsuited for analytic duty. He substitutes the phrase "heroic leadership," which he defines as:

> belief in leaders because of their personage alone, aside from their tested capacities, experience, or stand on issues; faith in the leader's capacity to overcome obstacles and crises; support for such leaders expressed directly—through votes, applause, letters, shaking hands— rather than through intermediaries or institutions. (Burns 1978, 244)

Burns maintains that heroic leadership is not simply a quality or entity possessed by someone, but rather a type of relationship between leader and led. He contends that the essence of the relationship, which engages the emotional needs of both hero and spectator, is short-term psychic dependency and gratification.

Here the working definition of *charisma* is a leadership quality that evokes an emotional reaction in followers. The *persona*—the personality or character of an individual—as well as the actual accomplishments of the leader bring forth the emotional response. (For a detailed analysis of charisma, see Willner 1984.) Charisma is less central to the character test than integrity because Americans are sometimes willing to overlook its absence in presidential candidates and presidents—something they have been unwilling to do with integrity. Still, voters do want to feel strongly about candidates and presidents, who are not always expected to inspire quasi-religious devotion but are expected to possess the kind of personal magnetism that can stimulate some degree of popular excitement and enthusiasm at the prospect of their leadership. Presidential aspirants and the incumbent are tested for their ability to create an emotional conviction of being presidential timber—deserving of the presidency and well-suited to its demands.

Walter Mondale, the 1984 Democratic presidential nominee, is only the latest example (an earlier example, familiar to older readers, is Adlai E. Stevenson II) of a candidate whose considerable qualifications could not overcome a distinct lack of inspirational magic. Journalists and the American public would not let Mondale forget how poorly he fared by comparison with the incumbent, Ronald Reagan. Not every successful presidential hopeful had this magic, but those who did found it easier to get elected and experienced less demanding evaluations once in office.

American conceptions and public expectations of presidential charisma can be traced to four presidents—Jackson, TR, FDR, and Kennedy. Only two of these presidents are routinely judged as great by historians—Jackson and FDR—with TR most often labeled near-great. Kennedy is usually rated no better than above average, but recent national polls suggest that the American public sees him variously as the greatest of American presidents and the president most would like to see in office now (Martin 1983, 574). Such contrasting judgments tell something of the difference between experts and laymen, but perhaps more of the impact of personal style on stature in the public mind. Following are descriptions of the four charismatic presidential characters.

Andrew Jackson. Of Jackson it has been said that his personal magnetism was powerful enough to convert avowed enemies into passionate supporters. Jackson biographer Arthur M. Schlesinger, Jr., describes him as a "noble and impressive figure," with a "grim and indomitable spirit"; a "majestic visage" who struck people with his commanding aura, his self-possession, and his shrewd, intuitive faculties. "He wrought," writes Schlesinger, "a mysterious charm upon old and young." Schlesinger quotes Jackson contemporary James Kirke Paulding: "He was indeed an extraordinary man, the only man I ever saw that excited my admiration to the pitch of wonder" (1964, 33). Said future president James Buchanan of Jackson: "Surely he was a great man, and his native strength, as well of intellect as of character, compelled every man to be his tool that came within his reach" (Schlesinger 1964, 33). These are remarkable statements, made by people who were not known for exaggeration or hyperbole. Apparently, Jackson's hypnotic impact by itself stirred conviction, belief, and support for him and his works. Jackson approximates classic charisma.

Theodore Roosevelt. Roosevelt's brand of charisma was more entertaining than Jackson's. By his colorful ebullience, his forcefulness, his cultivation of a Wild West, roughrider image, and his ostentatious display of energy and buoyant enthusiasm, Roosevelt made himself and the presidency seem at once potent, glamorous, and fun. He described his experience of the presidency as "ripping, simply ripping" and said of himself: "I do not know of any man of my age who has had as good a time" (Boller 1981, 180).

To his contemporaries, TR appeared to possess limitless vitality, audacious courage, and an iron will. People found him inspiring and amusing. William Allen White saw him as a "gorgeous, fighting, laughing, loving, hating, robust man" (Lowitt 1971). Richard Lowitt describes Roosevelt: "He had a strong and handsome face, a bristling mustache, a fire of youth, and an air of sincerity. A set of glistening teeth, quickly revealed when he burst into his well-known grin and uttered the famous 'dee-lighted' or when he soberly discussed the issues of the day, soon became a trademark of which cartoonists quickly took advantage" (1971, 180). British essayist and biographer John Morley called TR "an interesting combination of St. Vitus and St. Paul" (Boller 1981, 194).

And Rudyard Kipling, after meeting Roosevelt, said: "I curled up in the seat opposite and listened and wondered until the universe seemed to be spinning around and Theodore was the spinner" (Boller 1981, 194).

One of Roosevelt's leading biographers, Henry F. Pringle, writes of the unfounded rumors that TR was a heavy drinker: "It seemed impossible that such vitality could be natural. Men looked at his ruddy face, at his continued enthusiasms, at his gusts of anger or mirth or delight, and concluded that these were induced by alcohol" (1931, 401). Roosevelt's self-presentation led more than one critic to question his sanity. Upon TR's nomination for the vice presidency, Republican National Committee chairman Mark Hanna exclaimed: "Don't any of you realize that there's only one life between this madman and the White House?" (Boller 1981, 198). Though of a very different order than that created by Jackson, the purely personal impact Roosevelt had on the electorate was undeniably great. TR helped to put the presidency, in a state of decline since Abraham Lincoln, back at the center of American life.

Franklin D. Roosevelt. The even more extraordinary personal impact of Theodore's cousin, Franklin, is somewhat harder to disentangle from the despairing, fearful national atmosphere that colored the first impressions he created. Too, FDR's personal impact is confounded with his enormous substantive influence on the national concept of the presidency, which resulted from a record of accomplishment without peer in the twentieth century. These accomplishments contribute mightily to what has become a Roosevelt legend. But his personality seems no less responsible than his deeds for either his legendary status or his impact on the mass public of his time. "Roosevelt . . . so embodied everyone's notion of who 'the president' was," writes William E. Leuchtenburg, "that it seemed incomprehensible that anyone else could be president of the United States" (1983, 1). Describing General Dwight D. Eisenhower's stunned reaction to the news of FDR's death, Leuchtenburg cites an Eisenhower biographer: "Whatever his faults, [Roosevelt's] buoyant personality had been through twelve years of unparalleled crisis one of the positive assets of the whole Western World" (1983, 45). Harold L. Ickes, who served as FDR's interior secretary, said: "It seemed to be a quality of the Roosevelt character either to inspire a mad devotion that can see no flaw or to kindle a hatred of an intensity that will admit of no virtue" (Sullivan 1968b, 787). "There he was," writes Richard L. Strout, "the uptilted jaw, the tossed head, the big laugh, the great wave, the thunder of the crowd . . . Happy-days-are-here-again!" (1982, 12). Strout met "a large, smiling self-confident, magnetic man sitting in a wheelchair . . . the Roosevelt personality was part of our lives" (1982, 13).

The instrument that Roosevelt used to impress his personality on the lives of millions of Americans was the radio. He used it to "come into every home in the land as a trusted family friend at the fireside" (Hodgson 1980, 64). By projecting himself through the mass media:

> More than any previous President, Roosevelt . . . came to symbolize the nation as a familiar, everyday figure. He thus decisively enhanced that identification between the presidency and the nation that is one of the essential traits of the modern presidency. At the same time he personalized the presidency more than ever before, and so encouraged a double identification of the President with the presidency, and of the presidency with the nation, so that the President became for most Americans the living symbol of the nation in a direct and personal and emotionally vivid way as not even Washington or Lincoln had been. (Hodgson 1980, 65)

Robert Sherwood described Roosevelt as a "thoroughly and gloriously unpompous" man whose predominant qualities were "unconquerable confidence, courage and good humor" (1948, 9). Despite a "heavily forested interior," which was both complex and contradictory to those who knew him well, "he achieved a grand simplicity which will make him, I believe, much less a mystery to biographers than Lincoln was and must forever remain. . . . Whatever the complexity of forces which impelled him, the end result was easily understandable to his countrymen and to the world at large" (1948, 9).

In the process of setting the expectation that all future chief executives must be the primary shapers of their times—an expectation with which each of his successors, but few of his predecessors, had to deal (Leuchtenburg 1983, ix), Roosevelt established the model for what it means, in personal terms, to be presidential. FDR, with his patrician eloquence and charming, good-humored, informal, and self-confident manner, showed how to inspire a nation to believe in itself through belief in its leader.

John F. Kennedy. Kennedy, despite a comparatively lackluster record of performance as president, excites the popular imagination to the pitch of wonder and has come to symbolize the meaning of charisma. Kennedy, especially the legendary Kennedy, is the purest example of charisma as personal power aside from tested performance.

The memory of Kennedy has assumed grand proportions in the public mind in part because of his good looks and glamour, his youth and vitality, and his photogenic and stylish family. Kennedy also served as president fairly recently and is remembered by most members of the contemporary electorate. Furthermore, his assassination, a highly charged emotional event indelibly impressed on the national psyche by

75 straight hours of television coverage, created a legend laced with poignancy—a youthful hero cut down senselessly and tragically in his prime, turning dreams and promises to ashes.

The "real" John Kennedy, to those who knew him well, was a hard-nosed pragmatist with few illusions about himself or the world (Martin 1983). But he was also an electric personality whose appearances brought out the "jumpers," as described by James MacGregor Burns:

> The "jumpers" of 1960 hopped up and down, screaming in frenzy, as John F. Kennedy and his entourage approached during the presidential campaign of that year. One can doubt that these teenagers and subteenagers were whooping it up for Kennedy because of his stand on old-age pensions or on Latin American Policy.... He was handsome, with a boyish grin, [and] Kennedy's appearance and performance titillated them. That was enough. (1978, 247-248)

In 1983, on the twentieth anniversary of JFK's death, the mass media, in consultation with a handful of scholarly experts and average citizens, sought to explain the Kennedy magic. Said *Newsweek:*

> What his idolators and even some of his detractors have missed most of all, then and still, was his flair, his panache, his aspiration to great deeds, and his contagious confidence that they could be done ... he stood for hope in what some of the eye-witnesses in these pages regard as the last hopeful time in our national life. (Goldman 1983, 62)

Said *Time:*

> It is fascinating ... that the youngest elected President ... should be thus elevated, by the force of his presence, his vivid charm, to the company of the greatest Presidents, as if the inspirational power of personality were enough for greatness. Perhaps it is. Many Americans make the association ... [JFK was] a symbol—but of what exactly? Mostly of a kind of hope, the possibility of change, and the usually unthinkable idea that government leadership might intercede to do people some good. (Morrow 1983, 60)

Said one expert:

> I would say that his chief accomplishment was changing expectations of the presidency—changing them permanently. Public expectations of Presidents rose significantly under Kennedy and have never really receded to what they were before. (Brauer 1983, 53-54)

The Kennedy mystique affected the sentiments of a wide range of Americans, especially by providing the belief and hope that things could be made to happen. The most concrete evidence of Kennedy's inspirational influence was the change he wrought in attitudes toward the government. He stimulated an entire generation of college-educated people to believe that public service was a high calling. To the larger society he imparted credibility to the notion that the national government was a virtue, not a necessary evil. Kennedy was able to alter citizens' perception of government more because of who he was than from anything he accomplished as president. Kennedy clearly illustrates the powerful potential of personal magnetism.[3]

Other. Integrity and leadership magnetism head the list of personal qualities Americans instinctively seek in presidents, but other elements of the character test can be identified. Some qualities have occasionally rivaled the top two in significance to the electorate, though none has achieved quite the same clarity or consistent importance in the public mind.

The quality of moral idealism is epitomized by the benevolence Lincoln displayed toward his critics during the Civil War and toward the South in his plans for Reconstruction. Moral idealism is also illustrated by the rhetorical emphasis Wilson and Carter put on world peace and human rights. Other virtues expected of leaders can be summed up in such statements as Harold J. Laski's (1940) admonition that the president should be an "uncommon man of common opinions," Clinton Rossiter's (1960) assertion that the president should be "intelligent but not intellectual," and Erwin Hargrove's (1974b) argument that effective presidents must possess "democratic characters." In addition, it has been suggested that presidents must be, among other things, warm, positive, caring, honest, decisive, audacious, tough-minded, in tune with their times, and visionary.

Taken together, the criteria embodied in the character test reveal that great, or even minimally capable, presidents should have within themselves personal resources that enable them to transcend normal human limitations. They must be able to inspire and reinvigorate the faint-hearted, to do more work, to surmount more obstacles, to understand more complexities, to explain more clearly, to answer more tough questions, and to muster more courage and resolve than the average citizen. They must, in short, be exceptional characters.

The Power Test

The second test implicit in the concept of presidential greatness is the power test. Potency, the forceful and effective use of power, is a core feature of presidential greatness largely because the greatness concept evolved to help allay society's fears. While the character test identifies exemplary ways of being president, the power test concerns preferred ways of doing presidential work.

Americans are impressed more with vigorous and assertive than tentative or reluctant uses of presidential power. Both mass public polling results and the rankings of presidents by historians indicate that Americans prefer the "take charge" president who is willing to seize the initiative and try boldly to make things happen. According to a 1979 Gallup poll, citizens are most interested in getting strong leadership and forcefulness in office from their presidents, more so even than solutions to policy problems (Wayne 1982). George Gallup's 1960 observation that "inaction hurts a president more than anything else" still rings true (Edelman 1964, 78). Highly esteemed presidents, such as Washington, Jackson, Lincoln, and FDR, to a great extent owe their status to the concrete results they achieved. In addition, they have in common a penchant for the bold stroke, for making decisive moves, which enhanced their reputations. Behind-the-scenes operators like Polk or Eisenhower, whose accomplishments were significant but whose publicly displayed leadership styles lacked forcefulness, enjoy considerably less historical stature and require special explanation to be appreciated (see, for example, Greenstein's 1982 reinterpretation of Eisenhower).

The element of audacity within the power test is important because it often acts to stimulate such emotional states as inspiration and awe, overriding feelings of fear and hopelessness in citizens. Presidents who pass the power test cut through complexities and take decisive action, no matter how anxious the populace, how confused the issue, or how uncertain the experts. Firm use of power inspires and reassures by demonstrating that the president knows what to do and is willing to do it—somebody is in charge who is not afraid to lead. In a *Time* magazine interview, Richard Nixon said:

> Unless the President leads, nobody will. This is central to an effective presidency: the vision, the sense of direction, to see the map whole and to chart the basic course without leading the country aimlessly on one detour after another.... He must be able to crystallize our purposes, and he must not shrink from the use of power.... The presidency is a vehicle for the exercise of power. We choose Presidents to make things happen. (1980b, 35)

Generally, then, a president's stature corresponds to the strength, vigor, and assertiveness of presidential performance. Within the limits of ethics and prudence, the more ambitious the president's plans and the more aggressive efforts are to implement them, the more likely the president is to be regarded favorably.

One dimension of the power test—effective response to challenges to presidential authority—was demonstrated early in the nation's history by Washington's reaction to the Whiskey Rebellion and Jackson's handling of the South Carolina secession threat. In 1794, when western

Pennsylvania farmers rebelled against the federal excise tax on grain and forced a federal inspector to flee for his life, the action was interpreted as defiance of the authority of the federal government and its agent, the president. Washington called for the enlistment of an army, then he and Treasury Secretary Hamilton rode with the 12,000-man force toward insurrectionist territory. This display of power was sufficient to end the rebellion without the need to fire a single shot (Sullivan 1968a, 52). Similarly, when the South Carolina Legislature passed its Ordinance of Nullification, which declared federal tariff laws null and void in that state, and threatened to secede from the Union, President Jackson, despite his personal sympathy with South Carolina's complaint, responded to its defiance with ringing words and the threat of invasion. He said, "Disunion by armed force is treason. Are you ready to incur its guilt?" He then had a bill introduced in the Senate that would authorize the president to use force to sustain federal authority. Faced with the prospect of invasion, South Carolina rescinded its ordinance. Jackson's popularity soared (Braun 1968, 207-208).

Another dimension of the power test is bold initiative—asserting some previously unacknowledged power and claiming an inherent right to use it in the national interest. Such a claim of prerogative power was Thomas Jefferson's move to acquire the Louisiana Territory, a bold stroke whose dramatic impact on the national psyche of the time has few parallels in presidential history. Jefferson, who was surprised when Napoleon presented him with this extraordinary opportunity, had first to swallow his own constitutional scruples. He then moved quickly to build political support for the purchase under time pressure created by his justifiable fear that Napoleon might rescind the offer. When the act was done, the jubilant national reaction swamped the few expressions of criticism for Jefferson's action: the acquisition of new territories in the absence of explicit constitutional authority to do so (Tugwell 1960, 62).

Failures of the power test appear weak, impotent, and unworthy of the presidential mantle, particularly when the vigorous use of power is widely regarded as essential. Much of the public reaction to President Carter's handling of the Iranian hostage crisis is a recent case in point. The classic illustration is provided by the hapless James Buchanan, who is judged chiefly by his last four months in office. Buchanan adopted a conciliatory stance toward the states that had seceded from the Union following Lincoln's 1860 election. As a lame duck, he was reluctant to commit his successor to drastic courses of action, and, as a strict constitutional constructionist, he concluded that he lacked authority to compel unruly states to remain in the union and to act in seceded states. Sympathetic historian Thomas A. Bailey describes Buchanan's plight:

A non-legalistic Buchanan might have resorted to dictatorial decrees, as a war-vexed Lincoln did later, to stem secession and try to force the states back into the Union. But Congress was not in session during Buchanan's lame duck ordeal of 1860-1861. If he had promulgated laws from the White House when the lawmaking body was a mile away on Capitol Hill he would have subverted his beloved republican form of government and subjected himself to impeachment. He had no army with which to crush the South, and if he had tried to raise one by illegal means, how could he have prevented the Civil War by starting it? Until the guns began to boom, there was always the last-ditch hope of a peaceful settlement. (1966, 289-290)

However much a prisoner of circumstances beyond his control Buchanan might have been, and despite the fact that few meaningful options for decisive action seemed apparent, his reluctance to move boldly at a crucial moment brands him a failure from the perspective of the power test.

The Success Test

Displays of presidential character and of judicious but forceful uses of power create a leadership image for presidents. But to be judged great, presidents must also make things of lasting value happen. Successful results are the ultimate test of presidential competence and greatness. Morton Borden, editor of *America's Eleven Greatest Presidents,* writes:

What indices have scholars used, consciously or unconsciously, in making their choice [of great presidents]? Obviously they have not used public popularity, or political skill, or intellectual brilliance, or hard work and devotion, or adherence to democratic means. Many of America's greatest presidents had some of these qualities, but so did others who are considered average or poor. The fact seems to be that America's greatest presidents have been chosen on the basis of success: the degree to which each has solved or resolved the crucial issues of the period. (1971, viii)

Success is defined as the favorable, prosperous, or satisfactory outcome or result of an attempt or endeavor. *Effective* means having an effect, being adequate to accomplish a purpose, or producing a desired or intended result. As applied to presidents, the concepts of success and effectiveness are more elaborate and extended than their definitions imply. Although presidential success will be discussed further in later chapters, it is enough to say here that most Americans would probably agree that the ultimate purpose of the presidency is to make things happen and that the truest measure of a president is the results secured. The more obvious and widely impressive the results, the greater the perceived success and the higher the public estimation of the president. Topping the polls generation after generation are presidents whose results were the most tangible, unarguable, and nationally significant. The much larger number of presidents in the middle and lower ranges of esteem are those whose achievements seem less impressive or are simply less apparent. Rankings of those in the middle ranges, such as Polk, Cleveland, Truman, and Eisenhower, show some instability from one historian's poll to another. The stock of particular presidents may rise or fall as new information, the greater perspective of time, or the revisionist interpretations of supportive biographers become available.

The instability of presidential rankings highlights certain problems with the concept of presidential success. Citizens must make their judgments in the here and now, often before all relevant data are gathered or perhaps understood. Later, with the benefit of hindsight, citizens are likely to judge differently. Implied is that the definition of successful results is subject to change. The difficulty stems from the fact that it is current judgments, not the later, more refined, and dispassionate variety, that govern the level of public support for the incumbent.

Another problem with the presidential success concept is that as a basis for comparison of one president's achievements with other presidents', it does not make adjustments for circumstances. This has bearing on anyone's conscious or unconscious use of presidential exemplars in contemporary evaluation. Essentially, absolute magnitude of a president's attainments is an unsophisticated barometer of presidential success because it takes no account of differences in the historical constraints and opportunities faced by each president. Needed is some basis for establishing the degree of comparability between presidents, so that assessment of their achievements can be adjusted for circumstances. Scholars have begun to posit stages or cycles of political development, each associated with a different characteristic mix of political limits and chances confronting the national leadership (Rockman 1984; Skowronek 1984; Hargrove and Nelson 1984; Barber 1980). Skowronek, for example, envisions American political history as a series of shifting "regime sequences," in which political coalitions emerge to gain control of national political machinery (regime construction), sustain control for some finite period (established regime maintenance), and eventually lose control to a rising coalition able to establish greater legitimacy (enervated regime). His categories enable him to ask: "How is the quality of presidential performance related to the changing shape of the political-institutional order?" (1984, 89). Answering the question leads to adjusted comparisons of presidents. Pierce and Carter, who faced enervated regimes, could not possibly have matched the achievements of Jackson and FDR, who enjoyed the special opportunities of regime construction. Thus, in comparing Jackson with Carter, for example, the question is not "What did each accomplish?" but "To what extent did each respond effectively to the circumstances he faced?" If historians' rankings were based on answers to questions like the last, the orderings would likely differ substantially from their present configuration.

Little evidence exists that the problems with the presidential success concept are perceived as such by most Americans or that these problems cause anyone much anguish. Efficacy in the form of successful results, despite potential confusion in definition and application, remains the fundamental performance expectation American citizens have of their president.

Notes

1. In the March 19, 1986, issue of the *National Journal* (p. 786), the average approval ratings for Presidents Kennedy through Carter, based on all years served, and the rating for Reagan, calculated through March 1986, were reported. Kennedy, the only pre-Vietnam, pre-Watergate president included, had an average of 70 percent. Johnson averaged 55 percent, Nixon 49 percent, Ford 46 percent, Carter 47 percent, and Reagan 52 percent. Even though Reagan had an approval rating of 63 percent in the March 1986 Gallup poll, which exceeded the approval ratings of such popular presidents as FDR and Eisenhower after five full years of service (both had about 60 percent support according to the January 28, 1986, *New York Times*), his average level of support still reflects post-Vietnam, post-Watergate trends.
2. Smoller and Moore-Fitzgerald employed focus group interview techniques to explore the evaluative attitudes of ten randomly selected Bloomington, Ind., citizens toward presidential performance. The discussion protocol is reproduced in their working paper, "Citizens Evaluate the President" (Department of Political Science, Indiana University, 1981, Photocopy). Copies of the paper and the transcript of the discussions can be obtained from Professor Fred Smoller, Department of Political Science, Chapman College, Orange, Calif. 92666. My content analysis of the material was impressionistic rather than systematic. I simply read the transcript carefully and noted the repetition of themes supportive of the tests described in the text. I used my own coding project, which involves the published writings of several columnists who focus on the presidency, in the same way. Although my coding scheme is designed to yield statistically representative generalizations about the evaluative criteria the columnists employ, its focus differs from that of this chapter. Thus, my use of the columnists' writings here is based less on my formal scheme than on the impressions about cultural expectations that took shape in my mind as I read and coded hundreds of their columns. For this reason I have not reproduced the scheme here, but it can be obtained from me at the Department of Government, University of Texas, Austin, Texas 78712.

3. Writing in the "Political Focus" column of the *National Journal* (February 1, 1986, p. 356), Ronald Brownstein argues that the Kennedy image may figure in the revitalization of the Democratic party in the post-Reagan era. Noting that Kennedy is replacing FDR as the principal hero in the Democratic pantheon and that the public now considers Kennedy the greatest American president, greater by ever-increasing margins than Lincoln or Roosevelt, Brownstein reports that the Democratic party's "sharper young leaders" see in the Kennedy image a model for the future. Kennedy challenged the nation to sacrifice for the greater good, while Reagan encouraged self-interest. Kennedy "exhorted America to get moving again, and excited it with a muscular style of government. But he ... didn't seem to be pushing a major expansion of government's role as Roosevelt did before him and Lyndon B. Johnson after. Instead he encouraged and challenged and inspired individual citizens to do the moving. It was positive, but not paternalistic, government." Resurrecting the Kennedy theme may be just the way to trump the appeal of Reagan-style Republican candidates who oppose big government.

CHAPTER 3

Human Nature:
The Psychology of
Choice and Judgment

What is it about human nature that affects how candidates and presidents are evaluated? What are the implications for improving choice and judgment? An oversimplified concept of human nature provides a straightforward understanding of the determinants of human perception and information processing—the mental procedures that drive choice and judgment. Human beings in general are depicted as simultaneously *cognitive, affective,* and *normative,* displaying mental (thinking, analysis, logic), emotional (feeling, sensing, intuition), and ideological (valuative, preferential, judgmental) orientations toward life experience. Labeling and defining the three features as discrete entities, however, risks overlooking their highly interactive qualities. They work in unison to influence the perception of external reality and the internal processing of information.

A more sophisticated model is needed here to organize what is known of how cognitive, affective, and normative tendencies interact to shape perception, information processing, and, ultimately, choice and judgment. The model should also serve as a convenient structure for making sense of what research has learned of how Americans evaluate their political leadership. A model that can serve these purposes is *schema theory,* an increasingly influential strand of cognitive psychology. Accounts of schema theory and research, findings from political science on the evaluative stances of citizens toward the presidency, and results of my original research will be used to support three arguments:

(1) Gaining accurate perceptions of candidate characteristics and presidential performance is difficult at best. As a result, the quality of the information registered by citizens about candidates and presidents is inevitably reduced. And the quality of evaluations based on that information is necessarily affected.

(2) Despite the lack of reliable information, evaluation must proceed. Strategies for minimizing distortion potentials involve efforts to integrate belief, emotion, cognition, and information. Such integration can be a workable means for dealing with personal tendencies that influence choice and judgment.

(3) A person's vision of the presidency—beliefs about what the presidency is for and how it works—can decisively affect the success of integration. Of the three visions of the presidency to be defined and illustrated, the pragmatic vision stands above the humane and potency visions as an evaluative stance most likely to facilitate integration.

Schematic Information Processing

How do people organize their thinking about candidates and presidents? How do they distinguish between acceptable and unacceptable candidates and between good, fair, and poor presidential performance? The prevailing wisdom in cognitive psychology holds that the building blocks of all such cognitions are schemas, the intelligence that selects and interprets the information that is admitted to the mind (Goleman 1985, 75). Information that becomes available to the senses is not indiscriminately registered and processed. Perception is selective—an internal editor somehow decides what data will be recognized and what meaning the data will have (James 1983; Bruner 1963; Cantril 1963).

Schema theory is the most recent, but by no means the first, effort to understand and describe the workings of the internal editor. Many of schema theory's central premises, emphases, and insights can be traced to the earliest psychological writings. But its language is current, increasingly influential, and easily understood.

Schemas emerge from the human need to make sense of the world and to guide behavior, despite the massive amount of available information and the threats such information might present. A schema can be thought of as "a kind of informal, private, unarticulated theory about the nature of events, objects, or situations which we face. The total set of schemas we have available for interpreting our world in a sense constitutes our private theory of the nature of reality" (Rumelhart 1978, 13). Schema theory

depicts comprehension as a process in which new information is interpreted in terms of prior knowledge [or preconceptions]. Understanding
is achieved by recognizing that new information represents a particular
instance of a more general type. The news that President Carter has
decided to invade Cuba, for example, may be interpreted by some as
simply one more instance of a Democrat stumbling into war. Understanding the particular event comes about through the elicitation of a
general interpretive framework, or schema. (Kinder, Fiske, and Wagner
1978, 18)

Given a task (such as choosing among presidential candidates or
evaluating presidential performance), a person uses schemas to quickly
distinguish relevant from irrelevant information, to notice the important information, to expand upon any portions of it that may be skimpy
or confused, and to select an appropriate strategy for completing the
task. Schemas cause the person less work by providing less information
to process—they, in effect, reduce the cost of assimilating information.
Schemas thus economize, simplify, clear up ambiguities by supplying
missing data necessary to comprehension, and furnish the valuative
criteria used both to select and to appraise information.

Although called cognitive structures, schemas and schematic processes simultaneously engage cognitive, affective, and normative dispositions. Put another way, schematic theories identify information as
relevant for reasons of emotion and belief as well as for reasons of logic.
That the theories are value-laden is made clear by the fact that they
edit external information and supply the criteria for judgment (Kinder,
Fiske, and Wagner 1978). And when relevant information has emotional
significance, it lends a special potency to the schema. "Such emotions as
fear," argues Daniel Goleman, "hyperactivate schemas, making them
compelling centers of attention. Our angers, sorrows, and joys capture
attention, sweep us away" (1985, 82).

Schema theory is useful here because it emphasizes the interactive-
ness of thinking, feeling, and believing, and the impact of this relationship on perceptions of reality. Thoughts stir feelings and beliefs; feelings
and beliefs guide thoughts; and together thoughts, feelings, and beliefs
affect the meaning of information. Schemas afford a more realistic
explanation for how citizens choose among candidates and judge presidents than can such concepts as beliefs, cognitions, opinions, feelings, or
perceptions taken alone.

Schemas accrue from the sum total of an individual's life experience. The schemas held by a person at any given point are formed by
that person's particular life history (Goleman 1985, 75). Because of
schemas, people display habitual modes of perceiving and interpreting
the noticed portions of the outside world. Schemas are also content-

specific, with a separate schema developed for each type of important experience, large or small.

Memories are stored in schemas—the contents of a person's long-term memory are revealed by an inventory of schemas (Goleman 1985, 79). They can thus be called up for aid in selecting and interpreting new information. Taylor and Crocker (1981, 92) argue that a schema can be described as a pyramidal structure, hierarchically organized, with abstract or general information at the top and specific information organized under the general categories. A schema for the presidency, for example, might contain general concepts of what the presidency is for and how it works, which are rooted in some mixture of factual information, political values, and expectations derived from past presidents. From these general concepts, concrete knowledge of presidents and their performances, based upon the individual's observations and experience, is organized. Confronted with a voting booth or an opinion pollster, the individual uses the schema for guidance in reaching a judgment about a candidate or president. The schema first identifies which portions of the stimulus configuration, in this case which candidate or performance characteristics, are important enough to be evaluated and, thus, noticed. It then supplies the evaluative criteria against which to measure the adequacy of the evidence selected for appraisal. The individual's subsequent judgment represents the product of a tacit comparison between activated parts of the schema and those portions of the stimulus configuration picked for evaluation.

The operation of schemas may sound like a deliberative, analytic process. To the contrary, it takes place in milliseconds not minutes, and largely outside awareness, below the level of consciousness. Daniel Goleman cites cognitive psychologist Emmanuel Donchin:

> The notion that information processing is largely pre-conscious or not available to awareness is so clear to me that it seems self-evident. There's a huge amount of evidence that when we encounter an event of any sort there's an enormous amount of very fast parallel processing among many multiple channels. These channels are activated in an obligatory fashion, without any conscious control. It goes on continually, with incredible rapidity.... Awareness is a limited capacity system. We don't know—and don't need to know—about most of the stuff the mind does.... Figuratively speaking, 99.9 percent of cognition may be unconscious. (1985, 73)

Of special importance here is the fact that schemas can be, and often are, wrong as guides to action, interpretations of reality, or explanations of behavior. The potential for error stems from the tendency of schemas toward simplification, which, while essential for dealing with complexity, necessarily sacrifices some of the more subtle and textured aspects of reality. In addition, people have a limited capacity for simultaneously paying attention to different pieces of information, only about six "bits" or "chunks" at one time. Long-term memory is large, but short-term attention span is very narrow (Simon 1985, 302). Furthermore, mistakes can be expected because humans are not neutral information-processing machines and because schemas serve not only to explain the world but also to defend egos and express values (Katz 1963).

Several findings particularly relevant to the appraisal of leaders indicate the possibility of distortion in information processing. For example, people tend to concentrate on data that support their previously held positions, while screening out arguments that challenge them (Kinder, Fiske, and Wagner 1978). Also, citizens misperceive stands taken by leaders on policy issues in ways that reinforce and support their own views (Page and Brody 1972). Other human proclivities that can result in misrepresentation of information include the tendency to focus on that which is unambiguous (Fiske 1980); extreme or intense (for example, flashy political advertising; see Tversky 1977); or especially salient to personally important values or symbols (Kinder, Fiske, and Wagner 1978). A body of research guided by attribution theory (Kelley 1973) has uncovered various systematic tendencies toward error in the comprehension and interpretation of information. Attributions of abilities, opinions, and responsibility for outcomes to others are supported by evidence that is vivid, concrete, emotionally or symbolically interesting, and consistent with preconceptions. Rational or scientific evidence like statistics, facts, and figures tends to be ignored (Nisbett and Ross 1980). In addition, the actor usually outweighs the situation when information involving both is evaluated (Jones and Nisbett 1971; Ross 1977). Thus, in the assignment of praise or blame to presidents, strength of character and level of competence are likely to figure more prominently in evaluative conclusions than any mitigating circumstances, whether justified by the facts or not.

Schemas also are resistant to change and are seldom overturned by mere evidence alone (Nisbett and Ross 1980). Still, schemas are susceptible to revision. In a sense, they are theories that test themselves for goodness of fit with the external reality (Goleman 1985, 76). A schema that fails will be revised, assuming accuracy matters and inaccuracy entails too many costs.

Like other schemas, presidency schemas work to reinforce preconceptions, affirm personal interests and values, and express strongly held feelings as much as they do to register and process information as accurately as necessary. For most people, invalid presidency schemas inflict few meaningful penalties; valid ones, few significant rewards. Distorted presidency schemas can provide important psychic returns—the pleasure, satisfaction, or confirmation a person gets from interpreting an external event a certain way. For example, the doctrinaire ideologue's assessments of presidents must remain undisturbed by disconfirming evidence or cherished values will be contradicted.

For those who wish to minimize the potential for distortions in information processing or to exert some conscious choice over distortions, simply being aware of the unconscious tendencies humans have to misperceive represents a step in the right direction. A more aggressive strategy is to scrutinize tacit theories of the presidency—to ask what classes of information are stressed, ignored, created, or distorted, and why. Despite the preconscious manner in which schemas actually process information, large chunks of their contents can be exposed. Humans are, after all, capable of examining their behavior for what it implies about their thinking. They can also reflect on patterns of attention, feelings, and beliefs with some degree of objectivity. As a result, the human condition can be improved, and alternative understandings of the presidency are worth discussing.

Three alternative models or visions of what the presidency is for and how it works will be presented later in this chapter. How a person conceives of the mission of the presidency—what its purposes are and how they should be sought—fundamentally orients that person toward who can and who should be president, as well as toward concepts of effective or acceptable presidential performance. In schema theory parlance, an individual's interpretation of the presidency is the organizing principle of the individual's tacit theory, which identifies the categories of information important enough to notice and evaluate. A vision of the presidency blends cognitive, affective, and normative dispositions into a unique stance toward presidential choice and judgment.

Before considering the alternative visions, however, what political science has learned of how Americans evaluate candidates and presidents must be reviewed.

The Presidency in the Public Mind

According to Donald R. Kinder and Susan T. Fiske (1986, 209), a fully adequate description of "what Americans are doing when they appraise their president" has yet to be attained. The store of knowledge about the place of the presidency in the public mind is remarkably limited. The following review of scholarly literature is not exhaustive but does fairly represent the fragmented and preliminary state of learning on the subject.

Aggregate survey research (Mueller 1973; Stimson 1976; Brody and Page 1975; Kernell 1978), which has been concerned with accounting for rises and falls in public support for presidents, has yet to agree on an explanation, although Fiorina (1981) and Kernell (1978) offer strong evidence that presidential performance in such areas as peace, prosperity, and civil rights are important determinants. On the basis of an empirical investigation of a model of their own devising (the "promise and performance" model), Ostrom and Simon have shown that "public assessments of presidential performance are anchored in the real world; that is, approval of the president depends upon the quality of social, economic, and international outcomes experienced by the public" (1985, 354). They found not only that peace, prosperity, and presidential integrity influence the level of public support, but also that a president's legislative performance and actions toward the Soviet Union had an impact.

Ostrom and Simon's research also demonstrated that "the manner in which outcomes influence public support will depend upon the prevailing concerns and attitudes of the public," which are driven, at least in part, by the content and tone of media coverage (1985, 355). Change in public support corresponds to the degree to which public attention is focused, by media emphasis and other influences, on presidential performance in a given area.

Voting behavior literature concludes that citizens' decisions on who to support and who to vote for rely, to a significant extent, on party identification, group affiliations, and candidate positions on policy questions (Kinder 1982; Asher 1983; Converse 1975). Recent study in voting behavior suggests that incumbent candidates have been judged by voters primarily on the basis of retrospective performance, challengers to incumbents on prospective policy promises, and candidates running in nonincumbent races on probable future performance (Miller and Wattenberg 1985).

Political behavior research investigates various influences—time, events, candidate identities—on citizens' evaluations of incumbent and prospective leaders. Certain enduring concepts of what presidents should be like have been identified: they should be competent, trustworthy, and reliable (Miller, Wattenberg, and Malanchuk 1982; Kinder, Peters, Abelson, and Fiske 1980; Kinder and Abelson 1981). One study discovered that knowing a candidate's identity changed the priority of criteria citizens used to assess suitability for office (Kinder and Abelson 1981). Different candidates were judged differently according to who they were. Other research has shown that political events may alter citizens' perceptions of candidates (Lazarus 1982) and that television news content and order of presentation can affect citizens' judgments of specific situations (Iyengar, Peters, and Kinder 1982). The findings concerning media coverage are consistent with those of Ostrom and Simon (1985).

Gallup polls occasionally ask random national samples of Americans to identify their expectations of the presidency and presidents. A 1979 poll found that a majority of the public invested the major responsibility for policy making in the presidency, not Congress. Citizens said they prefer presidents who display strong leadership and forcefulness in office. Inspiring confidence and solving policy problems also are important (Edwards 1983; Wayne 1982).

Although various research traditions within political science have addressed related issues, no comprehensive, systematic effort has been made to explicate the place of the presidency as an object of evaluation in the public mind. If descriptions of alternative visions of the presidency are to be based on evidence and not conjecture, information is required that has yet to be assembled. For example, an understanding is needed of how people mentally classify presidential performance for purposes of evaluation. According to aggregate survey research, citizens are most concerned about presidential actions in the broad categories of peace, prosperity, civil rights, and integrity. Whether other areas of concern exist or how people define and organize their expectations within these categories has not been determined.

To appraise the facility with which alternative presidency visions integrate the components of human nature, information is needed on the interplay between thinking, feeling, and believing as they pertain to the evaluation of candidates and presidents. Again, only inference is possible, for no study has yet directly investigated the matter.

To define the alternatives in ways that reflect how informed citizens differ in their understandings of the presidency, data must be gathered about how significant differences are distributed among citizens. Most political science research, however, treats the public as an homogeneous mass; "it is assumed that all citizens have similar expectations about presidential performance and hold the president responsible for the same outcomes" (Ostrom and Simon 1985, 338). Apart from a handful of studies that distinguish citizens by party identification, the general public has yet to be divided into "theoretically meaningful" groups for study (Zukin and Carter 1982, 220).

Because the territory remains largely unmapped, I must rely primarily on some exploratory research of my own. Although my study is too limited to be considered the last word, it can serve here to frame some important choices that reflective citizens must consider.

New Research: The Patterns of Judgment

Visions of the presidency are not schemas. Instead, they can be thought of as representing the conceptual architecture of presidency schemas in that they point to the categories and hierarchies of importance to the internal editor. The descriptions of visions are based on responses to questionnaires that cannot directly tap the dynamic, intricate, largely unconscious workings of the mind that schematic processing represents. Questionnaire responses are snapshots, not movies.

The questionnaire used in my study measures what people acknowledge to be their grounds, or reasons, for judging presidents. The limitations of the questionnaire, however, permit only one measure of people's cognitive and normative dispositions toward presidential performance in general.

The affective or emotional component of judgment is not addressed. The items on the questionnaire are worded to refer to hypothetical and general, instead of genuine and specific, circumstances. They therefore lack the kind of realism that usually evokes emotional response: reactions to specific events and to the personality of the president engaged in events. The questionnaire results may not predict, and at times may prove to be inconsistent with, the responses the study's participants would give to actual instances of presidential performance, especially under conditions of emotional arousal.

Most existing research on public stances toward the presidency reveals very little about the dynamics underlying emotional reactions to the presidency, or anything else for that matter (Clarke and Fiske 1982). Although cognitive psychologists almost unanimously agree that cognition and emotion are intimately tied, they continue to debate the exact relationship between the two (Goleman 1985, 81). The connection between beliefs and emotion has also received little explicit research attention.

Evidence suggests that the presidency has emotional significance for most Americans. Conclusions about the role played by emotion have been drawn from public reactions to presidents and events and will be made from the questionnaire results. But the inferences should be recognized for what they are: speculative. No one has yet reached a complete understanding of emotion, the most significant determinant of choice and judgment.

Following is a description of the study I conducted: the research objectives, the questionnaire, the respondents, and the statistical techniques used to analyze responses and identify presidency visions. For further detail, see Appendix 1.

Research Objectives. In light of the fragmentation of information that exists about how people conceptualize the presidency for purposes of judging presidential performance, one important aim was to devise a way to get an overview of the grounds for judging presidents and the categories of presidential performance into which they fall. The structure of judgment exposes the way people mentally classify performance into categories they deem important enough to evaluate. Another aim was to learn of the contents within each of these categories, to probe for any subtlety, nuance, or complexity that might characterize the specific expectations people had.

The stated research objectives made it impossible to use data gathered by the Gallup Organization or by survey research centers at colleges and universities, which use standardized questionnaires designed with other purposes in mind. The questionnaires are administered to randomly selected national samples of citizens, and the responses are statistically representative of the population at large, which is a tremendous advantage. But such surveys neither ask enough questions about the presidency in particular nor pose questions in a way that sheds light on the structure and content issues of concern here. I was thus forced to design my own questionnaire and to generate my own sample of respondents.

The Questionnaire. To allow respondents to, in effect, define their own categories for judging presidents and to allow me to probe for details on the specific expectations within their categories, I had to ask many questions—enough so that the respondents' freedom to reveal their categories and expectations was not restricted by too small a selection of response opportunities. Accordingly, the original questionnaire contained 72 questions.

The questions were composed with the help of a theoretical structure, or model, culled from the scholarly and journalistic literature on the presidency that identified, in the broadest and most comprehensive terms possible, the traditional categories for judging presidential performance. For the respondents to define categories and identify expectations that would be truly their own and not merely selections from a limited number of choices, they would have to be presented with virtually all of the significant categories and expectations of presidential performance. Their responses would tell which of the options were important to them.

The response format of the questions was forced-choice. The layout of the questions looked like this:

I judge a president's competence by the extent to which:
strongly agree : : : : : : : : strongly disagree

The Respondents. Given the exploratory nature of the research and the developmental status of the questionnaire, it was logical to rely upon a small, statistically unrepresentative, and easily accessible sample of respondents, not a large, expensive, and random national sample. Two hundred four undergraduate students of American government, nearing completion of required introductory courses, served as the questionnaire's respondents. While younger and better educated than the mass public, this group does possess sufficient demographic, political, and ideological diversity to make any extreme distortion of the results unlikely.

The sample obviously does not represent the American electorate. But it is, in one respect, better suited for purposes here than a sample of the mass public would be. The students possess greater than average familiarity with the presidency, probably have reflected on the nature and requirements of presidential competence, and are characteristic of attentive subpublics, which pay some attention to politics and are thus likely to exert disproportionate influence on the purpose of governmental institutions and on the fate of political leaders. To a greater extent than can be presumed of the general public, attentive subpublics are likely to have reasonably well-developed visions of the presidency and are likely to profit from consideration of alternative visions. The students' responses tell something of the shape and nature of the alternatives.

Statistical Techniques. A mathematical technique called factor analysis was used to determine which of the 72 performance expectations were important to the respondents and how the important expectations clustered into patterns representing categories of presidential performance. Factor analysis is based on the correlation coefficients between the questionnaire items. Using a matrix of the correlations, factor analysis identifies those items that tend to hang together strongly enough to make up distinct, interpretable factors. Patterns of responses to the questions are established.

Factor analysis also identifies the strength of the association a particular item has with the factor on which it appears—an item's factor loading. Items that do not load strongly on one factor or another add nothing to the understanding of response patterns and can thus be safely ignored. Factor loading determines which items go together to make up a category and which do not. Weakly loaded items were eliminated from the analysis, leaving just 35 of the original 72 questions. Each of the surviving questions received an average ranking of three or higher on the response format, where a ranking of one indicates great importance; four, indifference; and seven, little importance. All surviving questions identify performance expectations that are important to a majority of the respondents.

Nine factor patterns of three to five items emerged. Implied is that, for the students who participated, the presidency is divided into nine performance categories, each containing several specific performance expectations. For purposes here, the most interesting results are found by comparing the relative importance of each of the nine performance categories with different subgroupings of the 204 students. What came forth is information about how informed citizens differ in their understandings of the presidency—the source of the descriptions of contrasting visions of the presidency.

Respondents were asked to provide standard demographic data about themselves (age, sex, party identification) and information concerning fundamental life values and self-described ideology with respect to domestic, economic, and foreign policy. The intention was to see if any characteristics were related to different understandings of the presidency. More precisely, the aim was to determine which, if any, individual differences were associated with significant differences in the priorities of importance assigned to the nine categories. Different priorities give evidence of different understandings.

Priority of importance was defined by the average item ranking within each category—the higher the ranking, the more important the category. I expected to find that party identification would be associated with the greatest differences in importance. I was surprised to discover instead that the greatest number of statistically significant group differences and the most striking discrepancies in category rankings occurred between subgroups who described themselves as liberals, moderates, or conservatives in all three policy areas. For the rankings of the nine categories for each ideology subgroup, see Table 3-1.

Words like *liberal* or *conservative* are touchy, controversial labels whose meanings are imprecise and unstable, changing with shifts in the political winds. For these reasons, I would have preferred to avoid their use. But for the sample of respondents, political ideology more than anything else distinguished evaluative priorities. Therefore, political

Table 3-1 Liberal, Moderate, and Conservative Rankings
of Presidential Performance Categories

Performance Category	Policy Liberals (N=86)	Policy Conservatives (N=89)	Policy Moderates (N=29)
General policy quality	3	1	4
General policy results	2	3	2
Crisis management	4	2	1
World peace	1	8	3
Economic flexibility and fairness	5	7	5
Political leadership	6	4	7
Economic policy consistency	8	5	6
Foreign policy potency	9	6	8
Domestic policy agreement	7	9	9

ideology will underlie the discussion of contrasting visions of the presidency.

Three Visions of the Presidency

The liberal, conservative, and moderate subgroups generally agree about the purposes of the presidency: to contend with issues of peace and war, to foster economic well-being, to promote domestic tranquillity, to provide leadership, and to formulate sound and effective policies. The respondents' concerns are with the sorts of things that give rise to the fears the presidency emerged to quell. Each subgroup considers all nine performance categories to be more than a little important.

Although, for example, policy liberals find foreign policy potency significant and policy conservatives acknowledge the importance of world peace, the different priority given to each of these categories is striking and reveals a fundamental distinction in how the subgroups expect the president to contend with peace and war issues. All give fairly high priority to the categories of general policy results, general policy quality, and crisis management, which is further evidence of agreement on what the presidency is for. But the questionnaire items within these particular performance categories are worded generally enough to mask sharply divergent group beliefs concerning how best to achieve policy results, what constitutes a quality foreign or economic policy, or how crises can most effectively be averted or managed. The rankings of the other categories, which contain questions specifically worded to include methods as well as broad aims, make plain the different beliefs. Disagreement over the ends of the presidency does not distinguish the visions of the liberal, conservative, and moderate subgroups (or other groups of Americans) from one another, but preferred means and symbolic tones, which can be inferred from rank-order priorities, do. The rankings given by each group to the nine categories reveal just how different the concepts are that they hold of appropriate priorities and strategies for using presidential resources. The results are contrasting visions of the presidency.

Policy Liberals: The Humane Presidency

For liberals, who in 1983 comprised approximately 18 percent of the national electorate, the best president is able to contribute to a pacific international climate in which the tensions between the United States and the Soviet Union are kept to a minimum, uses little or no military power, and is known as a spokesman for human rights. World peace is the first priority for liberals, and a high-quality foreign policy is one that encourages a peaceful international atmosphere and de-emphasizes U.S. strength and potency.

Liberals' rankings of foreign and economic policies suggest that they generally play down the importance of toughness, strength, perseverance, and dominance as strategies of presidential leadership. General policy results, which emphasizes economic outcomes, is rated number two. Liberals, like moderates and conservatives, want such economic indicators as inflation and unemployment improved, but their rankings of two other categories with economic policy content show that they prefer distinctly different solutions to economic problems.

Economic flexibility and fairness is ranked substantially higher than economic policy consistency. The flexibility category includes such statements as "he stands up to powerful economic interests to help people who have less" and "he adjusts his policies to changing economic conditions," while the consistency category stresses the importance of "staying the course" by adhering to policies promised in the campaign. Liberals recognize the need for both flexibility and consistency, as presidents struggle to strike a balance between the shifting polarities created by events and circumstances, but their priorites make their preferences clear. Whether because of normative commitment or a cognitive conviction that it is the surest route to economic results, liberals prefer a flexible policy, tilted slightly to the advantage of mass rather than elite interests.

The relative position of two evaluative categories that stress presidential assertiveness further underscores the liberal vision of a humanist presidency. Foreign policy potency, which enjoins the president to seek to dominate world affairs by using strength, ranks last. Political leadership, which requires presidential forcefulness on the domestic front, ranks sixth. Furthermore, the domestic policy agreement category, which requires the president to support and promote the values of the respondent, outranks foreign policy potency and is about on a par with political leadership. For liberals, the extent to which a president maintains respect for America's power in the world is simply less important than the extent to which they agree with the values implicit in a president's domestic policies. And that the president's values agree with theirs is almost as important to liberals as that the president be able to get those values implemented in the form of policies. In ways not true of moderate or conservatives, values matter to liberals. Though they acknowledge that strength and dominance have a place in the presidency, liberals prefer presidents who are flexible and responsive in tone and who use power and potency as last resorts. Though the presidency must sometimes contend forcefully with unpleasant realities, its primary purpose is to uplift and to nurture conciliatory, humane values.

Jimmy Carter

President Jimmy Carter, in his inaugural address, said:

> Our commitment to human rights must be absolute, our laws fair, our national beauty preserved; the powerful must not persecute the weak and human dignity must be enhanced. . . . We pledge perseverance and wisdom in our efforts to limit the world's armaments to those necessary for each nation's own domestic safety. . . . Our nation can be strong abroad only if it is strong at home, and we know that the best way to enhance freedom in other lands is to demonstrate here that our democratic system is worthy of emulation . . . [our strength is] a quiet strength based not merely on the size of an arsenal but on the nobility of ideas . . . We will fight our wars against poverty, ignorance and injustice, for those are the enemies against which our forces can be honorably marshalled. We are a proudly idealistic nation, but let no one confuse our idealism with weakness. (Carter 1982, 20-21)

Carter's use of the presidency and his self-presentation reflect the liberal vision as accurately as does his inaugural rhetoric. Despite a reputation for "excessive tactical flexibility" (Brzezinski 1983, 23), a self-description as a "fiscal conservative" (Carter 1982, 74), and a decision late in his term to press for domestic budget cuts and defense spending increases, Carter emphasized in words and in policy the priorities of the policy liberals. The primacy of world peace is reflected in the human rights theme of his foreign policy and in the specific achievements—the Camp David accords, normalization of relations with China, and the Panama Canal treaties—of which he is most proud. Carter also implied the importance of peace when he said: "Our failure to ratify the SALT II treaty and to secure even more far-reaching agreements on nuclear arms control was the most profound disappointment of my Presidency" (1982, 265).

Conservatives and moderates were sharply critical of what they perceived as Carter's naiveté, as evidenced by his admission that he had misunderstood the true nature of Soviet motivation prior to the invasion of Afghanistan and by his reference, in a 1980 debate with Ronald Reagan, to daughter Amy's concern about nuclear weapons. But Carter explicitly rejected the conservative world view and revealed his liberal vision:

> Instead of promoting freedom and democratic principles, our [pre-1976] government seemed to believe that in any struggle with evil, we could not compete effectively unless we played by the same rules or lack of rules as the evildoers. . . . I was familiar with the widely accepted arguments that we had to choose between idealism and realism, or between morality and the exertion of power; but I rejected those claims. To me, the demonstration of American idealism was a practical and realistic approach to foreign affairs, and moral principles were the best foundation for the exertion of American power and influence. (1982, 142-143)

Carter no less faithfully evinced the liberal subgroups' predilections toward domestic and economic policy. His initial attack on joblessness, soon followed by an abrupt shift to an anti-inflation emphasis, demonstrated flexibility to the point of widely perceived inconsistency, as Carter himself acknowledges. His failure to win congressional approval for such classic liberal priorities as welfare, tax reform, and a national health program were a "great disappointment" to him (1982, 84). His belief that he was, like Woodrow Wilson, "taking office at a time when Americans desired a return to first principles by their government" (1982, 59) and his display of nonimperial, democratic symbolism in the tradition of Thomas Jefferson also evoke the liberal ethos.

Carter's religious beliefs were a key factor in his self-presentation. By all accounts, they were genuine and ran much deeper than mere political posturing. In his memoirs, Zbigniew Brzezinski, Carter's national security adviser, recounts his difficulties in persuading Carter to leaven principle with sensitivity to the realities of power politics. Brzezinski describes a conversation he had with Pope John Paul II, which offers a glimpse of Carter's presidential self-image. Said the Pope: "You know, after a couple of hours with President Carter, I had the feeling that two religious leaders were conversing" (1983, 27).

Carter's estrangement from the establishment of the Democratic party, his espousal of such conservative issues as budget balancing and governmental efficiency, and his image as a technician with few clear priorities and little sense of history led members of the traditional New Deal-Great Society liberal democratic coalition to reject him (Leuchtenburg 1983). They would dispute his classification as a liberal. The label here, however, refers to a mode of interpreting the presidency as an instrument for use and as an object of evaluation, not to membership in a specific American political tradition.

Carter is the strongest advocate in recent history of the policy liberals' priorities. As the title of his memoirs implies, Carter found comfort in the face of the trials of his presidency by "keeping faith." He elaborates on his philosophy and describes the liberal vision in the following passage:

> For each of us there are focal points for our political faith—either the resilience of our diverse peoples, the wisdom of the Constitution and its derivative laws and customs, the national spirit of hope and confidence that has shaped our history, or the unchanging religious and moral principles that have always been there to guide America on its course. Sometimes we forget, and even deviate radically from our nation's historic path. But we soon remember the advantages of compassion for the weak, ethical standards, the beauty of our land, peace and human rights, the potential quality of our children's lives, and the strength we derive from one another as a free people—unfettered except by self-imposed limits. Then we are able to correct our mistakes, repair what we have damaged, and move on to better days. (1982, 89-90)

Policy Conservatives: The Potent Presidency

Conservatives, 36 percent of the electorate in 1983, show by their rankings that they interpret the presidency primarily as an instrument of power, not as a beacon of democratic inspiration. The ethos is Realpolitik, the intellectual "godfather" is Machiavelli, and the mode is "hardball." The performance category ranked highest by conservatives is general policy quality, which requires the president to have a "clear, well thought out approach to solving the nation's domestic problems," to "appoint domestic advisers who know what they are doing," and to have "a well-developed, long-term foreign policy design." The preeminence of this performance category suggests that conservatives want, above all else, to feel confident that the president is competent and is acting with a sense of purpose.

Placing crisis management second in priority implies the importance to conservatives of protecting life, liberty, and property. A president who puts great weight on moral idealism to preserve these basic rights makes conservatives uncomfortable. To them, power and self-interest, not altruism, govern the behavior of individuals, groups, and nations. The real world may occasionally be inspired by idealistic rhetoric, but it ultimately respects only power. The safety and security of the United States can only be protected by a president who is able to muster and discipline power to serve carefully wrought plans to advance the country's interests.

Like liberals and moderates, conservatives expect economic results, but they believe the path to desirable outcomes requires more strength and persistence than accommodation and flexibility. The potency theme is strongly demonstrated in the order of conservative priorities below the top three performance categories. For example, economic policy consistency is placed above economic flexibility and fairness, and political leadership—the ability to "take charge of the government"—is the fourth-ranking performance test. Conservatives believe a president must set a clear-cut course and stick to it, deviating only for strong cause. They prefer a president who creates a competitive power advantage at home and abroad over one who displays domestic flexibility and fairness or nurtures a pacific international climate by stressing the moral basis of American foreign policy. Political dominance is much more important than adherence to conservative ideology on domestic questions. As a result, policy conservatives can be described as less ideological than policy liberals. Conservatives want to respect the presidency rather than be inspired by it. And the feeling of respect is brought on not by doctrinal purity but by strategic savvy and successful cultivation of power, which define the conservative vision of the presidency.

Richard Nixon

The presidential prototype for the conservative vision is Richard Nixon. His published writings, including his presidential memoirs (1978), *The Real War* (1980b), *Leaders* (1982), *Real Peace* (1983), and *No More Vietnams* (1985), set forth this vision in elaborate detail. His desire to be taken as "a serious man," his protestation that a president is better off being respected than loved, his distrust and visceral distaste for "trendy" idealism, his cultivation of "cold, impersonal calculation" and strategic craftiness, his elevation of analysis over emotion, his penchant for the unexpected "bold stroke" that maximizes competitive advantage and strikes awe and respect in onlookers, all echo the vision revealed by the conservatives' rankings of the performance categories.

In *Leaders*, Nixon quotes from Max Lerner's introduction to an edition of Machiavelli's works and agrees with what Lerner says:

[We] still shudder slightly at Machiavelli's name [because] of our recognition that the realities he described are realities; that men, whether in politics, in business or in private life, do not act according to their professions of virtue. . . . Machiavelli today confronts us with the major dilemma of how to adapt our democratic techniques and concepts to the demands of a world in which as never before naked power politics dominates the foreign field and determined oligarchies struggle for power internally. Let us be clear about one thing: ideals and ethics are important in politics as norms, but they are scarcely effective as techniques. The successful statesman is an artist, concerned with the nuances of public mood, approximations of operative modes, guesswork as to the tactics of his opponents, back-breaking work in unifying his own side by compromise and concession. Religious reformers have often succeeded in bringing public morale closer to some ethical norm; they have never succeeded as statesmen. (1982, 327)

Not only Nixon's philosophy, but also his presidency, mirror the priorities, themes, and tones implicit in the conservative rankings. The predominant objective of the Nixon modus operandi was control. Nixon sought control of events by carefully constructing "game plans." Winning required "policy quality" (White 1975; Safire 1975; Kissinger 1979).

Best known is the foreign policy grand design reflected in his choice of conceptual strategist Henry Kissinger as his national security adviser. Nixon's unprecedented Annual Foreign Policy Reports contained "a conceptual outline of the President's foreign policy, as a status report, and as an agenda for action" (Kissinger 1979, 158). Equally thorough plans were drawn for everything from structuring the president's time so that he could save himself for the "big plays" to coping with the press and handling other public relations problems (White 1975, 154) to controlling the federal bureaucracy, a brilliant scheme that, but for Watergate, might have imposed unprecedented political discipline on that vast machinery (Nathan 1983, 43-56).

Nixon's fondness for aggressive and potent presidential leadership is legion. Domestic and international political dominance were among the highest priorities for his administration. Nixon gave an inkling of his principle of leadership during an interview with William Safire. In response to Safire's question, "What motivates people?", Nixon said, "People react to fear, not love—they don't teach that in Sunday school, but it's true" (Safire 1975, 8). In *The Real War,* Nixon offers his rationale for foreign policy potency:

Americans prefer to conduct their peacetime contests in the international arena by Marquis of Queensberry rules. For the Soviet leaders, however, the same rules apply in peace as in war, and those are the rules of the street-fighter: anything goes. To meet their challenge

> the American President must use all the power at his command in an
> effective and responsible way. . . . This requires that he think realisti-
> cally, not naively; that he never give our adversaries something they
> want unless he gets from them something we want; and finally that he
> accept the reality that moral perfection in the conduct of nations
> cannot be expected and should not be demanded. . . . He needs to know
> how power operates, and he must have the will to use it. (1980b, 249)

Many doctrinaire conservatives felt that Nixon betrayed conservative ideology in certain respects, particularly in seeking détente with the
Soviet Union and rapprochement with the People's Republic of China.
Like Carter, Nixon was no doctrinal purist, and he could not pass the
litmus test of correct positions on specific policy questions. But take his
conservatism as a state of mind and as a way of viewing the presidency,
and Richard Nixon comes closer to epitomizing conservative priorities
than even Ronald Reagan. Both domestically and internationally, Nixon
played hardball as president, basing well thought out and potent policies on cold hard facts. For policy conservatives, Nixon acted in the only
credible way a president could to succeed in the real world.

Policy Moderates: The Pragmatic Presidency

The conservative vision of the presidency clearly contains elements
of pragmatism, but that is not its dominant tone. The juxtaposing of
conservative priorities implies a certain emotional undercurrent, a nagging fear of seeming weak, a sense that any impulses toward empathy or
softness suggest weakness and must thus be ruthlessly disciplined and
controlled.

Conservatives' rankings of performance categories with items that
imply empathy, sympathy, or responsiveness—such as economic flexibility and fairness, world peace, and domestic policy agreement—rank
last. For conservatives, a president must, in Nixon's words, "bring to his
work a cold, impersonal calculation" that would be inconsistent with the
emphasis of such sentiments.

Liberals, too, betray an emotional investment in the presidency, not
only by their passion for human rights and their empathy for the
underprivileged, but also by placing morality above potency as criteria
for judging presidential performance.

Policy moderates, who were a plurality of the American electorate
in 1983 (40 percent), show little interest in sentiment. Indeed, their
distinguishing characteristic is a certain degree of emotional detachment from either the idealism or the potency totems of the presidency.
Moderates stress final outcomes and are more open to experimentation
with alternative ways to achieve them. Following is a description of
pragmatic philosophy:

[Pragmatism] was an attempt to apply the scientific method to the perennial questions of philosophy. The pragmatist does not merely believe his ideas are right in the manner of an ideologue; he tests them by their consequences. If the consequences are other than those predicted by his ideas, he changes his ideas accordingly. He is saved not by belief but by works. His motto is: by their fruits shall ye know them. (Beatty 1982, 12)

In their rankings, moderates differ more sharply from conservatives than from liberals, but their priorities imply something other than simply a mixture of liberal and conservative perspectives. The top choice of moderates is crisis management, with items such as "he heads off conflict before it becomes dangerous" and "he considers alternatives carefully and does not take unnecessary risks," which erect prudence and caution as preeminent tests of the presidential mettle. Moderates, not particularly impressed by shows of potency or empathy, gave low priority to both power and ideology performance categories. Their vision is pragmatic and suggests a presidency that limits the emergence or expansion of undesirable consequences.

Moderates require less evidence of dominant leadership than conservatives and less evidence of humane concern than liberals. To avoid or control international crises, pragmatists believe it is wiser to seek an atmosphere of peace than to use force. To achieve economic and other policy results, moderates display a slight preference for flexibility over consistency; they rank economic flexibility and fairness fifth and economic policy consistency sixth. The close rankings, however, demonstrate a willingness to alternate between the options as circumstances may dictate.

Like liberals, moderates give low priority to such assertiveness categories as political leadership, foreign policy potency, and economic policy consistency. Like conservatives, they care least about whether the president articulates a domestic policy with which they are in ideological agreement. For moderates, displays of high moral purpose (important to liberals) and of toughness and decisiveness (important to conservatives) are not high priorities, unless they are needed to accomplish a goal. Avoiding disasters and getting results, primarily by means of presidential prudence and flexibility, are the top priorities. The moderate vision of the presidency is low-key, almost passionless.

John F. Kennedy

The mindset, if not always the performance, of the pragmatic presidency finds its clearest recent expression in the administration of John F. Kennedy. This is ironic, for Kennedy has been described as a confrontational cold warrior who went conservative hard-liners one better and as the epitome of the charismatic liberal president. His memory continues to touch and inspire people all over the world, and in a 1979 poll the American public rated him the greatest president in American history (Martin 1983, 574). For all this public acclaim, Kennedy is much less impressive to revisionist historians and political scientists (see Wills 1982). One critic brands him a belligerent cold war ideologue who was especially dangerous for disclaiming any ideology and affecting a detached pragmatism (Miroff 1976). But whatever Kennedy truly was or did, existing descriptions of his behind-the-scenes presidential style and his personal outlook represent the moderate, pragmatic vision of the presidency recounted here.

In their multigenerational biography of the Kennedy family, Peter Collier and David Horowitz describe John Kennedy's political outlook as he sought the Democratic presidential nomination:

> He was pragmatic, testing the limits, but not getting caught on any limb of commitment that might be sawed off from behind. In the same way that he hated to wear hats, which, although part of a time-honored political uniform, he felt didn't "fit" him, he was wary of stepping into any programmatic political philosophy that might not become him. While he had gotten free from the conservative identity his father tried to force on him, he was not much changed from the newly elected Senator who told an interviewer of having gotten letters from Massachusetts constituents chiding him for not being a "true liberal" and said, "I'd be very happy to tell them that I'm not a liberal at all." The identity he embraced had less to do with political ideas than with political sensibility. "I'm a realist," he said to the reporter when pressed for a label. (1985, 291)

Biographer Ralph G. Martin says Kennedy was a "man without much obvious passion" who preferred "facts, unadorned and objective" and who avoided "abstractions, kept clear of political theory, and used ideas only as tools." Kennedy did not change once installed in the presidency. For example, when Henry Kissinger spoke to him of the need for "conceptual schemes" of foreign policy, Kennedy was unable to keep his attention on the matter. Kennedy considered himself neither an intellectual nor a liberal. According to Martin, he was, instead, "the classic pragmatist. He valued ideas only if they promised results" (1983, 304).

Events such as the Bay of Pigs, the Cuban Missile Crisis, and racial conflict in the South forced crisis management to the top of Kennedy's list of priorities. Following the Bay of Pigs disaster, he installed a cautious decision-making system, based on written expressions of decision options, in which haste was avoided and advice sought from low-

level functionaries to cabinet officers. But Kennedy shunned the counsel of those who were too ideological, too earnest, too emotional, and too
talkative. Like Nixon, he distrusted emotion. Unlike Nixon, with whom
one senses a fear of opening the floodgates, Kennedy gave the impression of having a matter-of-fact desire to keep from distorting reality. His
cautious approach to the presidency is illustrated by his reaction to
advice that he follow Truman's example of rousing the people's ire
against Congress to get his legislative proposals moving. Said Kennedy:
"There is no sense in raising hell and then not being successful. There is
no sense of putting the Office of the President on the line of an issue,
and then being defeated" (Martin 1983, 367). It also went against
Kennedy's grain to engage in "emotional begging, pushing and fighting
for votes in Congress" in the manner of Lyndon Johnson or Ronald
Reagan (Martin 1983, 367).

Kennedy was as low-key in victory as in defeat. After the successful
resolution of the Cuban Missile Crisis, he was exhorted by aides to make
a televised speech claiming credit for deflecting the Soviet challenge.
Kennedy's response: "Khrushchev has eaten enough crow. Let's not rub
it in." As for the national euphoria that followed the relaxation of
tension caused by the confrontation, he commented, "That will wear off
in about a week" (Martin 1983, 471).

Devoid of hatred, skeptical of idealism and self-righteousness, un-
impressed by pomp, tending toward mockery of his overhyped charisma,
possessed of a wry sense of humor, and capable of criticizing his own
performance, Kennedy is said to have never gotten carried away by
anything in his life. Despite the very different impressions he made in
the minds of admirers and critics, the man behind the symbol was, by
all accounts, a curiously passionless, aloof, pragmatic, and cautious
president in demeanor and, for the most part, in performance. By and
large, Kennedy was representative of the moderate vision of the presidency.

The Alternatives: A Matter of Perception

Each of the three contrasting visions of the presidency is rooted in a
different concept of what presidents should attend to first. Each implies
different assumptions about which of the alternative strategies for using
the presidency are most likely to be effective. Each conjures a different
feeling about the appropriate tone of the presidency and a unique image
of what constitutes good presidential form: an aura of idealism, of
strength, or of pragmatic competence. As a guide to choice and judgment, therefore, each makes the same reality look different. The descriptions of the alternatives offer clues to how each vision works to

integrate believing, reasoning, and feeling behind selective perceptions and interpretations of the presidency.

The humane vision believes the intrinsic worth of human beings is of the highest value, reasons that idealism and pacifism are the surest ways to sustain a nation and a world worth living in, and feels inspired by a leader who serves its assumptions or estranged from one who threatens them. Proponents of the humane vision thus oppose military adventurism like the 1983 U.S. invasion of the small Caribbean island of Grenada, are sympathetic to the nuclear freeze movement, have high hopes for arms reduction talks with the Soviet Union, and respond with dismay to tough presidential talk like Reagan's use of harsh language against Third World nations known to support terrorist activities.

The potent vision believes that in a ruthless world fear and self-interest motivate most people, reasons that only strategic cunning, backed by power and strength, can prevail in such a world, and feels secure and respectful of a president who plans carefully and uses power effectively or feels scornful and fearful of one who does not. Followers of the potent vision support the Grenada invasion, worry that arms reduction talks do little more than raise false hopes among Americans, and respond enthusiastically to Reagan's "America is standing tall again" rhetoric but grow skeptical and disenchanted because of Reagan's failure to back up his promise of swift and effective retaliation for terrorist attacks against the United States with more than occasional action.

The pragmatic vision believes the world to be an unpredictable place filled with contradictory interests and motives, reasons that only cautious flexibility will provide the maneuverability needed to contend with uncertainty and diversity, and feels a healthy respect for evidence of skill, poise, and competence and has a mild disdain for posturing of any stripe. Adherents to the pragmatic vision see the Grenada invasion as a somewhat pathetic instance of overkill, with few results beyond a short burst of jingoism. They believe that the nuclear freeze movement is well-intentioned but will not succeed and is thus a waste of time, and that arms reduction talks are worth pursuing but cannot be expected to produce miracles. Furthermore, they believe Reagan's threats and Carter's moralistic pieties do little good and may do some harm. In any event, neither reflects the appropriate rhetorical tone for the presidency.

Proponents of each view defend their reactions to events on rational grounds. But as the examples are intended to show, the responses are formed by a combination of belief and emotion, which subtly codes and textures the logic of the reasoning.

Conclusion

The Role of Emotion

One school of thought, identified with the academic study of emotion, has a plausible hypothesis about the relationship between cognition and emotion: the "emotion system" is the original source of cognitive structures like schemas or presidency visions and the primary provider of blueprints for cognition, decision, and action (Tomkins 1962, 282-304). All cognition is coded by emotion (Izard 1977, 155), a position with which many contemporary cognitive psychologists might agree.

Constructs like presidency visions do appear to be grouped cognitively in a fashion consistent with their affective relevance to the individual (Scott 1969). Human emotions—fear, anger, hope, love, disgust, interest, joy, excitement—might thus be expected to influence choice and judgment by their effect on how the presidential world is understood and directly in the form of gut reactions to presidential events. One psychologist, Robert Zajonc (1980), argues that two largely independent systems of evaluation are at work in the human psyche: a relatively slow, detailed, cognitive system used, for example, when people are asked to judge objects or behavior in which they have no immediate emotional investment; and a cruder, faster, and less complex affective system fueled by objects or behavior that trigger impulse and emotion. Zajonc also believes that affective reactions usually dominate cognitive ones, a theory the record of public reactions to presidential events tends to uphold. For example, public support for Carter declined precipitously and remained low after it became apparent there would be no rapid solution to the Iranian hostage crisis. At the time, the drop in support was interpreted as the result of public anger and frustration with Carter's inability to get the situation resolved. Much later, however, after Carter had left office and the tension had subsided, more balanced views emerged, such as that expressed by a participant in the Smoller and Moore-Fitzgerald focus group discussion:

> I feel that his goal was to save lives. And by him being able to achieve it even though we had to sort of get slapped in the face, I think that ultimately the way that he handled that was probably the only humane way he could have done it. (1981, 3)

Emotion plays a decisive role in the evaluation of leaders. The available evidence suggests that of the three human orientations—cognitive, affective, and normative—emotion is the least susceptible to deliberate control, yet has the most clear-cut influence on evaluation in action. It becomes necessarily a central focus of any effort to integrate the three orientations in an approach to choice and judgment.

The nature of emotion is two-sided. Given unbridled vent, it is the enemy of responsible evaluation. It can destroy access to a person's cognitive powers, obstruct views of reality, and yield foolish, impulsive, ill-considered decisions. On the positive side, for someone who can learn to harness it, emotion can facilitate intuition. Emotion's potential in this regard is suggested by the following:

> Special states of consciousness characterized mainly by the emotions (especially certain combinations of interest and joy) have the capacity to facilitate the phenomena of intuition, tacit knowing, and the receptive mode. . . . An emotion provides certain "information" to the organism, but this information (e.g., a certain pattern of pleasantness, tension, impulsiveness and other experiential phenomena) unlike the abstractions of cognitive processes, has a direct relationship to sensory events. The information contained in emotion is nonlinear and nonrational, and emotion cues foster intuitive knowing as well as analytical-intellective processes. Thus emotion and cognition are sometimes contrapuntal—they may be in opposition or in harmony. In either case, emotion alters perception and cognition. (Izard 1977, 157)

Emotional reactions to presidency-relevant sensory events are best treated as additional, potentially useful information, not as definite indicators of immediate action. Emotional responses can stimulate and supplement those more purely rational cognitive processes that, by the standards of science and by the traditional conceptions of good citizenship, should ideally precede choice and judgment. To learn to recognize and interpret information provided by emotions, it must be routinely and self-consciously examined. This is more easily said than done, however, for mistrust and suppression of emotion are hallmarks of the rational, objective, scientific method. Emotionalism is also frowned upon by the civic culture (Edelman 1964, 137). Furthermore, a certain distaste for citizen indulgence in gut reactions is implicit in the criticism of public expectations of the presidency.

Holding back emotions serves useful purposes during delicate procedures like brain surgery or while conducting experimental research. The barriers to legitimizing emotional data, however, restrict political evaluation and the workings of the presidency because they needlessly deny access to potentially relevant information. The logical aim is integration—a synthesis of cognitive, normative, and emotional evidence prior to making decisions. Emotions should be put to constructive use, as the information supplied by them is needed for successful choice and judgment.

The Case for Pragmatism

Presidency visions represent alternative understandings of the presidency and sharply different treatments of emotion. Of the three, the pragmatic vision of the presidency is best able to perceive reality accurately and contend with the influence of emotion. The pragmatic vision is thus the most workable structure around which to organize a personal approach to evaluation. Its priorities, notably crisis management, most directly address the system-threatening problems likely to arise in a chaotic world. The pragmatic vision encourages greater experimentation for finding solutions to problems and its mindset is better equipped to allow both presidents and citizens to view the world as it really is.

A description of the chaotic nature of the political world was recently penned by William H. Riker (1982). Following a score of years of reflection, during which he and his students energetically sought to develop a predictive science of politics, Riker concludes that long-term prediction is well-nigh hopeless because of the incoherency and instability of political reality. In the real world, outcomes are unstable and, thus, unpredictable. The only patterns that can be discerned are those of uncertainty and change, incoherency and flux. Riker's chaos model of reality is an accurate description of the view from the White House. The need to contend effectively with persistent, threatening uncertainty is precisely why the presidency came into being. One mandate of the presidency is to cope with those unexpected and new problems for which easy and known solutions do not exist (Corwin 1957).

The conservative and liberal visions each are less acceptable approaches to the use and the evaluation of power. Their flaws are rooted in their emotional undercurrents, which play larger and less well-managed roles than in the pragmatic vision. The conservative vision imposes order on chaos by forcing disciplined adherence to carefully laid plans. The conservative desire for demonstrations of potency, while unarguably necessary on occasion, may fuel instead of extinguish the fires of chaos. Essential is the ability to distinguish the necessary from the provocative, no easy task for anybody but especially difficult for those afraid to show weakness. The liberal vision is anchored in the fundamental democratic values of the nation, with ideals that uplift, inspire, and nourish the human spirit and offer solace in the face of chaos. In its extreme, the liberal vision is doctrinaire in ways that tie a president's hands and blind a citizen to complexity. Pacifism is desirable in the abstract but can be easily misunderstood as weakness, at home or abroad, to the detriment of peace and other liberal priorities. Its overemphasis on the domestic front, for example, helped to erect a huge welfare establishment without an adequate economic base. The result has been a political backlash against the very humane values it sought to entrench. An emotional commitment to do the right thing too often overlooks the prudent thing, which does less harm in the long run.

By contrast, the emotional stance of pragmatism—a combination of cautious skepticism, distaste for posturing, and thirst for results—leaves it freer to use the strengths of the other visions while not falling prey to their weaknesses. Pragmatism also instinctively tends to examine emotion as intuitive data whose relevance is testable rather than as master to be served or as threat to be suppressed. A clear understanding of emotional evidence is necessary for successful integration. "Pragmatism," says William James, its principal intellectual spokesman, "unstiffens all our theories, limbers them up, and sets each one at work." It has "no dogmas, and no doctrines save its method," which is "the attitude of looking away from first things, principles, 'categories,' supposed necessities; and of looking toward last things, fruits, consequences, facts" (1974, 47). Pragmatic presidents have more options, and pragmatic citizens fewer illusions. Both are less in need of the idealism and potency icons of the presidency and more inclined to do what is necessary to cope with problems or fit the historical era. Pragmatic citizens are less likely to be swayed by presidential posturing or symbolism alone—no small advantage in the age of the media presidency. They are more likely to tolerate and support the flexibility requisite to political leadership in a chaotic world.

Unfortunately, pragmatism is not free of limitations. One of its dangers as a presidential strategy is that it has a certain tinge of fatalism, which can lead its proponents to overemphasize the existential here and now and to forgo efforts to control chaos with grand designs, such as those Nixon devised, that plan for the future. Another is to misread the moral significance of events, treating value-laden issues as inconvenient but morally neutral problems. Franklin D. Roosevelt's incarceration of Japanese-Americans in concentration camps during World War II and John F. Kennedy's early indifference to the civil rights question are cases in point.

Recognizing that human limitations cannot be entirely overcome by either leaders or followers, however responsibilities are interpreted and approached, the problem becomes one of choosing the most workable from among imperfect alternatives. The pragmatic vision, which shares the aims but not always the priorities or the means of the liberal and conservative visions, is the best vehicle for integrating belief, emotion, cognition, and information behind a personal approach to evaluation.

CHAPTER 4

Evaluation in Action:
Carter "Loses," Reagan "Wins"

Rejected at the polls and widely regarded as an ineffectual president during his single term in office, Jimmy Carter was involuntarily
retired to his hometown of Plains, Georgia, and political oblivion in 1981
at the age of 56. Hovering near 60 percent approval in public opinion
polls as the 1984 election approached, 73-year-old Ronald Reagan was
returned to office in triumph, carrying 49 states and winning a record
525 electoral votes. Even his critics felt compelled to describe him as a
successful president.

What accounts for the striking difference between Carter and Reagan? The standard reply is that Reagan was a leader who got results and
Carter was not. The answer offered here, however, is somewhat different. Reagan was a leader, all right, but his high standing in the public's
esteem is explained not so much by his concrete presidential achievements as by his good fortune, charm, and intuitive grasp of public
relations. Evidence presented in support of this answer will also illustrate how shared understandings (culture) and common psychological
dispositions (human nature) orient and skew evaluation in action. A
description will also emerge of the lengths to which presidents must go
in the media age to scrape together a governing consensus of support.

The Records Compared

The tricky and imprecise business of comparing presidential
records is especially difficult here because one record is complete and

the other is not. Furthermore, the records of the current president and his immediate predecessor must be examined without benefit of historical perspective. Accepting the standard definition of *record* as the specific, concrete results a president achieves, ignoring the fact that time often changes the meaning of a presidential record, and limiting the comparison of records to Carter's one term and Reagan's initial term, a case can be made that Reagan does not stand head and shoulders above Carter. Their different reputations cannot be attributed to differences in concrete achievement alone.

As president-elect, neither Carter nor Reagan seemed conspicuously well-prepared for the office of the presidency. Both electoral successes were historical anomalies. Carter was a nontraditional outsider whose nomination would have been impossible but for drastic changes in Democratic party nomination and convention rules, and whose election owed much to public displeasure with Ford's pardon of Nixon. Reagan was the representative of the far right of the Republican party, a candidate who could not win in the judgment of moderate Republicans, but who had the good fortune to run against Carter at his lowest ebb in popularity. Also to Reagan's advantage, election day fell on the one-year anniversary of the Iranian hostage ordeal. An ABC News/Harris Survey conducted in July 1980 showed a 79 percent disapproval rating for Carter's handling of the situation in Iran.

Although Reagan's having served as governor of California was thought to have afforded better preparation than Carter's experience as governor of the more provincial Georgia, neither man had significant exposure to Washington or the federal government prior to his election. If candidate Reagan was a smoother, more engaging public personality, candidate Carter was felt to be more intelligent and known to have a greater appetite for hard work.

By the end of four years in office, each had compiled a significant legislative box score, a cornerstone of the presidential record. Reagan's principal legislative achievements—substantial reductions in the growth rate of spending on entitlements and other social services, and the Economic Recovery Tax Act of 1981, which cut the individual income tax rate by 25 percent—were reached during the first six months of his term, the traditional honeymoon period. By attaining his legislative goals in Congress, Reagan helped dispel the belief that America was ungovernable (Smith 1984) and helped demonstrate that the presidency is indeed "possible" (Bonafede 1985). Reagan based the claim that he arrested the momentum of the New Deal and established a political revolution of historic proportions on his legislative achievements. His legislative and budgetary strategies represent important innovations in the use of presidential resources, which may prove to be the most durable consequences of Reagan's successes. Actual policy impact has been less significant and more ephemeral than is widely believed, a point made in *The Reagan Record* (Palmer and Sawhill 1984). The book offers information that has been extensively reported but little noticed: federal spending, as a percentage of gross national product, increased during Reagan's first term;[1] the retrenchment of government has been far less revolutionary than either supporters or critics contend;[2] and Reagan was unable to sustain a legislative coalition sufficient to expand his program after the first six months and has since been repeatedly forced to compromise. Since 1981, the congressional leadership, not the White House, has controlled the budget process. In light of these facts, the image of Reagan created by his legislative record is an impressive achievement in its own right. Rarely has a president succeeded in establishing such a favorable reputation from such limited legislative success.

For Carter, nearly the opposite is true—rarely before has a president extracted so little credit from what is in fact a solid legislative record. Carter's box score is considerably larger than Reagan's and includes both domestic and foreign policy matters. Carter resolved a number of long-simmering issues that previous presidents had avoided because of the political costs and uncertain payoffs. The Panama Canal treaties, for example, assuaged an historic resentment toward the United States in Central and South America. The need to address the problem had been recognized by presidents since Eisenhower (Lewis 1981). The Civil Service Reform Act of 1978 was the first major overhaul of the federal personnel system since the Pendleton Civil Service Act of 1883 and represented a long-overdue modernization of the merit principle and the structure of the civil service. A five-part energy policy package, passed after 18 months of laborious and heated congressional wrangling, contained only about half of what Carter wanted. The legislation, however, represented the first tentative step the United States had taken toward making a national commitment to conserve energy (Johnson 1980, 293), a step whose importance had been recognized, but not acted upon, by previous presidents. Carter's legislative achievements generated few votes and little political support. Still, the long-term consequences of specific legislative enactments may well turn out to favor Carter over Reagan.

The state of the national economy and the president's ability to keep it healthy are other traditional, and often crucial, elements of the presidential record. The national economy was seriously troubled during both the Carter and the Reagan administrations. Unemployment remained high. During his tenure, Carter presided over double-digit inflation, which he was unable to bring down. Reagan accrued a spectacular budget deficit brought on by his success in winning defense spending increases, and his refusal to support countervailing tax increases. Although experts disagree about whether high inflation or large budget deficits do the most long-run harm (Stein 1984), the public has had little difficulty deciding which was worse. As the 1980 election approached, Carter's "handling of the economy" was weighted negatively by 86 percent in public opinion polls (Harris 1980). In sharp contrast, Reagan, as the 1984 election neared, received "excellent" or "good" marks on his handling of the economy from 61 percent of a random sample of Americans (*National Journal,* October 27, 1984, 2058). The media reaction was similar. The August 18, 1980, issue of *U.S. News and World Report* described Carter as a failure at managing the economy. The consensus on Reagan's performance in the media was, in the words of a *New York Times* headline, "Good but Mixed" (Kilborn 1984, 13). Uncertainty was expressed about the effects of huge deficits over time, but Reagan was applauded for reducing inflation.

A case can be made that budget deficits are as dangerous as inflation (Stein 1984) and that, although the precise degree of responsibility a president holds for any economic indicator is rarely certain, Reagan was more directly to blame for deficits than Carter was for inflation (Stockman 1986). Carter, however, was criticized substantially more by the press and the public than was Reagan. Although the impact of inflation on individual citizens is more obvious and dramatic than budget deficits, it does not adequately explain the vast difference in public judgment of the economic management of these chief executives.

The handling of foreign relations, a centerpiece of presidential assessment, is the last major category of the presidential record to be considered here. Carter's strongest performance—and Reagan's weakest—was unquestionably in the area of foreign policy. In addition to the Panama Canal treaties, the Carter administration managed the successful negotiation of the second Strategic Arms Limitation Treaty (SALT II), which, while never ratified by the Senate, continues to influence U.S.-Soviet relations. SALT II addressed the important issue of arms control and serves as the foundation on which continuing negotiations depend. Carter can also boast of the Camp David accords and the ensuing Egyptian-Israeli peace treaty, which was described as "far and away the most substantial advance in the direction of a comprehensive Mideast settlement in the entire . . . history of the Arab-Israeli conflict" (Johnson 1980, 292).[3] In addition, U.S.-Soviet relations remained comparatively relaxed during the Carter years. He avoided serious confrontation and maintained an open dialogue with the Soviets until the December 1979 invasion of Afghanistan. Furthermore, not one American soldier died in combat while Carter occupied the White House, a record few presidents can match. Except for the failed attempt to rescue American hostages in Iran, which resulted in accidental loss of life, Carter did not engage U.S. forces in action and escaped the stigma that would haunt LBJ, Nixon, and, to a lesser extent, Reagan. In the tradition of Woodrow Wilson and the canons of democratic morality, Carter mounted an ambitious and idealistic human rights initiative, potentially most important for its long-term significance. Said *New York Times* columnist Tom Wicker: "His disputed and sometimes derided human rights policy . . . began the task of restoring decency and generosity to a world approach that had come to rest too heavily and ineffectively on muscle, money and blood" (1981, 18).

Carter did have his faults in the area of foreign policy, however. He displayed a naiveté in acknowledging his misunderstanding of Soviet motives when Afghanistan was invaded. His call for a boycott of the 1980 Winter Olympic Games, held in Moscow, was considered futile by many. And he was criticized for his equivocal response to the revelation in August 1980 that a brigade of Soviet combat troops was based in Cuba.

At first term's end Reagan had no list of specific accomplishments comparable to Carter's. Reagan administration officials would claim to have reestablished worldwide respect for the United States and to have restored military parity with the Soviet Union through a tremendous increase in defense spending. Reagan undeniably created a new and, to most citizens, a more popular tone in American foreign policy. He reasserted U.S. leadership of the noncommunist world and adopted a harsh rhetorical stance toward the Soviet Union. Arms control negotiations faltered, and no agreements were reached. In some repects, the tension level between the two countries was greater than at any time since the Cuban Missile Crisis of 1962.

Reagan showed himself willing to use military power: At the request of the Organization of Eastern Caribbean States, he sent American forces to Grenada in October 1983. Determined to discourage communist encroachment in Central America, the administration backed the government of El Salvador and the guerrillas in Nicaragua with U.S. military and economic aid. Reagan's commitment of U.S. Marines to a peacekeeping mission in Lebanon resulted in significant loss of American life during a terrorist bombing, an incident his critics believed he could have avoided. For his dependence on military solutions to foreign policy problems, Reagan paid a price in American lives and increased anxiety among allies and citizens, some of whom feared he might provoke nuclear war with the Soviets or entangle the nation in a Vietnam-like conflict in Central America. Although public estimation of his handling of foreign affairs remained positive throughout his first term, Reagan was clearly less surefooted in foreign policy than in domestic policy. He could claim to have reversed the decline of American military power and world prestige, and to have solidified the North Atlantic Treaty Organization (NATO) alliance, but not to have assuaged world fears of Armageddon.

Although complete reckonings of the Carter and Reagan records have not been presented here, the abbreviated review does support two conclusions. First, using the standard set by great presidents, neither record is exceptional. Second, the Carter reputation is much worse and the Reagan reputation far better than can be explained or justified by their respective records. Some future historian might well wonder at the dramatically different public reactions each man stimulated, given their concrete achievements. That historian's judgment will turn, of course, on perspectives and policy effects not now discernible. Future generations might end up viewing either president as great or as a failure.[4]

However, only those who experienced the Carter and Reagan presidencies will feel the difference that explains the divergent reputations of these men. The fact is that to a majority of the present generation of Americans, Reagan seemed successful and Carter did not. Reagan managed to create one sort of general impression, while Carter labored under quite another. The key to short-run reputation is impressions and their management. This assertion involves no attempt to depreciate, downgrade, or trivialize an ability to create an impression of success in the public mind. Instead, the aim is to put such an impression into perspective and to seek its lessons for those who would examine it.

The Short-Term Success Test

In light of earlier discussions about the role of perception and emotion in judgment, the claim that success has as much to do with impression as with actual performance or results should not be surprising. The distance between citizens and the presidency, the disinclination of most Americans to master the intricacies of presidential functioning, and the fundamentally emotional meaning of the presidency in the American political culture all argue that this claim is to be expected.

The appearance of success is not necessarily different from, or less valuable than, the reality; they are usually related. The successful management of mass impressions is a political skill as important to "real" success as is the formulation and implementation of policy. Without public support, a president has little chance to leave a mark. To his credit, Jimmy Carter had an impact despite the extensive disenchantment he generated as early as six months into his term. But it surely does not reflect well on him that he was unable to elicit the support, appreciation, and credit commensurate with his actual attainments. The blame cannot be placed entirely on an unappreciative electorate, stingy with its praise and ignorant of the significance of what he did.

Impressions do get more emphasis than they should. This argument will be clearer following a discussion of three distinct impressions that constitute the short-term success test. A president, to be perceived as successful in the here and now, must create and sustain impressions: (1) of standing for something clear and unequivocal; (2) of knowing how to implement policy stands; and (3) of being a loved and respected leader. Whatever the record may show and whatever history eventually concludes, Ronald Reagan created these impressions while in office and Jimmy Carter did not.

Standing for Something

The impression of having a clear-cut sense of direction, a well-defined political philosophy, and a straightforward, widely understood position on issues is, for many, the essence of leadership. Leaders are needed to tell others what to do, to push for action in one direction instead of another. Position taking is how they do this. The president's willingness to take a confident stand, to clearly identify with the stand taken, is a crucial source of feelings of reassurance and inspiration that leadership exists, in part, to provide. At a visceral, emotional level, merely proposing a course of action and appearing confident about its validity contributes to the impression that a president is successful. A president who is unable to convey a powerful sense of direction invites uncertain and anxious reactions in onlookers, which leads to rejection and the label of failure. These reactions are instinctive and primordial, preceding ideology or conscious rationalization.

A president has managed to create an impression of standing for something when any citizen or bureaucrat imagines that a successful prediction can be made about how the chief executive will respond to whatever issue or event might emerge. When consumer advocate Ralph Nader advised President-elect Jimmy Carter to find ways to make people in government—from the cabinet on down to the lowest functionary—feel as if Carter were "looking over their shoulders all the time," he was, in effect, telling Carter to make known definite policy positions. When a president stands for something, supporters and subordinates believe they know instinctively what should be done. And they are more likely to do it.

Another indication that the presidential message has gotten across is when the political debate, as conducted in the media, in Congress, and in informal discussion, adopts the president's perspective, language, and definition of the problems confronting the nation. If a president can sell a particular point of view on the national agenda, winning acceptance for proposed solutions will be considerably easier. Opponents are forced on the defensive and must confront and contest the issues on the administration's terms.

Again, Reagan won and Carter lost. Reagan came to be the clear embodiment of his own expression of political conservatism in the national consciousness. He also managed, from the earliest days of his first term, to sell his definition of the issues, as the following excerpts from an editorial written a year into his presidency suggest:

> It is his unyielding advocacy of a particular philosophy that has given him the hardcore support that has sustained his career at the top levels of American politics for a long-running 16 years. . . . By sticking to his guns, he has forced his issues to the top of the national agenda. It has taken time, but the debate in Washington is now on the ground that Reagan has chosen; about the costs of big government, high taxes and the federal superstructure. That is not what Congress and the country would be chewing about this winter, were not Reagan the stubborn and principled character that he is; the "Horton the Elephant" of American politics. (Broder 1982, sec. 1, 20)

Reagan sustained his ability to sell his definitions despite frequent, well publicized, and widely criticized departures from behavioral consistency with his issue positions.

Prior to the 1980 election, conventional wisdom held that a true believer of the extreme left or right of either major political party could not win the presidency—a view bolstered by the fortunes of candidates Barry Goldwater and George McGovern in the 1964 and 1972 elections. Reagan's election and first-term popularity provide strong evidence to the contrary and suggest that a clear stand is a real asset, especially when projected by an attractive personality and a sophisticated political strategy.

The importance of taking a stand was made painfully clear early in the Carter presidency. Although professing a genuine respect for Carter's considerable talent, decency, and personal charm, James Fallows, who served as Carter's chief speechwriter, offered a critical observation in an *Atlantic Monthly* article entitled "The Passionless Presidency":

I started to wonder about the difference between a good man and an inspiring one; about why Jimmy Carter, who would surely outshine most other leaders in the judgment of the Lord, had such trouble generating excitement, not only in the nation but even among the members of his own staff. One explanation is that Carter has not given us an idea to follow.... I came to think that Carter believes fifty things, but no one thing. He holds explicit, thorough positions on every issue under the sun, but he has no large view of the relations between them, no line indicating which goals (reducing unemployment? human rights?) will take precedence over which (inflation control? a SALT treaty?) when goals conflict. Spelling out these choices makes the difference between a position and a philosophy, but it is an act foreign to Carter's mind. (1979, 42)

Carter's self-styled image as an engineer who could draw up a blueprint for attacking any imaginable problem did not communicate a sense of comprehensive, intelligent control. Instead, citizens believed that Carter was unable to distinguish the important from the trivial, that he lacked a crystallized vision of what he was in office to accomplish. This first provoked disquiet, then anxiety, and, ultimately, abetted by failure to meet other tests, an "ugly air of negativism" in the public mind (Johnson 1980, 293). Because lack of support took root relatively early in Carter's term, later perceptions of his accomplishments were affected. As a result, those successes Carter was able to achieve did not count to his credit in the eyes of the public. This is, in part, why a respectable legislative record seemed irrelevant; why the *New York Times,* in an editorial endorsing Carter for reelection (1980, 22E), felt compelled to remind readers that "the President's legislative record is better than is commonly acknowledged" and why political columnist David Broder wrote that "Jimmy Carter's programmatic output against what [he] promised in the campaign [reflects] achievements more impressive than one would conclude from popular commentaries" (1979b, D7).

Unlike Carter, Reagan did not confuse the public about his priorities. He thus avoided the frustration, anxiety, and ire that can result from uncertainty when it is fostered by the president, who is expected to set a clear-cut course. Because Reagan's political philosophy was sharply etched, his legislative results could be logically perceived and understood (Greenstein 1983). As unmistakable expressions of what he stood for, his accomplishments made sense to an electorate undisturbed by confusion. Therefore, they counted.

Knowing What to Do

Creating and sustaining the impression of success requires a president to appear capable, to seem in command of an efficient and effective political enterprise that is able to locate and use the levers of power.

Management of the presidency is an intricate business that largely escapes public attention, but certain aspects are visible and create impressions that shape the president's reputation for competence.

Jimmy Carter seemed inept, weak, and out of his depth, a well-intentioned man who was just not up to the job. On the other hand, Ronald Reagan initially struck most Americans as a surprisingly poised, sure-footed professional who knew how to make things happen, a man whose smoothly functioning political organization was busily orchestrating a historic change in the federal government. Neither impression was fully accurate, but both illustrate the importance of three visible indicators of short-term success: having a game plan, avoiding early mistakes, and maintaining good professional relations.

Have a Game Plan. First, Reagan seemed to have a game plan and Carter did not. The Reagan team concentrated nearly all its attention and effort in the first six months on economic policy, a highly advertised priority that was consistent with the president's campaign promises and that addressed public anxiety about runaway inflation. Other matters were simply shunted aside, to such an extent that "after one month in office, the new president's fortunes were publicly staked to a number of high-risk promises predicting lower unemployment and inflation rates, faster economic growth and balanced budgets" (Heclo and Penner 1983, 27). The plan of attack was presented in budget and tax legislation proposed to Congress, and these measures became the focus of presidential pronouncements and media and public attention.

By comparison, the early months of the Carter administration seemed aimless. The original strategy was to increase public support through the president's symbolic emphasis on openness and trust (Glad 1980, 413), but complaints arose that the Carter presidency was becoming one of empty gestures rather than decisive action. In response, Carter proclaimed in April 1977 that the energy crisis was his number one priority. In the meantime, he pushed ahead on other policy proposals, including a job funding measure and an economic stimulus package. In all, no fewer than 60 priority legislative measures were put forth by the Carter White House during the first year alone (Glad 1980, 423). Too many initiatives, a top priority whose alleged urgency seemed unconvincing in light of the abundance of other proposals, and inadequate legislative groundwork made Carter's political strategy appear ad hoc and incoherent. The president himself seemed amateurish and uncertain of his priorities.

Avoid Early Mistakes.   Second, Reagan avoided early, well-publicized gaffes and Carter did not. Although the electorate has a history of forgiving the isolated presidential misstep, like Kennedy's Bay of Pigs fiasco or Eisenhower's U-2 embarrassment, people grow restive when they perceive a pattern of presidential blunders. Such a pattern is particularly unsettling during the all-important initial year when the nation is taking the new president's measure. Ideas about the president formed then are hard to shake, if they ever can be, given the power of stereotypes.

Reagan not only kept from making significant mistakes but also created a winning first impression with his summer of 1981 legislative successes. He gained momentum and a reputation for competence that was sufficient to drown out early-term criticism of his handling of foreign policy. It would also sustain him in the public mind later when, as inevitably happens, success proved harder to come by. Following the first half of 1981, the American people were prepared to give him the benefit of the doubt.

Carter, on the other hand, enjoyed no comparable early success to shield him from a number of rebuffs and embarrassments, which included the public bickering between the cabinet and White House staff, the controversial nomination of Theodore Sorensen as CIA director, and the indignation of members of Congress caused by the administration's failure to consult with them on top priority energy legislation. By the end of Carter's first year in office, his leadership was characterized as incompetent, and the question of whether he knew what he was doing was openly discussed.

Maintain Good Professional Relations.   Third, the impression of competence is enhanced by the appearance of good working relationships between the president and other power centers. As recently as the time of Eisenhower, a president could maintain strong popular support without establishing a favorable professional reputation in Washington (Neustadt 1980). Now, however, the president's ability to sustain personal rapport and effective working relations with members of Congress and the media is taken as evidence of shrewdness and firmness by the general public as well as government insiders. Habitual conflict, especially when caused by ignorance, provokes uneasiness and raises doubts about the quality of presidential leadership.

Again, Reagan wins and Carter loses. Despite a House of Representatives controlled by the Democratic party and a working press dominated by liberals, Reagan struck up cordial relations with both. Any disadvantage he had because of his Washington outsider status was more than offset by his personal likeability and charm and by his adept liaison operations. The press made much of the Reagan style, perhaps because of its sharp contrast with the Carter aloofness. House Speaker Thomas P. O'Neill, Jr., was quoted as saying he liked Reagan personally, despite his staunch disagreement with the Reagan program. The media expressed frustration with Reagan's inaccessibility and, as a result of his frequent press conference misstatements, portrayed him as uninformed on the issues. But Reagan deflected the charges lodged against him with lighthearted humor and affability, which seemed to diminish the sting of criticism in the public mind.

Reagan also benefited from the sympathetic national reaction to the March 1981 attempt on his life. That event, which left him critically wounded, allowed him to display his most appealing personal qualities and characteristics, which put him in a very special, esteemed position in the public consciousness. With a bullet in his chest, Reagan walked unassisted into the hospital, joked with the surgeons about their political affiliations, and remained optimistic throughout his ordeal. Reagan's handling of the assassination attempt and its impact on people's feelings shifted public expectations in his favor. Reagan would enjoy an extension of the honeymoon period, which affected his treatment at the hands of both the press and Congress. Normal relations would eventually resume, but despite the highly controversial nature of the policy debate during the first Reagan term, the tone of political discourse would remain unusually civil and good-humored, never sinking to the level of bitterness and acrimony characteristic of the Nixon, and to a lesser extent the Carter, years.

Unaided by either personal charm or fortuitous events, Carter was left to contend with a decidedly less favorable emotional climate. He alienated members of the press and Congress in ways that appeared gratuitous and naive, lending credence to the charge that he was out of his depth as president. To many close observers of the presidency, Carter seemed innocent of even the most basic principles of good legislative relations. He installed Frank Moore as head of congressional liaison, a decent but inexperienced Georgian unfamiliar with legislative practices at the national level. White House staffers developed a well-deserved reputation for insensitivity on Capitol Hill. They were known to treat members of Congress brusquely and failed to return phone calls promptly, if at all. In his memoirs, Carter states that his refusal to play traditional patronage games was a conscious and deliberate decision. However noble his motives were, and however egotistical or petty those who took offense were, their reaction was predictable to a casual student of human behavior, let alone of congressional politics. Carter himself routinely neglected to confer with congressional leaders on policy matters of special concern to them. At first, he rarely did the necessary personal lobbying on important legislation, thereby needlessly complicating the chances of passage. Other presidents—Eisenhower, Kennedy, and Nixon among them—have found it distasteful and difficult to engage in direct personal stroking and pressing. But in Carter's case the reluctance was extreme and, unarguably, damaging. The White House did not even show the traditional courtesy of consulting the Democratic leadership on appointments for individuals from their own states, which served to alienate House Speaker O'Neill and others whose support and goodwill were sorely needed.

Illustrative of Carter's difficulties in establishing a good working relationship with Congress is his handling of pork-barrel water projects dear to those legislators in whose states and districts they were to be located. Carter's proposed revisions to Ford's fiscal 1978 budget included a tentative decision to eliminate 19 water projects. Congressional reaction was furious, not only because members wanted to protect the projects but also because of the administration's method of informing members about the decision. Although in the campaign Carter had promised to reduce wasteful and hazardous federal programs and to protect the environment, he moved more quickly than expected. Members, if they received word of the proposed cuts at all, did so only shortly before the plan was officially presented to Congress. And some members complained that they had been told that projects in their states would not be affected, only to discover that they were (Glad 1980, 419).

Although Carter improved his legislative operation significantly in his second year in office, he never fully overcame the resentment created in the early months. Inside observers marveled at Carter's apparent willingness to jeopardize the whole of his legislative hopes over such comparatively trivial matters as prior consultation and political courtesy. To professionals, pushing a low-priority issue like pork-barrel water projects seemed not worth the risk of offending those whose votes would be needed on other, far more important legislation. Carter intended his refusal to yield to "politics as usual" to be taken as an important symbolic stand and to be interpreted as determination and political courage. To most citizens, however, it was prima facie evidence of naiveté and incompetence. The press helped the public form a lingering and, to a large extent, inaccurate impression that Carter did not know how to work with Congress.

Although, from the beginning, the media had been somewhat put off by Carter's emphasis on ethics and morality, he had for the most part been granted the traditionally gentle honeymoon treatment. Despite his mounting troubles with Congress, his standing in the polls remained relatively high throughout the spring of 1977, and press criticism was not unusually severe. In mid-July, however, the Senate Governmental Affairs Committee began an investigation into the circumstances of a $3.4-million personal loan Bert Lance, Carter's director of the Office of Management and Budget and close friend, negotiated from a Chicago bank while he served as an officer in a Georgia bank. This inquiry into Lance's banking practices, the first major scandal of the administration, set the stage for a sharp deterioration in Carter's treatment by the press, which began to play up the incompetence theme as well. Carter emerged from the first summer of his presidency with an image problem he would never completely rectify.

Enjoying a Privileged Cushion

A *privileged cushion* is an unusual kind of public credibility that leads citizens, media, and political professionals to instinctively treat the president with kid gloves. In addition, the president is given the benefit of the doubt, which serves as protection from loss of public support that mistakes, inactions, or vicissitudes might cause. A privileged cushion derives from a combination of three factors. The first is a favorable first impression stereotype based on early demonstrations of leadership and competence. The second is a presidential knack for winning others over, for reasons having as much or more to do with personal warmth, charm, and physical attractiveness than with actual performance. The third is the creation of what becomes a self-sustaining conviction in the public mind—that the president has wide public support, enough so to survive on reputation during periods when support is unstable and enough so to dishearten and effectively declaw critics.

Presidents such as FDR, Eisenhower, and Reagan burrowed into the public consciousness until they seemed like living institutions to most American citizens. Reagan, with an anxious national climate at the time of his first inauguration, his early legislative successes, the attempt on his life, and his winning ways, quickly established himself as a brand-name president, which was unthinkable before the 1980 election. The American people thus no longer considered him on probation—subject to critical examination and evaluation. As a result, public esteem and, to a lesser extent, public support for Reagan came to be less directly contingent on short-term reactions to his day-to-day performance than was the case for Carter. Reagan's shortcomings and mistakes were more likely to be tolerated and had significantly less impact on either his professional reputation or his public prestige. Consequently, Reagan could get away with things that Carter surely would not have.

A privileged cushion is a major leadership resource, for it extends the honeymoon atmosphere of assuming the best, softening critical scrutiny, and suspending skepticism and disbelief. Given the ominous support trends of the late twentieth century, the presidency may no longer be able to function effectively under the present constitutional arrangements unless the incumbent can generate a privileged cushion. Although such a cushion is only partly a function of good performance and hard work (along with personality and luck), it is still appropriately viewed as a short-term measure of presidential success. It reflects the creation of a widespread public impression that in important respects the president has proven abilities, is therefore successful, and need only avoid glaring disasters. The American electorate had formed this impression of Ronald Reagan by the summer of 1981, and even his resolute critics, like *Washington Post* columnist David Broder, were willing to acknowledge it. Broder in 1984 wrote: "At the level of personal leadership . . . there is no doubt that Reagan has brought strength and vitality to an office which had begun to appear distinctly diminished" (p. 6).

The most intriguing and mysterious component of the privileged cushion is the personal impact of the president upon the populace. Merely to be liked by the American people is no guarantee of their support or approval. Surveys have shown that more people have liked the president than have approved of his performance (Edwards 1983, 224). Instead, the reasons why a particular president is liked determine whether "liking" translates into a privileged cushion of support. Carter, for example, was admired for his earnest decency and other moral qualities, but they were a thin shield against attacks on his competence. He was considered a good man but not a good president. Reagan, on the other hand, was liked and respected for reasons that enhanced his credibility and made him much less vulnerable to criticism. Although Reagan escaped neither criticism nor a lengthy period of declining support during his second year in office, the general impression that he was in command of a viable institution seemed unaffected by his support problems. Carter was not perceived as in command despite the fact that his approval rating was higher than Reagan's at the close of their respective second year in office. Impressions and polls do not always correspond.

What was it about the Reagan persona that helped him to sustain the impression of support during periods of decline, to escape the consequences of criticism, and to rebound strongly in the polls by term's end? He may not have gotten results with charm alone, but his unflagging optimism, buoyant good cheer, and genial affability blunted the harshness of criticism and minimized the erosion of public support. Critics found themselves disarmed by the Reagan treatment, and many softpedaled their judgments for fear of seeming too carping or shrill. Many political columnists realized that the public would not tolerate harsh attacks on Reagan. Even Reagan's frequent press conference misstatements were not forcefully challenged. A retired and somewhat bitter Jimmy Carter complained that the press found Reagan's failure to "check the facts" before making statements "kind of amusing," while Carter was "blasted" by the media when he made "the tiniest substantive error" (1984, 12).

Apparently weary after four failed presidents, the public was hungry for upbeat news and was beguiled by Reagan's cheerful certainty that his plans would work. But Reagan's way of being himself, rather than his policies, won for him the kind of instinctive support that appeared to transcend issues and self-interest. Even those who stood to lose the most from the Reagan initiatives—the elderly, the poor, minorities, farmers—were favorably disposed toward him. Such a bipartisan privileged cushion had not been seen since the time of Eisenhower. Early in the election year of 1984, Democrats believed that Reagan was vulnerable on the issues, but they feared the impact of his popular personality. Said Ohio Democratic representative Dennis E. Eckart: "He has such a reservoir of good will, even among people who feel inimical to his interests, that it will be difficult to translate [issue vulnerability] into votes" (Cohen 1984, 469).

What evidence indicates the presence of a privileged cushion? The most obvious potential sign, the level of approval a president enjoys in public opinion polls, can be misleading. For one thing, the average level of support, regardless of performance, has declined for all presidents since Kennedy. Both the peaks and the valleys of approval are much lower than they used to be, a phenomenon attributed to the lingering effects of Vietnam and Watergate. But whatever the reason, it changes the meaning of any given level of support. Not even a cushioned president is likely, in the foreseeable future, to approach Eisenhower's eight-year average support level of 75 percent. Carter's 47 percent average is closer to the contemporary norm.[5] Furthermore, even cushioned presidents cannot escape brief periods of weak support, particularly when the economic news is bad. Reagan's midterm support level of 41 percent, registered during an economic recession described by Democrats as the worst since the Great Depression, was lower than those of his four immediate predecessors. Unlike Carter, Reagan would rebound strongly from his midterm slump. But Reagan's four-year average is closer to Carter's than to Eisenhower's, despite Reagan's cushioned status. Finally, approval percentages are based on polling questions that do not measure respondents' impressions of how much the president is supported or esteemed by others. Those who disapprove might well believe that a president like Reagan is a brand name—a unique political character who is enthusiastically supported by most other Americans, even if not by themselves.

Despite the important qualifications, support polls do provide certain inferential evidence of the presence or absence of a privileged cushion. For example, the trend of public support over time shows the extent to which a president's support is affected by short-term reactions to performance. The support trends of Reagan, Carter, and Nixon are plotted in Figure 4-1. Although Reagan's line displays the familiar V pattern of strong early-term, low mid-term, and increasing end-term support, it is smoother and less choppy, with fewer sharp peaks and deep valleys, than the Carter and Nixon lines. It suggests that Reagan's support was less directly and immediately contingent on short-term reactions to his performance, that he enjoyed a certain leeway, or

Figure 4-1 Public Support Trends for Reagan, Carter, and Nixon

Reagan's approval rating compared with Carter's and Nixon's after 45 months in office.

	Approve	Disapprove
Reagan 10/84	54%	35%
Carter 11/80	31	56
Nixon 11/72	62	28

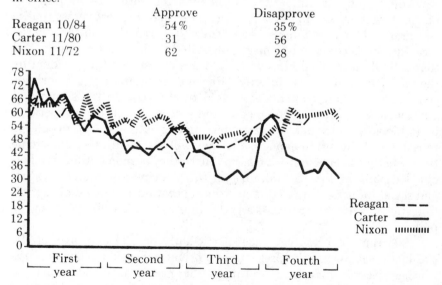

Source: "In Perspective," *National Journal*, October 27, 1984, p. 2058. Data from Gallup Organization Inc. Copyright 1984, by National Journal Inc. All Rights Reserved. Reprinted by Permission.

benefit of the doubt, not accorded to Nixon or Carter. Comparison of the Reagan and Nixon trends also emphasizes a point made earlier: it is not so much the absolute magnitude of support that distinguishes the cushioned president as the stability and resilience of support. Nixon enjoyed a higher average level of support during his first term, but his trend line reveals more peaks and valleys. Reagan's standing with the public was somewhat less probationary than either Nixon's or Carter's.

Another inference about Reagan's cushioned status that can be drawn from the trend line in Figure 4-1 concerns the steep increase in support toward the end of his first term. An end-term surge is not unusual, but substantial increases (in this case, pushing support to the 60 percent level) are usually associated with some significant presidential success, such as the Camp David accords or a U.S.-Soviet summit. Reagan, however, had no major accomplishment during his third or fourth year. In fact, he was coming under heavy fire in the press for massive budget deficits, unfair economic policies, and such foreign policy failures as the terrorist bombing of the Marine outpost in Beirut, Lebanon. Not only did Reagan avoid the sharp drop in support that often accompanies a presidential misstep or highly publicized bad news, he actually continued his upward trend.

Poll results also allow the president's reputation to be put into perspective. For example, Reagan's actual level of support across time is less grand than might have been expected, given the impressions he created that a strong public mandate existed for him and his works and that he had established himself as a remarkably successful president by the fall of his initial year in office. Reagan's reputation began with his claim of a mandate, which was bought by Congress in the summer of 1981, widely reported in the media, and entrenched through repetition in millions of informal conversations among citizens. Get people to repeat something often enough, and they will eventually assume it to be true, whether it is or not—a classic illustration of momentum psychology. Reagan's ability to capitalize on the principles of communication and social influence—to define his own reputation and make his definition stick—is in many respects a better indicator of his cushion than the polls.

The tone of press coverage, particularly critical coverage, of the president also reveals the presence of a privileged cushion. The proposition that Reagan got away with things other presidents could not have is supported by the nature of his media treatment. As early as February 1982, for example, liberal *New York Times* columnist Anthony Lewis asks: "Why the kid gloves for Reagan's presidency?"

Blunder, incoherence and policy disaster increasingly mark Ronald Reagan's presidency. The reporters and editors who watch official Washington know how bad it is, but they are not really saying it on television or in the papers. They are still giving Reagan a cushion. . . .

Lewis then recites such evidence of Reagan's incompetence as record budget deficits, a recessionary economy, an incoherent Middle East policy, indecision on strategic weapons, and mishandling U.S. reaction to the imposition of martial law in Poland. He concludes:

No one can doubt what the press would be doing to Carter under such circumstances. It would be savaging him as incompetent and vacillating. It would be treating him with contempt, mocking him in stories about "killer rabbits." It would be writing darkly about the disarray in Washington. But that record is not Carter's; it is Reagan's, every item of it. (1982, sec. 3, 10)

Robert J. Samuelson, writing in the December 11, 1982, issue of the *National Journal,* makes a similar point:

The fashion now is to regard Reagan as a political giant, much in the mold of Franklin D. Roosevelt, attempting to shift the course of American politics. But the duller truth is that the policies pursued by Reagan have differed only in degree, not in direction or emphasis, from those followed in the final days of the Carter administration. To wit: tighter money, more defense spending and less domestic spending. (1982, 2122)

Early in 1984, columnists and others were commenting about Reagan's charmed ability to avoid paying the political price for actions that would have severely damaged Carter or other presidents: the loss of 241 American lives in the terrorist bombing of the Marine headquarters in Beirut, the refusal to permit the press to accompany American troops on the Grenada invasion, massive budget deficits, widespread uneasiness with U.S. policy toward Central America, and the withdrawal of Marines from Beirut to offshore battleships, an event conservative *New York Times* columnist William Safire labeled "Reagan's Bay of Pigs" (1984, 6). While most analysts marvelled at his adroitness at escaping the political fallout, Reagan was not free from diligent and concerted media criticism. If the tone was less negative and less savage than comparable evaluations of Carter, it was still sharp and increased in intensity as his first term drew to a close. For a time at least, the situation was reminiscent of the disdain in which Eisenhower had been held by political professionals (Neustadt 1980). But despite the widespread disapprobation of the cognoscenti, Reagan and Eisenhower managed to sustain high levels of popular support.

For example, the public reacted with indifference to the most consistently labored and arguably best deserved criticism leveled at Reagan: that he was overreliant on advisers and poorly informed about the complexities of the major issues. *U.S. News and World Report* ran a feature entitled "Reagan: Firm Leader or Part-Time President?" that questioned Reagan's aloof management style (March 19, 1984, 31). *Newsweek* criticized the "Disengaged Presidency" (September 7, 1981, 21), and *Washington Post* columnist Lou Cannon, a longtime Reagan watcher, wrote in *Reagan* of the "delegated presidency." Cannon called Reagan an "intellectually lazy" president who "did not do his homework," with potentially disastrous consequences, especially in defense policy (1982, 372). Syndicated columnist Edwin M. Yoder, Jr., characterized Reagan as our "first constitutional monarch, leaving the faults and worries to subordinates" (1984, 22). And at the beginning of Reagan's fourth year in office David Broder wrote: "Reagan remains today, as he was when he came to the presidency, indelibly resistant to the challenge of serious policy analysis. . . . Across all the major areas of government policy, Reagan is a man still dealing with a 3 x 5 card's worth of substantive analysis" (1984, 6).[6]

Despite a professional consensus that Reagan was dangerously out of touch with the intricacies of government and too dependent on aides, little discernible impact was made on his standing with the citizenry. Moreover, Reagan's professional reputation as the man who proved that the presidency was still possible was not tarnished. He remained "Teflon-coated"—nothing stuck to him. He slipped punches and dodged bullets like no president in memory.

Carter was criticized for his tendency to pay too much attention to detail while losing sight of the overall goal. Carter's first secretary of health, education, and welfare, Joseph A. Califano, Jr., wrote: Carter was "the highest paid Assistant Secretary for Planning that ever put a reform proposal together" (1981, 403). Editorial writers reiterated that Carter was preoccupied with particulars throughout his presidency. Unlike the criticism of Reagan's disengagement, criticism of Carter's overinvolvement did him real damage. Reagan got away with his most fundamental error, but Carter did not.

Support trends and muted criticism suggest a privileged cushion, but the best indicator is a brand-name reputation. Reagan's brand name was "The Great Communicator"—he possessed rhetorical and self-presentation skills that enabled him to sustain enthusiastic support across partisan lines and to win acceptance for his own self-interested redefinitions of political success. In addition, he presided over a collection of brand-name policy initiatives, which embodied "The Reagan

Revolution." Reagan's reputation shaped perceptions strongly enough to sometimes override the reality of weak public support or flawed performance. Presidential scholar Fred Greenstein illustrates the point:

> But is Reagan as effective a communicator as has generally been assumed? . . . close analysis of the 1980 election results does not support Reagan's use of the inevitable claim of just-elected politicians— that their victory carries with it a mandate for their policy proposals. Although experienced politicians discount such presidential claims, members of Congress, bolstered by near uniformity in mass media accounts and by partially engineered constituency pressure, clearly were persuaded at the time of the 1981 tax and expenditure cuts that the president was riding high. One reason they were persuaded was that it was difficult to believe that such an effective communicator had not won the public over. . . . From the good will he engendered, it was not hard to conclude that the legislators' constituents backed the specifics of his proposals and would be prepared to accept their consequences. (1983, 174)

A similar, but more credible, aura of political invincibility clung to Reagan as the 1984 election approached. The *National Journal* quoted a House Republican:

> I can't believe how down the Democrats are about the election. They have several good issues, like fairness, racial polarization—which will prove especially important in the South—the arms race, Central America, Lebanon and others. (Cohen 1984, 470)

Democrats confronted what would prove to be the hopeless task of convincing the public—and themselves—that Reagan's reelection was not inevitable before they could address the many promising campaign issues Reagan's policies made available to them.

By creating the impressions that he stood for something, that he knew how to wield the levers of power, and that he was politically unbeatable, Ronald Reagan passed the short-term success test with flying colors. Jimmy Carter, on the other hand, failed because he seemed to lack a sense of direction, an understanding of how to use presidential power, and an ability to generate a durable, loyal public following.

Neither Carter's nor Reagan's picture fairly represents an accurate interpretation of reality. Carter, it can be argued, had a surer sense of priorities, a better handle on the presidency, and a broader basis of public support than he was credited with. His first priority was world peace, and his attainment of an arms agreement with the Soviets, the Panama Canal treaties, the Camp David accords, and a worldwide concern with human rights belie the charge that he did not know how to make important things happen. Although he lost the 1980 election, he did receive more than 35 million votes—hardly evidence of an utter inability to generate and maintain support.

As for Reagan, he was not so unflinching in pursuit of his priorities, not so adept at bending the machinery of government to his will, and not so politically invincible as is usually imagined. In many instances Reagan substantially altered his plans and priorities in response to political pressure, calling his firm stand into question. Following his early victory on tax and budget cuts, Reagan effectively lost control of the budgetary process to Congress (Smith 1984) and otherwise displayed less dominance over the machinery of government. Reagan evinced an impressive ability to sustain popularity and support, but his invincibility was largely illusory, as his low midterm support scores show.

The point here is neither to embellish Carter nor to diminish Reagan, but to suggest that conventional impressions of each man do not necessarily reflect an objective assessment of the complex facts. Many of the tendencies to distort in human information processing are at work, including oversimplification, stereotypes, overvaluation of the actor at the expense of the situation, highly selective perception, resistance to information that disconfirms entrenched beliefs, and the influence of emotions. Thus, even if the three components of the short-term success test represented reasonable and sufficient measures of the quality of presidential performance, the prospects for their sober, even-handed application are not great.[7]

The components of the test, however, are clear expressions of the emotional needs great leadership fulfills. The need for relief from anxiety is met by a leader who serenely points the way down a clear path. The need for confidence, optimism, and hope is met by a leader who knows what to do and how to do it. And the need to feel secure is met by a leader who, like the most outstanding presidents, fits the collective sense of what a president is and nestles into the collective psyche as a brand-name president.

The comparative fates of Ronald Reagan and Jimmy Carter reveal a need to modify the truism that Americans judge their presidents harshly. Instead, there is a double standard. Presidents who are able to create the emotionally reassuring impressions that satisfy the short-term success test are judged favorably and gently, their missteps and foibles overlooked. They are afforded a more reliable and bountiful supply of the fuel that energizes the presidency: public support. Presidents who fail the test can expect to be held to much stricter, much less forgiving standards of performance and accountability. For them, support is more contingent, more brittle, and less instinctively generous. In a sense, their presidencies are undercapitalized.

Adverse Consequences

Given the public's interest in a viable presidency, undercapitalization, as illustrated by the support fortunes of Jimmy Carter, represents trouble. Although some presidents truly do not deserve support, nobody wins when a president fails. Paradoxically, overcapitalization, of the sort exemplified by Reagan's privileged cushion, can also work against the best interests of the political system. Thus, the presidential experience of neither Carter nor Reagan can be considered optimal. This case can best be made by reviewing certain adverse consequences of the short-term success test. The first stems from the fact that the test creates the wrong incentives for action that can cause an imbalance in the allocation of presidential energies. Presidents are encouraged to overemphasize the symbolic dimensions of leadership at the expense of the less visible and colorful, but equally important, requirements of policy analysis and management. At worst, a kind of goal displacement can result. To concentrate exclusively on creating favorable impressions is to risk "failing to resolve the crucial issues of the period" (Borden 1971, viii).

Standing for something clear and unequivocal may help make things more understandable for inattentive citizens, but it can also oversimplify and thus distort a complex reality for citizens and presidents alike. Being a forceful, competent leader who can make things happen in the real political world is, to be sure, a relevant test of the presidential mettle. But in practice, it encourages presidents to devise high-risk, quick-fix, go-for-broke political strategies to create an early impression that they know how to get results. Early legislative successes, for example, often result in hasty, ill-conceived policies yielding undesirable outcomes. The unexpected costliness and widely perceived ineffectiveness of many Great Society entitlement programs and the huge federal budget deficit brought on by the supply-side tax cuts are recent cases in point. The momentum psychology that facilitates quick political success, which does not guarantee long-term policy effectiveness, often works against the quiet, less impassioned reflection most likely to yield workable policy.

The third component of the short-term success test, attainment of a brand-name status and a privileged cushion of public support, is a legitimate measure of an important presidential skill. In addition, a president who achieves this status finds the presidency more manageable. But an unintended consequence, well illustrated by the Reagan presidency, is the discouragement of hard-nosed appraisal of the actual performance of the cushioned president. The benefit of performance feedback is denied the president, who thus will not learn from mistakes made. If undercapitalization promotes a desperate effort to shore up a governing consensus of support, overcapitalization invites a different, but equally undesirable, response: overconfidence and self-satisfaction. Neither is likely to yield maximal performance. To win a privileged cushion is to risk succumbing to a false sense of presidential security, to imagine that solving political support problems is tantamount to having finished the job. To lose is to feel tempted to concentrate all available energies and resources on gathering support. Either way, something important is likely to be neglected.

Another problem with the short-term success test is that the impressions that comprise its criteria are made early in the public mind, as early as the first year, and strongly resist new evidence and change thereafter. The test thus induces a kind of premature closure, based too heavily on first impression stereotypes. Public notions that Carter was a loser and Reagan a winner took root as early as six months into each man's presidency and had a dramatic impact on subsequent public judgments, which was to some degree independent of their performances after first impressions were formed. With only moderate exaggeration, in the public's eyes, Reagan could do no wrong and Carter could do no right. Ultimately, Carter received less credit and more blame than his record warranted, and Reagan just the reverse. The value of encouraging citizens to remain open to new evidence and to apply the same realistic standards to all presidents is not merely an idle and idealistic concern for fairness. Instead, it is a pragmatic attempt to shape expectations that encourage presidents to use their resources wisely—something unlikely to happen in either undercapitalized or overcapitalized conditions.

The most telling criticism of the short-term success test is that it is incomplete. A president can create the required impressions and pass the test without necessarily advancing such aims as a stable structure of world peace, a sound domestic and international order, or an equitable and orderly domestic society. Standing for something, knowing how to lead, and enjoying widespread support may be necessary, but they are rarely sufficient to meeting the ultimate presidential responsibility for containing or resolving significant national problems.

If the premise that judgment should employ criteria that, if met, are likely to advance the fundamental purposes of the presidency is accepted, then a most difficult task must be confronted: identifying and defining such criteria.

Notes

1. In "Spending Rose Sharply in 'Reagan Revolution'" (*New York Times,* February 2, 1986, 12), Robert D. Hershey, Jr., reports that government spending is now substantially higher as a percentage of gross national product—nearly 25 percent—than the 22½ percent that prevailed in 1981. He cites former Reagan OMB economist Lawrence A. Kudlow, who maintains that the budget differences in the Carter and Reagan administrations "are much less than meet the eye." Other analysts contend that the political debate has obscured the budgetary realities by failing to allow for the relative sizes of the various budget components. "Referring to the scores of highly visible programs that have been cut, including food stamps, some housing and energy subsidies and even Medicare, John Makin, the director of fiscal policy studies at the American Enterprise Institute, declared, 'It makes for a lot of noise, but that's not where the big bucks are.'"

2. In an interview with *Newsweek* editors and reporters (April 21, 1986, 58), former Reagan OMB director David Stockman makes a similar point: Reagan's place in history "won't be as a revolutionary. I think it will be as a conservative who ratified the status quo, in terms of the size of the government, the degree of welfare state functions. The basic kinds of policy commitments did not change. Maybe [their] extreme manifestations have been discredited, but the basic policies have been reinforced, maybe in a slightly less expensive form." The subtitle of Stockman's (1986) memoirs: "Why the Reagan Revolution Failed."

3. The American people apparently agree. A *New York Times* poll conducted in 1985 asked a random national sample of citizens to rate the government's handling of five foreign policy situations on a scale of 1 to 10. The public gave the Camp David negotiations the highest rating at an average of 6.45, followed by the invasion of Grenada at 5.66, the Iranian hostage crisis at 4.95, the bombings of the U.S. Embassy in Lebanon at 4.18, and the response to the Soviet downing of a South Korean commercial airliner at 3.96 (Clymer 1985, 6). Carter can also be credited with cementing Egypt's realignment into the Western camp, keeping that country from adopting a pro-Soviet or neutralist stance. Some specialists believe Carter's achievement was equaled only by the Nixon overture to China in presidential foreign policy actions since the Second World War.

4. One respected analyst, David Broder, a frequent, principled critic of the Reagan administration, nonetheless predicts that Reagan will ultimately be viewed as a president of "historic dimension." His reason: Reagan engineered a series of policy changes that do constitute a long-term revolution in government. He shifted the initiative for domestic policy from Washington to the states. He forced the Soviet Union to reconsider its military strategy and relationship with the United States. And his judicial appointments can be expected to produce a large-scale change in social policy ("Reagan Revolution Leaving Its Marks," *Austin American Statesman,* December 23, 1985, A6). Broder also credits Reagan's historically high popularity, his grace as chief of state, and his role in bringing the Republican party into parity with the Democratic party. A major point of this chapter is that if Reagan is viewed positively by history, it will be for very different reasons than those that explain his first-term popularity.

5. See Chapter 2, note 1.
6. In Chapter 5 I will argue that Reagan's management system may actually be a significant innovation, one of several strategic inventions of his administration that may be of more historic importance than his policy initiatives. Media criticism of Reagan's ignorance of the complex realities of public issues had little impact on Reagan's standing with the public.
7. The relationships between the short-term success test, the cultural tests of Chapter 2, and additional criteria to be discussed in following chapters, can be found in Appendix 2.

CHAPTER 5

The Grounds for Judgment: Competent Presidential Processes

Having examined the preconscious influences that affect choice and judgment in action, the focus in this and the next chapter is on espoused grounds: the traditional yardsticks against which candidates and presidents are measured in informed political discourse. Espoused grounds, as discussed by political scientists and journalists, are the sorts of reasons attentive citizens give for choosing and judging as they do. Collectively, these reasons are called conscious rationalizations, both to distinguish them from preconscious influences and to emphasize that they often reflect a kind of "reconstructed logic" (Kaplan 1964) or "espoused theory" (Argyris and Schon 1974). That is, they are adduced after the fact to justify choices and judgments that may actually have been made for different, maybe less popular or less carefully considered, reasons.

Espoused grounds thus are incomplete as sources of explanation for particular choices and judgments. This, however, does not detract from their importance, for the traditional grounds for choice and judgment do influence evaluative behavior, even if not exclusively. Furthermore, public discussion tends to concentrate on espoused grounds rather than preconscious influences. And perhaps most importantly, they represent hypotheses about what presidents must be and do to make the presidency work.[1] For all these reasons it is surprising that the traditional grounds are rarely subjected to analysis and criticism of the sort to be offered here. Such examination might yield some modest improvement in the quality of their use.

The purpose of this chapter is threefold. The first is to label and define the grounds for judgment. The second is to inquire what, if anything, is wrong with them. The third is to propose and define *competent presidential processes* as a partial solution to the problem with the traditional grounds for judgment—that they do not offer a workable here and now basis for assessing incumbent presidents.

Subjective and Objective Criteria

What are the traditional grounds for judgment? Although their definition and classification can be approached in various ways, here they will be divided into two broad categories: subjective and objective, with subcategories organized under each heading. Under the subjective heading are three entries: leadership style, ideology, and self-interest. Under the objective category are short-term results and long-term results.

The subjective category subsumes criteria that belong to the thinking, or evaluating, subject, not to the object of thought or evaluation. The first of the subjective criteria is leadership style—a president's characteristic mode of self-presentation as leader. Reminiscent of the character test discussed in Chapter 2,[2] leadership style involves an elusive combination of personal appearance and demeanor, which fits culturally inspired concepts of what it is to be presidential. Judgment in these terms is a partial function of affection or other positive feelings. Leadership style is considered a subjective criterion because its evaluative sentiments spring from within and because people often differ in their reactions to a particular leadership style. But its employment here as a conscious, cognitively rationalized basis for judgment rests on the conclusion that an incumbent who looks and acts presidential, as defined by the culture, has a greater chance to be effective. Unfavorable comparisons of Carter with Reagan provide evidence of the importance of style to citizens and the media.

The second criterion is ideology—beliefs about the appropriate ends of government and the proper uses of executive power. Three kinds of presidency-specific belief systems were described in Chapter 3 as contrasting visions of the presidency, with emphasis on the interaction of ideology with emotion and cognition. The emphasis in public discourse, however, is usually on rationalization. Belief systems are typically represented as internally consistent explanatory systems that entail and justify necessary conclusions about the moral desirability of a president's means or ends, as distinct from purely pragmatic effectiveness at using means or achieving ends. Thus, business conservatives, for example, might have difficulty crediting FDR with political success because to them what he did was simply wrong. Similarly, strict constitutional constructionists might not look with approval on the methods of Thomas Jefferson, Andrew Jackson, or Abraham Lincoln. Though they might grudgingly acknowledge the value of results like the acquisition of the Louisiana Territory, the conversion of the presidency into the people's office, or the preservation of the Union, these strong adherents to ideology cannot shake the conviction that the means used by the president stretched the Constitution beyond recognition and were thus wrong.

The third subjective ground is self-interest—typically a conscious, rationally calculated conclusion about a president's contribution to an individual's or group's well-being, as the individual or the group defines it. The measure is often, but not exclusively, economic well-being. A familiar illustration is pocketbook voting (Does my paycheck buy more now than it did under the previous administration?), although dispute continues over whether voters base their decisions on individual or aggregate economic well-being (Kinder 1981; Kramer 1983). Another example is the tendency to judge on the basis of presidential position taking in support of the group or interests with which one identifies— often a single-issue interest group, like farmers, Chicanos, feminists, religious fundamentalists, or oil industry tycoons, that advances ideological justifications for its causes. But in its purest form, the motive for an offer or denial of support to a president rests on advocacy or service to the comparative advantage of the group's interests relative to others.

The objective criteria for evaluation of presidential performance concern results: the extent to which a president is able to secure (or is perceived to have secured) consequences important to the evaluators. The value of the result is a subjective matter, but the term *objective* is being used here to mean being or belonging to the object of perception or thought. What is being evaluated is the object of the presidency, particularly the skill with which the president uses the object as measured by the ability to make something happen. Making something happen is taken as evidence implying skill; skill for its own sake is the value on which judgment turns. Results may or may not confirm ideological or self-interested expectations. They may be short-term political results of the sort indicative of the short-term success test described in Chapter 4, like getting legislation through Congress or creating a wave of national optimism. Or they may be more lasting results, like acquiring the Louisiana Territory or winning World War II. Judgment rests on a president's perceived or actual responsibility for an outcome, for that is the measure of competence.

Objective criteria tend to be the focus of professional presidency watchers—historians, political scientists, columnists, journalists, political professionals, members of Congress, and others who place particular value on the skill with which the levers of power are wielded, and prize and respect the ability to make things happen, regardless of what they are. Many liberal academics and political columnists, for example, acknowledged and admired the skillful use of the presidency by the Reagan administration while they simultaneously deplored many of the results it got. Results in general, as opposed to any specific result, may also convince apathetic citizens that someone capable and responsible is in charge who is able to solve problems.

Evaluating the Grounds for Judgment

If the grounds for judgment as they appear in contemporary political discourse have been adequately classified and defined, the question then becomes: What, if anything, is wrong with them, as seen from the standpoint of the public interest in a viable presidency? In fact, criticism has been leveled at each. For example, mass public expectations for results have been roundly criticized—by academics and journalists—as too demanding and thus unrealistic. People are said to expect too much, largely because they do not understand the limits and constraints of the "impossible" (Barger 1984), "no-win" (Light 1982) presidency.

A second, more intractable problem is that the lasting consequences of presidential achievements are rarely apparent until long after the president has left office. They are often simply not knowable in the here and now, which helps account for the instability of historians' rankings of great presidents below those who reign at the very top. And even if results are discernible right away, perceptions of their value or importance are subject to dramatic change as time passes and other consequences become apparent. For example, James K. Polk and Theodore Roosevelt both got results that were hailed and applauded by most of their contemporaries. Polk took possession of the California and New Mexico territories in a war with Mexico, and Roosevelt helped foment a revolution in Central America that enabled him to acquire land suitable for the construction of the Panama Canal. But these actions also instilled resentment that continues to plague U.S. relations with Latin America. They may even contribute to the current responsiveness of certain Central American nations to the influence of the Soviet Union and its regional client states. Similarly, John F. Kennedy boldly forced the Soviet Union to back down in the Cuban Missile Crisis, which was perceived as good by anxious Americans. But the humiliation increased

Soviet determination to undertake the most massive military buildup in recorded history. By 1984, the Soviet Union had achieved military parity, if not superiority, to the United States, and Americans confronted with an ominous and expensive arms race might well now wonder if Kennedy could not have found an alternative solution. These examples represent hindsight, to be sure, but they also illustrate the slippery nature of immediate results as grounds for judgment.

The practical solution has been first to ignore those long-term consequences that cannot be perceived, and second to substitute short-term political results for lasting results as the here and now test of the presidential mettle. But the problem is not optimally resolved by such a substitution. Political success is apparent in the here and now, but it does not guarantee long-term policy effectiveness, as suggested by the ultimate failure of many New Deal and Great Society programs or by the large budget deficits brought on by the supply-side tax cuts. A president can make all the right political moves and still fall short of resolving the crucial issues of the times.

Both lasting results and quick political success have the considerable advantage of objectivity—they bear, in principle, a definable and discoverable relationship to the object of evaluation: the skill with which a president performs. However, they suffer from the uncertainties of timely measurability (being able to see the important result during the period when evaluation of the president must take place) and ultimate relevance (assurance that the result perceived turns out to have the promised or expected significance in the long run). Either kind of result is therefore difficult to use fairly and intelligently, let alone definitively, in the here and now as a basis for judgment.

The subjective standards, on the other hand, can be applied meaningfully in the here and now. But they have problems of their own, which stem less from any intrinsic irrelevance or illegitimacy than from their susceptibility to the distortions of human nature as they are applied in practice. For example, ideology, in principle, supplies a value grounding that is essential for any meaningful evaluation. In practice, however, it too readily and too frequently degenerates into dogmatism, which narrows and distorts perception and thus precludes openness to new evidence, particularly disconfirming evidence. The argument presented in Chapter 3 suggests that the more intensely and emotionally anchored the ideology, the more likely it is to govern judgment to the exclusion of other criteria. The greater its priority, the more likely it is to stunt perception and desensitize the perceiver to the nuances and complexities of the evaluated object. The extremist actions of true believers, whether right-to-life advocates who firebomb abortion clinics or antiwar zealots who trashed and burned universities during the Vietnam era, supply worst-case illustrations and help to account for American society's guarded view of the normative dimensions of human nature. Ideologues who play by more conventional political rules, such as Christian fundamentalist political action committees, are not generally noted for their evenhanded interpretations of politics or their balanced assessments of presidential performance.

As a source of guidance as to right and proper presidential means and ends, ideology is clearly an essential component of informed judgment. Democratic ideology, for example, is imbedded in the Constitution and is a cornerstone of American political culture. Enduring concepts of right and wrong are indispensable to both social harmony and individual adjustment. But ideology is only one of the requisites to informed judgment. And as an intense, exclusive, or high-priority evaluative criterion, it is especially prone to flaws when put to use.

Self-interest is another indisputably relevant criterion in principle. Problems emerge in practice, however, from too great or too exclusive an emphasis by too many individual evaluators. Presidents, who must usually seek the middle ground on a host of issues, confront increasingly numerous coalitions of disaffected minorities (Mueller 1970) who collectively withdraw the support necessary for political viability. Carter described the well-organized special interests as "a growing menace to our democratic system of government" (1982, 80), a sentiment Reagan must have experienced as he sought to sell a revised tax code and a deficit reduction plan early in his second term. Self-interest may be, as Hobbes, Locke, and assorted modern social choice theorists have asserted, the dominant motive for civic participation. But taken to extremes, it can undermine efforts to sustain a durable social collective like a nation-state. Citizens must thus be enlightened by due regard for the interests of others, if only to sustain commitment to the collective order and to forestall rebellion, civil war, or other forms of social disintegration.

Gut-level reactions to a president's leadership style or mode of self-presentation cannot help but influence judgment. In a democracy, the acceptability of a president's personal style and presidential style is a legitimate basis for judgment. Because the president and citizens share an emotional as well as contractual relationship, and because the overall effectiveness of the president depends heavily on the ability to inspire public confidence and trust, it can only make sense to measure a president in part by the ability to inspire faith in the hearts and minds of citizens.

Problems with the subjective standard of leadership style are caused not by any lack of inherent suitability, then, but by misinformation and overvaluation. Given, for example, that concepts of acceptable leadership style originate in part from the need citizens have for deliverance from anxiety-producing problems, an obvious potential exists for overemphasizing the potency of the presidency, leadership mystique, or assertive posturing. The framers of the Constitution also raised a problem: how to read accurately anything so elusive as character or such components of character as self-presentation. This problem is magnified in the media age by the deliberate manipulations of public relations tactics and by the distortions of mass media editing. The average citizen has found it increasingly difficult to penetrate symbolic packaging and electronic imagery to get to the real human article.

In Chapter 6 an argument is made that the subliminal reactions that humans in general experience in response to one another can yield insights into character and thus serve as valuable guides to presidential selection. How valuable depends on moderating the influences of culturally inspired meanings and expectations and on access to reliable and valid information. Both contingencies are relevant here and should serve to restrain enthusiasm for leadership style as a reliable basis for judgment.

None of the three subjective criteria for evaluation suffers, then, from quite the same sorts of intrinsic dilemmas that beset the objective grounds. Each has, in principle at least, a legitimate part to play in judgment but is susceptible of error when used. One additional shortcoming of the three criteria has not yet been mentioned: their very subjectivity. They operate solely according to the internal lights of the thinking subject or the individual citizen, and they have no necessary connection to the object of evaluation—presidential performance. A citizen needs to know little or nothing of the presidency to judge on grounds of ideology, self-interest, or leadership style. As a result, the subjective criteria are incomplete as grounds for judgment. How can judgment be reasonable if the workings of the presidency, which are being judged, are left utterly out of account?

In view of all the potential and actual problems, the claim that perfect judgment is nearly impossible seems well substantiated. But one thing is certain: neither the objective nor the subjective grounds will go away. Both individually and in interaction with one another, they will continue to influence the evaluation of presidential performance. The hope is that explicit reflection on their shortcomings will sensitize the electorate to the more egregious possibilities for misuse.

Although none of the grounds can be eliminated, it might prove useful to supplement them. By comparing how the strengths and weaknesses of each match up with those of the rest, something appears missing—a meaningful link between here and now judgment, on the one hand, and the actual operation of the presidency, on the other. Needed is a criterion suitable for use in the here and now that avoids the problems of subjectivity and ultimate relevance. A consciously designed and continually useful yardstick that requires familiarity with the mechanics of presidential functioning, intended to stand the test of time, might be satisfactory.

Competent Presidential Processes

To link here and now judgment with the actual operation of the presidency in a way that addresses the problems identified, another criterion must be devised—one that is, in a sense, self-correcting as new presidential experiences come forth. The existing and growing body of knowledge about presidential competence, a collection of experience-based insights into how presidents can most effectively use their resources, should be systematized as meaningful grounds for here and now judgment.

Competent presidential processes—the strategic savvy with which presidents wield the levers of power—have long been a focus of writings about the presidency by political scientists and journalists (Rockman 1984). From Neustadt's (1980) treatise on how persuasion overcomes constraints, to Heineman and Hessler's (1980) distillation of management lessons learned from Carter's mistakes, to Larry Berman's (1982) dissection of the decision making that culminated in the tragedy of Vietnam, to Greenstein's (1983) volume on Reagan's innovative uses of presidential resources, a line of analysis emerges concerning how and how not to make the presidency work. Similarly, the columns of such editorial journalists as George Will, William F. Buckley, James Reston, David Broder, Tom Wicker, Joseph Kraft, Dom Bonafede, Hugh Sidey, and Lou Cannon are filled with commentary on the strategic smarts of recent presidents.

These writings amount to an impressive corpus of analysis about how to make the presidency work. They represent the best insider and outsider thought on the effective use of executive resources. Most contain implicit or explicit evaluative statements on the performances of particular presidents, from which generalizations about competence are drawn. But so far as I can discover, no one has suggested that the insights offered by these writings be refined, classified, and cast into propositions suitable for use as grounds for judgment. The resulting competent process standards (CPS), based on fairly extensive knowledge of what has and has not worked in the past, could achieve the status of systematic, empirically grounded hypotheses concerning what presidents should do now to get results later.

Using the past to connect the present and the future can be a way to escape the distorting momentum psychology of quick political success as a basis for here and now judgment and to modestly increase the likelihood that the grounds for judging current performance will not seem irrelevant in retrospect, when all the results are in. Citizens reinterpret past presidents, such as Truman and Eisenhower, more often than they should have to, even with the limitations of information and historical perspective.

The potential advantage of competent process standards over the criterion of quick political success hinges on their testable relationship to long-term results that most perceive as desirable. The effort to discover this empirical relationship necessitates examination of the record of presidential experimentation. Competent processes are thus subject to continual refinement and redefinition in the light of new presidential experience and thus address the problem of subjectivity— inattention to the actual workings of the presidency. Those who stay abreast of the codified record of experimentation will be exposed to state-of-the-art insight into presidential functioning.

Of course, the future usually disproves any convention. Presidents are continually finding new methods of using their power, as Reagan's innovative and seemingly successful modes of contending with the media, the bureaucracy, the citizenry, and the responsibilities of office, attest. Hypotheses are inherently at risk of being refuted. But far from undermining their value, their falsifiability is their strength because they can be corrected and renewed. Though hypotheses may later be proven wrong, they were demonstrably the best that could be drawn up at the time—a claim to legitimacy that impulsive reactions to quick political success cannot match.

The ultimate meaning and value of any presidential achievement remains open to partisan dispute and historical revisionism. The most competent process standards can hope to do is to reduce the instability of judgment that is attributable to momentum psychology. For example, Eisenhower, judged by informed contemporaries as a bumbling if popular incompetent, is now being reconsidered as an astute, "hidden hand" president, largely because of an inchoate redefinition of what constitutes presidential competence (Greenstein 1982). A special focus on competent processes can bring the debate over redefinition into sharper focus. But they cannot help determine, for example, whether Eisenhower failed the moral test of using his popular strength for progressive purposes, a value judgment reached by James David Barber (1985, 514). The example underscores the fact that competent process standards are supplements, not substitutes, for values and other relevant grounds for judgment. But surely citizens cannot be hurt by a disciplined exposure to the operation of the presidency. For most people it is this exposure, and not moral compasses or value groundings, that is missing.

The State of the Art

To illustrate competent process standards, exclusive focus will be on the major innovations of the Reagan presidency—those that are very likely to influence the performance of presidents to follow.[3] The Reagan administration has been unusually creative in its approach to the operational presidency. As suggested in Chapter 4, its strategies may be more lasting than its policy impacts. Whether future presidents will be able to duplicate Reagan's success is uncertain because the element of surprise in using new strategies and the Reagan charm will be missing. And whether Reagan's policies will produce the long-term changes he intended is unclear. In any event, Reagan's approach represents the state-of-the-art practice in the effort to produce such changes. Therefore, the prevailing hypotheses about what presidents should do to maximize their chances for lasting results are based on his innovations.

The basic philosophy of strategic effectiveness, from which competent process standards derive, is captured in the following excerpt from a recent analysis of presidential management:

> There is no mystery about the strategic approach to government. It involves laying out the host of possible objectives; understanding the connections among them; choosing your priorities among them; defining the roles and responsibilities for your top officials; assessing the impact of outside forces ... assessing the limits on your resources; establishing discrete steps that should be taken within a specific time frame to achieve the priority objectives; and leaving enough play in the joints to take into account the unexpected. (Heineman and Hessler 1980, 16)

The Assumption of Power

An important strategic innovation of the Reagan administration was its overall approach to assuming the reins of power during the months prior to the inauguration and during the initial year of incumbency. The first 6 to 12 months of a presidential term have always been recognized as a crucial testing time—for establishing good first impressions and for certain additional opportunities and pitfalls endemic to new beginnings.

First, the president's opportunity to achieve quick political success is at its peak then. Presidents since Kennedy have proposed most of their legislation in their initial years and found the greatest percentage of legislative approval in the first three months (Light 1982, 42-45). The early months find the media more anxious to stress the positive than they ever again will be (Smoller 1986). Presidential popularity soars and rarely, if ever, dips below the 50 percent mark (*National Journal*, May 19, 1984). Even the federal bureaucracy, often a source of resistance to presidents, is eager to demonstrate its willingness to serve (Heclo 1977). For a brief moment, the forces of pluralism—Congress, media, public, bureaucracy, interest groups, and issue networks—are willing to suspend their own priorities and entertain the president's.

Second, the first year is dangerous, for it invites mistakes. New presidents are necessarily ignorant of key facets of the job. Most analysts agree that little adequate prepresidential training is available. Inescapably, the newcomer must learn on the job. As numerous theorists of the cycles of the modern presidency have observed, the learning curve consumes at least 18 months (Neustadt 1980; Kessel 1975). By this time, the special opportunities will have expired, a paradox Paul Light describes as conflicting cycles of increasing effectiveness (as experience builds) and decreasing influence (as opportunities diminish). Some of the most important decisions will be made when the president is least capable of deciding wisely (Hess 1976, 16-25), risking reputation, prestige, and prospects for achievement.

Third, transitions take place frequently. In the last 40 years, eight presidents have served. Because transitions are expensive, inefficient, and disruptive, a premium is placed on being able to manage them effectively. Professional presidency watchers take note of the newcomer's public relations abilities, media skills, and acumen at avoiding highly publicized mistakes. But the focus of those concerned with competent processes is the extent to which a new president gets control of the governmental machinery: the legislative and budgetary processes, personnel, and the bureaucracy. Most recent presidents have not handled themselves particularly well in any of these areas, neither early nor late in their terms. The Reagan administration, however, took unprecedented control of them all early by abandoning three cornerstones of presidential resources management: (1) get as much legislation introduced and passed as possible during the first months in office; (2) make appointments quickly and delegate most of the responsibility for personnel selection to cabinet members; and (3) abandon the budgetary process as a first year presidential priority because it is so rigid.

The Reagan forces created a new standard for taking control of the government. Six competent process standards, derived from the Reagan experience, concerning what presidents should do first to get results later follow, with a brief discussion of each.

CPS 1   To maximize the chances for legislative success and positive long-term legislative consequences, the president should devise proposals with extreme care and keep the list of proposals short—to a bare minimum.

The experience of liberal activist presidents like Wilson, FDR, and LBJ suggested that competent presidents sought speedy approval for lengthy lists of progressive legislation. Reagan upheld the norm of taking advantage of the receptive honeymoon climate by striking quickly but challenged the assumption that more is better. The bare minimum standard is a result of widespread professional respect for the administration's astuteness in winning approval for a major reduction in domestic spending and the Economic Recovery Tax Act of 1981 (Pfiffner 1982; Heclo and Penner 1983). It also reflects increasing acceptance of the idea that only unusual circumstances—the national despair and panic engendered by the Great Depression or the post-assassination atmosphere that encouraged passage of the Great Society programs—can be expected to prompt massive legislative action. Some movement of support is detected in the direction of the stages theory of political development, discussed in Chapter 2, which says legislative and other presidential aspirations should fit the historical epochs in which they are sought. But this first competent process standard stems primarily from various structural and circumstantial factors—some new, some just newly realized—which can be expected to constrain the size of legislative agendas in the foreseeable future.

In the absence of compelling circumstances that make it seem appropriate, a lengthy list of legislative proposals risks clouding the mass public's comprehension of the president's sense of direction. The comparative experiences of Carter and Reagan support this assertion. A related issue is that the chances for failure increase as the agenda grows. Avoiding highly publicized failure is crucial in the early stages.

The influence network surrounding the legislative process has become so fragmented, complex, and competitive that presidents must undertake a massive mobilization of resources on every important congressional vote to have a chance to build a winning coalition (Light 1982; Hodgson 1980). The declining influence of parties in Congress, the rise of well-financed single-issue interest groups and political action committees, the proliferation of congressional subcommittees with overlapping jurisdictions, and the increased autonomy of individual members of Congress, all place severe limits on the number of issues in which a president's modest store of political capital can be invested. Only the highest priorities are pursued.

The Reagan administration has also found avenues of policy influence other than the legislative process through which to steer the direction of government. By affecting the course of policy implementation in the executive branch, a president could neutralize unwanted legislation or set a new course without benefit of enabling legislation. The existence of viable alternatives to the legislative process reduces its importance in establishing policy direction.

If Reagan's success accounts for the bare minimum component of CPS 1, Reagan's failure—the budget deficit consequences of the 1981 tax cut—explains the presence of the "extreme care" clause. As mentioned earlier, quick political success does not guarantee long-term effectiveness. The extreme care clause reflects the growing conviction that considerably more thought and preparation should precede legislation, particularly when highly technical questions are involved, and the recognition that presidential candidates rarely have sufficient time to undertake careful studies of policy proposals during the campaign. An increasing body of opinion believes that the failure of the New Deal, the Great Society, and the supply-side tax cuts to yield the intended or expected results stemmed from insufficient attention to forecasting probable outcomes. If potential problems had been identified, the proposals could have been refined accordingly, prior to passage and implementation. It might be supposed that the fewer programs proposed, the greater the likelihood that they will be well conceived, but the consequences of the 1981 tax cut suggest this is no certainty. Reagan proponents have argued that the tax program was well thought out but not fully implemented, and thus not properly tested. Some have also suggested that the large budget deficits were anticipated and intentional— a device for creating pressure for greater domestic cuts. The emphasis on policy planning and preparation as a test of presidential competence is increasing in prominence. If preparation is to take place at all, it will likely have to before the pressures of campaigning and the legislative struggle, which is by nature emotionally charged, begin. Given the emergence of professional presidential candidates, like Nixon or Reagan, who devote years and decades of their lives to running and preparing for the presidency, this may not be an unrealistic expectation. Policies do not, of course, "spring fully formed from the overtaxed brow of the President or even from his immediate entourage" (Polsby 1984, 5). Instead, they tend to originate with people not employed by the ultimate decision makers, such as technical experts, policy analysts, researchers, bureaucrats, interest group members, or congressional committee staffers. But presidents, as those who incubate, advocate, and bear historical responsibility for the consequences of policies, are the logical ones to undertake the job of reflecting on what might go wrong and seeking to head it off at the design stage. The incentive is provided by heightened expectations for policy quality and a corresponding deemphasis on the legislative box score as the sine qua non of presidential success.

> CPS 2   To maximize control over policy implementation, the president should centralize the personnel appointments process in the White House and take the time to ensure that strategically important subcabinet positions are staffed with loyalists first and experts second.

Even before the Reagan administration demonstrated the value of this competent process standard, presidents who did not exert effective influence over the bureaucracy invited trouble. Executive branch processes have lives and momentum of their own and can easily pass a president by. The appointments process can be used to position individuals in the bureaucracy who will ensure that the laws are carried out in a fashion consistent with administration priorities. In this sense, an administrative strategy can serve as an alternative to legislation. The importance of people who can be counted on in the bureaucracy may seem obvious, but it was not to such recent presidents as Kennedy, Nixon, and Carter.

Reagan did not invent the loyalty test; it dates at least to Andrew Jackson's spoils system. But because of the Civil Service Reform Act of 1888, which sought to instill a nonpartisan attitude in civil servants, and negative public attitudes toward political favoritism, modern presidents before Reagan felt compelled to avoid large-scale efforts to place loyalists in key posts. The Eisenhower administration's attempt to identify a pool of loyal Republicans for appointment to important subcabinet positions came under intense public criticism and was abandoned (Mackenzie 1981, 120). Presidents Kennedy, Nixon, and Carter, convinced by arguments that it was good management to do so, left the selection of most key officials to their cabinet officers. Kennedy was unable to persuade some, including Robert McNamara, to accept cabinet positions without the authority to make appointments. Nixon, who came to regard the bureaucracy as a bastion of Democratic opposition to his policy initiatives (Aberbach and Rockman 1976), regretted his decision to delegate appointments authority. "I just made a big mistake," he is reputed to have said (Evans and Novak 1971, 70). He would seek to recover lost ground by means of an administrative strategy that combined intimidation of opposition bureaucrats (Nathan 1983, 39) with White House intervention in agency policy behavior (Randall 1979). Carter's actions led both his advisers and outsiders to conclude that he had, in effect, "given away the government" (Heineman and Hessler 1980, 165). Carter's difficulties with departments such as Health, Education, and Welfare would be attributed to the same mistake Kennedy and Nixon made.

One tangible result the Reagan administration achieved by openly and deliberately reversing the traditions in the appointments process was an unprecedented degree of personal loyalty to the president among a large number of strategically located officials in the federal bureaucracy (Pfiffner 1982). The candidate review process was centralized in the White House under E. Pendleton James, whose rank of assistant to the president was the highest ever accorded a personnel director. Although the Reagan cabinet did not have an unusual number of loyalists or Reagan-style conservative ideologues, almost every appointee below the cabinet level was a true believer. A study conducted by the National Academy of Public Administration (1985) found that an absence of prior governmental experience and a record of opposition to the agency of appointment supplemented ideological loyalty to the president as selection criteria (Starr and Weathers 1985, 25).

Reagan confronted much less obstructionism than had Nixon or Carter and could move quickly to influence the daily implementation of existing laws by executive agencies. One example involves the qualification standard used by the Social Security Administration (SSA) within the Department of Health and Human Services (HHS) to determine the eligibility of individual citizens for disability benefits under the Social Security laws. SSA and HHS were prime targets of the Reagan administration's efforts to cut spending and reshape welfare policy. By placing new political appointees into leadership positions within SSA, the administration was able to compel agency career officials to use much more restrictive eligibility standards for awarding disability benefits—ultimately eliminating some 500,000 individuals from eligibility. Despite the fact that in numerous cases federal courts held that improper standards were used to disallow benefits, the agency steadfastly refused to accept those decisions as binding and continued to disqualify aid recipients. Although individuals who were disqualified could expect to be reinstated by the courts, they were forced to undergo the expenses and rigors of litigation, a process many were ill-equipped to undertake (Pear 1985, 1).[4] Whatever the moral or legal ethics involved, this example clearly illustrates the tight political control of policy behavior of a federal agency and the value to a president's program of careful attention to midlevel appointments. Despite considerable outside pressure from disgruntled program constituents and the federal courts, the appointed leadership in SSA remained loyally determined to do the president's bidding.

The care and thoroughness with which candidates were screened for loyalty created something of a bottleneck, and the Reagan system would be widely criticized for the slowness with which many positions were staffed. Many agencies and departments were left to function with key leadership positions unfilled until late in the first or early in the second year. Administration spokesmen pointed to the value of deliberation and the press of other business, such as the budgetary initiatives (Pfiffner 1982). Their defense is persuasive in light of the results.

> CPS 3 To maximize early control of the budgetary process, the president should devise and quickly implement plans for revising the previous president's final budget as comprehensively as policy objectives require.

Given the importance of the nation's economic well-being to the president's political fortunes, the massive structural budget deficits that will confront the nation for the foreseeable future, and the crucial impact of national fiscal policy on the country's economic health and the deficit, presidents will inevitably be forced to give top priority to getting control of the budgetary process. Although such legislation as the Budget and Accounting Act of 1921, the Reorganization Act of 1939, and the Employment Act of 1946 has increased the statutory involvement of the presidency in the annual budget cycle and in fiscal policy generally, presidents since FDR have varied significantly in the extent to which they have emphasized the budget in their governing strategies and have immersed themselves in budgetary details. Presidents like Eisenhower and Kennedy involved themselves only selectively, while Johnson and Ford were actively and intimately engaged (Hill and Plumlee 1982; Mowery, Kamlet, and Crecine 1980). As the importance of the budget has increased, presidential freedom to choose how involved to get in the process has declined. With the passage of the 1974 Congressional Budget and Impoundment Control Act, aimed at strengthening congressional control over the budgetary process, it may have disappeared altogether. The significance of a president's grasp of the budgetary process has increased as a measure of professional competence (Hill and Plumlee 1982; Haider 1982) with recognition that to budget is to govern (Pious 1979) and that budgets are policies with price tags attached (Wildavsky 1979).

The budget is important, and its management is a key test of presidential skill. But before 1981, presidents were not expected to get much real control of the budgetary process until the third year in office. On the day a new president is inaugurated in January, one annual budget is in force, another is being debated in Congress, and a third is in the early stages of preparation by the Office of Management and Budget (OMB) within the executive branch. Each budget reflects a complicated negotiation process involving virtually every agency of government and requires 19 months from conception to enactment. A new president will not have presided over an entire 19-month cycle until the third year in office. Furthermore, the federal tradition of incrementalism favors small rather than major changes in existing budget base lines and three-fourths of recent budgets have consisted of uncontrollable entitlement categories, such as Social Security cost-of-living adjustments. The reasons for modest expectations for early presidential control of the budget process are clear. At best, it seems, an impact can be made on the budget in the planning stages, which goes into effect on October 1 of the new president's second year.

On March 10, 1981, only 49 days after taking office, Reagan submitted to Congress a complete revision of Carter's fiscal year 1982 budget, proposed just before he left office and due to become effective on October 1, 1981. Reagan's budget included large defense increases, large tax cuts, unprecedented reductions in domestic programs, and even reductions in the fiscal 1981 budget (Pfiffner 1982, 12). Within six months, Reagan had achieved most of his budgetary goals. This performance is the origin of CPS 3. Reagan's feat is perhaps the most fundamental alteration of what can be expected of presidents in modern times. It now seems possible for a president to make significant, not merely cosmetic, changes in all three budgets in the works on inauguration day. Presidents now must seek control upon entering office and not wait until late in the first term.

How did Reagan do it? Published analyses suggest three major sources of explanation. First, the budget was, for all practical purposes, the administration's only priority during the initial year. Except for the appointments process and the media relations strategy, the talent and energy of the key players were focused on revising and winning passage of a substantially reshaped fiscal 1982 budget (Heclo and Penner 1983). So exclusive a concentration of presidential resources was novel, and Reagan showed himself willing to stake his reputation on this single, high-risk gamble.

Second, the administration benefited from a supportive public. A larger than expected 1980 margin of electoral victory, a national consensus that the economy was out of control and in a state of crisis, an equally widespread conviction that runaway government spending was a major source of both inflation and massive budget deficits, and an emerging acknowledgment that some sort of drastic action was inevitable, all contributed to the public's willingness to accept Reagan's plans. By means of a carefully orchestrated public relations campaign, the president intensified the climate of urgency and was able to harness it to his budgetary proposals. His February 5, 1981, televised address, in which he warned of an "economic calamity of tremendous proportions" if his initiatives were not passed, was followed by a speech to a joint session of Congress February 18 in which his program for economic recovery was presented. In other presidential speeches and in lectures and TV appearances by cabinet officers, the need for Reagan's program was reiterated (Pfiffner 1982, 14).

Third, an internal strategy, aimed at quickly reworking the fiscal 1982 budget and selling the changes within the administration and in the Congress, simultaneously unfolded as the president ran his public relations campaign. The plan, concocted by the president's top advisers and implemented by OMB director David A. Stockman, emphasized speed, comprehensiveness, and audacity. Immediately after the election, a study began of agency budgets to identify potential targets for cuts. Stockman, a former congressman and a close student of the budget, led a 12-person transition team into OMB just three weeks before the inauguration. The strategy group instructed Stockman to cut $40 billion without touching defense or domestic "safety net" programs. Stockman's team worked around the clock with the very OMB staffers who had completed the Carter budget and produced a preliminary budget, which was used to persuade newly appointed cabinet officers to accept large cuts in their departmental budgets (Greider 1981). After the internal lobbying, the final revised budget was prepared for submission to Congress in early March. Stockman had managed to finish the equivalent of several months' work in only a few weeks.

Stockman mounted an intense and ambitious lobbying effort on Capitol Hill, where an unexpectedly receptive climate prevailed. The members had, of course, noted the president's public relations campaign and were not indifferent to his margin of victory or his popularity in their states and districts. They were also sensitive to the crisis atmosphere surrounding the economy. But most important, the opposition was caught off guard by the sweeping, comprehensive nature of the proposed changes (Greider 1981). So abrupt a departure from custom took it by surprise. Even the politically adroit special-interest lobbies could not respond effectively to proposals that were so expertly and zealously defended and that initially seemed to require sacrifices from all interests and, thus, to favor no one in particular—which, in effect, delegitimized the usual obstructionist strategies based on self-interested political horse-trading.

The coup de grâce was a brilliant exploitation of congressional budgetary procedures established under the 1974 Budget Act, which, ironically, had been intended to strengthen Congress's budget power at the expense of the president's. Fred Greenstein notes:

> Only a shrewd strategist of the current Congress could have conceived the plan to achieve expenditure cuts by employing the reconciliation provisions of the congressional budgeting procedures ... thus permitting a single vote on an omnibus bill that had the effect of reducing or eliminating programs that inevitably would have survived had members of Congress been forced to vote on them singly. (1983, 17)

Whether future presidents will be able to duplicate Reagan's strategies or results remains to be seen. But little doubt exists that the Reagan forces redefined both the timing and the scope of presidential budget aspirations, thereby establishing new hypotheses concerning how to get control of the government's purse strings.

The Media

The subject of a president's approach to contending with the media is not limited to the first year of the first term, although strategy begins then. What constitutes savvy presidential practice in media relations is not clearly defined. Professional writing and commentary before Reagan reflect the sensitive nature of this issue.

On the one hand, any president's pragmatic interest is in securing positive, friendly media coverage. Favorable treatment is usually sought by managing the flow of news through the White House press office, controlling potentially damaging news leaks, cultivating individual reporters and editors in hopes of getting the president's point of view across and, occasionally, seeking public sympathy through complaining of unfair, distorted, or simplistic coverage. The Nixon administration went so far as to wage a systematic campaign, employing Vice President Spiro Agnew as the point man, aimed at discrediting the press in the public mind.

On the other hand, most practicing political professionals, as well as journalists, acknowledge and believe in the First Amendment. They hold it as an article of democratic morality and professional ethics that presidents are obligated to disclose any information not demonstrably damaging to the national interest. The public's right to know is protected by a free press functioning as a democratic watchdog. A natural conflict arises: Full disclosure can be politically damaging, but incomplete or self-serving disclosure threatens to undermine democratic accountability. Few modern presidents have succeeded in reconciling these inconsistent imperatives. Professional presidency watchers are accordingly vague and imprecise when trying to define what it means to deal competently with the media. Few success stories are available for them to look to for guidance.

The Reagan strategy defines a standard of competence where one did not previously exist. It does so by providing the only success story in recent times. No one tactic undertaken by the administration to contain the press is unprecedented, but the well thought out, comprehensive, and successful strategy it employed is.

> CPS 4   If press coverage is to help, not hurt, the president, control over access to information and the subject matter and content of presidential statements must be exercised by the administration, not the White House press corps.

The premise of the administration's strategy was that reporters' pursuit of information, by its very nature, disrupts administration plans and hinders the president's ability to communicate his basic message. In the process, the institution of the presidency itself is weakened:

> Mr. Reagan's aides say they came into office mindful that the last four Presidents had been politically defeated or driven from office and convinced that the press's reporting had contributed to their downfall. The emotional press treatment of the Iran hostage crisis during the Carter Administration has never ceased to haunt them. (Weisman 1984, 36)

The media strategy joined the budgetary initiatives as the central preoccupations of Reagan's most powerful aides and remained so throughout his first term. They held regular public relations strategy meetings to keep the press from calling the shots. They studied the coverage of events and devised means for shaping future coverage. Laurence I. Barrett, White House correspondent for *Time* magazine who was permitted to attend a few strategy sessions, had this description:

> One big concern permeated all those sessions: how events had played or would play on the air and in print. What items on the schedule should be turned into "photo ops"? Should the President have a question period with the press today? If he does, what story should be "sold"? Is the briefing material ready to prepare Reagan for his next magazine interview? (1984, 442)

Subsidiary aims to forge a consensus on public relations among White House principals and to impose discipline elsewhere in the administration were of special importance because of information leaks (Kirschten 1984, 154-155). Despite some early disclosures unflattering to the administration, by term's end, an atmosphere had been created in which there were "few sins so grievous as public relations gaffes." White House staffers prided themselves on the favorable spin they could put on news deliberately released and on the ability to give the press "a gentle nudge in one direction or another" (Kirschten 1984, 155).

In addition to such advantages as Reagan's ability to project his likable personality and strong convictions, and the general public's ambivalence toward the media (Bonafede 1986), the strategy group possessed another important asset: its determination not to be trapped by excessive respect for the public's right to know. Even presidents who had disliked the press and suffered hostile relations with it felt obliged to treat it as a surrogate for the public, meeting reporters on a regular basis and responding to questions with a fair measure of forthrightness. Abetted by the conviction that being too responsive to the press weakened the presidential institution, the Reagan team felt justified in devising and implementing a strategy that significantly departed from the traditional norm.

The centerpiece of the strategy was simply to keep the president away from reporters, which meant far fewer full-scale press conferences than were typical of his predecessors, who averaged one news conference a month. Reagan held three in his first eight months and fewer than 30 (compared with Carter's 59) during his first term (Safire 1981, B6). Although the president could not be completely isolated, the primary purpose of the strategy was to ensure that Reagan was seen and heard in the most advantageous circumstances and settings when he did make himself available to the press.

The most obvious example is the brilliant orchestration of television exposure, which was used to dramatize and sustain presidential themes, to control the content of daily coverage, and to deflect potentially damaging criticism. In an interview with the *New York Times*, Michael K. Deaver, who served as deputy chief of staff and master political choreographer of the Reagan presidency, offers an illustration:

> Up until this president, you had housing starts going up and Jimmy Carter would go into the East Room and announce the figures. We went out to Fort Worth, and in front of a scaffolding with carpenters working in the background Reagan says "housing starts are up." With 80% of the public getting its news from TV, the guy in the audience says to his wife "My God! They're building houses again." (Smith 1985, 14)

A similar example, provided by Steven R. Weisman, illustrates the Reagan approach to deflecting criticism and promoting the administration's perspective on the news:

> [During a summer 1984] week of theme trips to a wildlife refuge, a national park, and other similar sites ... Mr. Reagan asserted repeatedly that his environmental record was better than generally recognized, and reporters repeatedly asked why, then, he had just appointed Anne M. Burford [who had been forced out of the Environmental Protection Agency for favoritism to business in the toxic-waste cleanup program] to an advisory board on oceans and the atmosphere. [Replied Reagan:] "If I answer that question, none of you will say anything about what we're here for today. I'm not going to give you a different lead." In other words, he did not intend to say anything that would displace his environmental message as the lead paragraph of that day's story. (1984, 72)

The Reagan administration also has effectively reformatted the traditional presidential press conference and invented new, controlled settings for presidential meetings with the press. The live television news conference, invented by John F. Kennedy, dampened the candor and freewheeling quality of presidential-press encounters somewhat, but the tradition of genuine give-and-take for the most part survived. One analyst, columnist William Safire, describes the televised news conference as "the greatest advance in America's form of democratic government in the last generation" because it provided for the United States the kind of "spirited accountability" of prime ministers to their critics in parliamentary systems and made it visible to the American people (1981, B6). In part because of Reagan's penchant for startling, factually inaccurate statements in unrehearsed settings, administration media specialists decided to redesign the press conference format. In a series of changes spread over the entire first term, they rescheduled conferences from afternoons to evenings during prime time (so a large audience could see them and not be unduly influenced by national news summaries, which tended to focus on gaffes), required reporters to raise their hands and refrain from shouting for recognition (to reduce the circus-like, adversarial atmosphere characteristic of predecessors' news conferences), and encouraged Reagan to exploit his own humor and charm in deflecting hostile questions (said Communications Director David R. Gergen: "His sense of humor and smile, when dealing with the press on television, is worth a million votes" [Kirschten 1984, 154]). The press sessions became East Room "ceremonial extravaganzas, complete with red carpet and glittering chandeliers" aimed at giving the public a "false impression of conviviality and shared purpose, with Mr. Reagan joking and calling on reporters (many of whom he hadn't met personally) by their first names." The result has been to reduce the role of reporters to the level of "actors, or even props in a presentation over which he has wielded nearly total control" (Weisman 1984, 73, 83).

The Reagan administration also responded with controls on access to reporters' complaints that insufficient opportunities existed for informal interchanges with the president that would reveal his thinking on issues. Late in the first term, the president began meeting with groups of White House reporters for off-the-record "Q and A" sessions over cocktails. The beauty of this device, according to the administration, was that it created an atmosphere that inhibited tough questioning and encouraged empathy with the president's point of view. Even an ardent critic might be expected to feel an obligation to a friendly couple like the Reagans after having accepted their hospitality and basked in their charm. Some reporters declined to attend because of the restrictive ground rules, and one, William Safire, wrote a column denouncing what he saw as a ploy to manipulate the press.

Another practice that reporters found vexing, but which added to the control of access, was the "cupped ear" interview. While using this technique, the president could appear responsive and sympathetic to press queries yet also avoid any unplanned disclosures. As the president moved from the White House to a waiting helicopter on the lawn, he would pause briefly to answer questions shouted by reporters cordoned off some distance away. With the din of the propeller whirring deliberately in the background, he would cup his ear as if straining to hear the question. He was then free to answer forthrightly, answer a question other than the one posed, or strike an amiable, "sorry, I can't hear" posture and stride off with a smile. When faced with complaints about access, Deputy Press Secretary Larry Speakes could accurately claim that the president frequently stopped and answered unscheduled questions, thus displaying an accessibility for which he was insufficiently credited. Speakes could also note the fact that the president was, indeed, hard of hearing. Reporters, well aware that they had been bamboozled and trumped, could only gnash their teeth.

The control devices reduced the adverse impact of the press on Reagan's political fortunes and changed the nature of information the public received about his administration in comparison with his predecessors'. Whatever the implications for the public's right to know, Deaver's claim that the Reagan presidency was a "media presidency," one that would "shape the communications strategies of all future presidencies," met with little argument (Smith 1985, 14).

The Organizational System

Organization is the manner in which the president, the people around the president, and the work routines and procedures are used to maximize the chances for long-term success. At issue is not the entire executive branch, but primarily the president's immediate staff and work environment. Choices are made about what the president will do and what will be left to others, how to supervise the work of subordinates and how to use their advice. Few aspects of the presidency are more subject to personal discretion. As president, one can do as one pleases in establishing organization.

The precise relationship between a president's short-term organization and long-term success is difficult to specify. Specialists continue to debate the optimal strategy for managing the presidency. Until recently, the prevailing wisdom was that presidents could not expect to succeed without extensive, personal involvement in all aspects of decision making and attendant presidential processes, including the acquisition of information, the clarification of options, and the supervision of subordinates. Only the president, argued Neustadt (1980), had the perspective and the incentive to do these things effectively. The wisdom in serving as the hub of a many-spoked wheel has been seriously questioned recently because a deep level of personal involvement is physically impossible (Sperlich 1964) and because alternative approaches have been recognized as having their strengths (Johnson 1974; Greenstein 1982). Most can agree on certain minimal organizational requirements for effectiveness. For example, presidents and other executives are well advised to establish processes that do not filter out important information; they should not fall prey to "groupthink" (Janis 1972) and other threats to the quality of decision making; and they should establish procedures of coordination aimed at minimizing confusion and conflict (Quirk 1984). Experts disagree over other crucial questions, however, such as: How much does a president need to know of policy intricacies to decide wisely? When should instinct, intuition, or ideology prevail over experts and facts in deciding? How much delegation of presidential authority is too much? Far from being issues of mere procedure and management, these questions address the fundamental nature of presidential responsibility.

As discussed in Chapter 4, the media and other informed opinion believed neither Carter nor Reagan made optimal choices concerning work procedures or the extent of his personal involvement in policy details. Carter's approach, critics said, was far too self-reliant, involving an unwise use of his time and resulting in confused priorities and unnecessary internal conflict. Reagan's approach, on the other hand, was too disengaged, making him a part-time president insufficiently informed on the issues and overdependent on advisers (Quirk 1984).

Whatever the merits of the criticisms, the Reagan approach represents an innovative and clearly defined theory of presidential responsibility, as well as a deliberate strategy for using the presidency to achieve long-term results. Although critics believe he has been lucky and has achieved short-term success in spite of his organizational system, Reagan and his supporters credit the system itself in large part for his success thus far and expect it to help place Reagan in a lasting and lofty position in presidential history. Time, of course, will tell. But as of now, Reagan has the most carefully developed, the most innovative, and the most up-to-date strategy for managing the presidency.

> CPS 5   To achieve lasting results, focus on those matters important to history (for example, course-charting, position-taking speeches) and on those matters only the president can attend to (for example, sustaining public support, making decisions, persuading). Keep the president out of everything else.

Prior to Reagan's implementation of a minimalist presidency, academic argument in support of such an approach was sparse. Only Stephen Hess, of the Brookings Institution, offered a rationale for a strategy like Reagan's:

> I propose a redefinition of the tasks of Presidents, those activities that they must perform and that cannot be performed by others. The corollary is that the many other tasks currently performed badly by presidents must be performed elsewhere ... [The president's] major responsibility, in my judgment, is to annually make a relatively small number of highly significant political decisions—among them, setting national priorities, which he does through the budget and his legislative proposals, and devising policy to ensure the security of the country, with special attention to those situations that could involve the nation in war. (1976, 10-11)

In brief, the Reagan approach had four components: extensive delegation, collegial decision making, presidential specialization, and presidential distancing. Reagan delegated authority through a system of cabinet councils—originally seven in number, reduced to two in the second term. The president served as "chairman of the board," presiding over an hierarchical flow of analysis and information channeled through the councils. A group of three close advisers—Edwin Meese III, James A Baker III, and Michael K. Deaver—initially managed the process. Management would later be centralized in the hands of a single chief of staff, Donald T. Regan. Numerous additional modifications and personnel changes would be made. In particular, the foreign policy machinery would be tightened and systematized as the first term wore on. But the key players—close advisers and cabinet officers—would always be generalists rather than experts or ideologues, on the theory that "expertise could be hired while management skill and common sense could not" (Cannon 1982, 309). Furthermore, ideologues were considered most valuable at the operating levels, a conclusion reflected in the use of the appointments process. The central figure—the president—would remain aloof from daily operations.

Despite the comparatively formal policy machinery under the president, the decision-making process at the top was remarkably collegial and informal (Greenstein 1983, 182). Reagan made the final decisions, but he did so with the help of a small group of close advisers—through a process he called roundtabling—who were responsible for clarifying the options and briefing him on the merits of an issue. Meetings and memorandums were the key mechanisms for educating the president on his choices (Kessel 1984, 163-165). While others gathered and analyzed information and framed the options, Reagan was free, in George E. Reedy's words, to "resolve the policy questions that will not yield to a quantitative, empirical analysis" and to "persuade enough of his countrymen of the rightness of his decisions so that he can carry them out without destroying the fabric of society" (1970, 29). The crucial choice-framing responsibilities, which can predestine decisions, are precisely what Reagan has delegated and what other presidents have been unwilling to delegate. By electing to trust certain carefully chosen advisers to do the bulk of this work, Reagan departed significantly from previous presidential practice.

Reagan's job was to make the major decisions and sell them: to the public, the Congress, and the media in forums ranging from face-to-face encounters in the Oval Office to telephone campaigns for key congressional votes to nationally televised speeches. He performed with consummate skill, earning the title "The Great Communicator."

Presidential distancing was reflected in Reagan's detachment from a personal management role in the policy process, in his noninvolvement in the hard, intellectual work of generating, refining, and cross-checking the options from which decisons were made, in the comparative infrequency of his press conferences, and in his relaxed, "9-to-5" approach to what previous presidents and the public had come to regard as the toughest job in the world. Distancing suited Reagan's personal predilections and created an atmosphere in which he could work comfortably.

As Lou Cannon wrote: "Heightened tension would not have made of Ronald Reagan a better president, and Reagan knew it. He did not want his personal harmony disturbed" (1982, 376). The liberating factor for Reagan was his advisers, who were able to protect him successfully from the dangers of detachment—dangers warned against by Neustadt in *Presidential Power* (1980). Noting that Reagan appeared to have a genuine gift for casting major supporting actors in positions that backed up the "leading man," Fred Greenstein concludes that Reagan "teaches future presidents that it is feasible and even desirable to shape their official family to their distinctive needs, whether or not in doing so they organize the White House in a manner that defies orthodox organization theory" (1983, 181).

Two of the four components of the Reagan organizational strategy—extensive delegation and distancing—were virtually unprecedented, in that no previous president had taken either to such lengths. Collegial decision making and presidential specialization had been used before with mixed results. Kennedy employed a collegial approach to generally good effect. Nixon had specialized, focusing most of his attention on foreign policy. His achievements were impressive, but his neglect of other matters helped bring about the Watergate scandal.

The four components together, however, amounted to a new invention, which could be defended on several grounds. Delegation, for example, is unavoidable for any president, given the demands of office and the physical limitations of human beings. Problems attributed to it in the past had more to do with misplaced trust than with intrinsic flaws. A president capable of identifying and supervising the right supporting talent can and should reduce the burdens of office to manageable, human proportions. Pivotal issues only the president can deal with would be addressed in an unharried, contemplative atmosphere. Collegial decision making is supported by both democratic theory and the results of psychological research. A group with proper guidance is likely to make better decisions on average than any single individual working alone, given that the available pool of energy, nerve, ideals, attention to detail, and cognitive power is multiplied (Janis 1972). Presidential specialization in a system based on division of labor reflects the superiority of bureaucratic forms over traditional forms of organization, as distinguished by Max Weber. Specialization permits the exploitation of unique talent and the cultivation of specialized expertise, both hallmarks of effective performance. And in the age of the media presidency, with the importance of public support and the relative lack of formal presidential authority, a successful president must also be a specialist in persuasive communication. Future presidents will have to possess the media skills of a Kennedy, a Roosevelt, or a Reagan. To be effective, they will have to invest the bulk of their time and energies in rhetorical pursuits. Finally, distancing, in addition to permitting a more measured pace, is both smart management and good politics. As Stephen Hess argues, it can help to reverse the flow of problems and decisions into the White House by recentering them in agencies and departments. The Reagan experience shows that the political fallout from unpopular decisions or consequences is much less damaging to a president if they are perceived as the doings of errant subordinates. Ultimate responsibility can be gracefully accepted by a president without causing a severe drop in political standing. Reagan's distancing taught the public and the media to expect less of him and more of his underlings, thus reducing his vulnerability without diminishing either his authority or his stature.[5] In fact, distancing actually increased his stature by giving him the aura of an elevated court of appeal. The incident of David Stockman's public disclosure of skepticism about the Reagan economic theory is illustrative. When lack of faith in a policy is expressed by a key adviser who helped implement it, a corresponding loss of public faith in the top man would be expected, along with a demand for an explanation from the president. Instead, Reagan simply took Stockman "to the woodshed"— allegedly reproving him for his breach of faith. By responding as an aloof authority figure, Reagan finessed the problem and conveyed a serene, self-confident definition of his status that the public seemed to accept with approval.

Criticism of the Reagan organizational approach, which emphasized the president's overreliance on advisers and ignorance of policy details, was more an indictment of Reagan's failure to do his part and fair share in the system he devised than of the system itself. However inevitable and valuable extensive delegation, the president must be "familiar enough with the substantive policy debates in each major area to recognize clearly the signs of serious, responsible argument" (Quirk 1984, 142). Although the president need not be an expert in every policy area, an understanding and familiarity is required of how experts and policy analysts reach conclusions, what their prevailing theories and models are, why they have succeeded and failed in the past, and what basic positions and arguments support alternative solutions to problems. Only by being informed, through careful, thoughtful study, can a president tell which advisers are making sense and when to rely on instinct or ideology because the facts and figures are no longer helpful.

Reagan has been criticized repeatedly by observers of all political persuasions, with apparent justification, for his lack of knowledge on issues. This, however, is not a fatal flaw and need not detract from the potential of the organizational approach pioneered by the Reagan administration. Numerous short-term benefits have already become apparent, and long-term benefits have been predicted. Future presidents are likely to imitate Reagan's approach, the state of the art for presidential organization.

The Policy Process

The last of competent presidential processes to be cast as an evaluative standard addresses how a president can help muster a winning coalition behind highly controversial policy choices later in the term, after the honeymoon period is over. A president may no longer be able to get exactly what was originally intended but remains responsible for getting something, particularly for problems that will not wait for solutions.

In the broadest sense, the question is whether the policy-making elements of the national system—Congress and the presidency—are capable of dealing with and resolving significant problems without the special circumstances created by the inauguration of a new president. This issue goes to the heart of the viability of the policy machinery, which tends to deadlock after the initial burst of responsiveness to a new president wanes. Reagan's experience suggests that the machinery does not come unstuck even following a landslide reelection or with high levels of public support. Despite a 65 percent approval score six months into his second term, Reagan was unable to evoke the kind of responsiveness that characterized his first year in office. As a result of the Twenty-second Amendment to the Constitution, which limits presidents to two terms, the second-term president is a lame duck and suffers a notable loss of potency.

The cycle of declining influence stalls not only the president, but the entire government. It leaves problems to fester and achieve crisis proportions. Crises have traditionally been the only alternative to new beginnings capable of creating an atmosphere in which collective action in response to problems was possible. These realities have prompted many of the cries for reform of the national institutions and procedures (Robinson 1985). Unless other workable alternatives are invented within the existing structures, reform may have to be brought about.

Midway through the first Reagan term an invention was concocted, a desperate measure of last resort. As a result, a $170 billion package of tax increases and Social Security benefits cuts was passed by Congress and signed into law by the president—before the Social Security trust fund was to run dry. The legislation did not solve the problem, but it did resolve the immediate crisis. The invention was to move the debate outside the normal legislative process. "Responding to the obstacles inside the constitutional framework [Congress and the president], created a new form of government" (Light 1985, 8).

The full story of this invention, complete with an insightful analysis of its significance, is told by Paul C. Light in a book entitled *Artful Work: The Politics of Social Security Reform* (1985). Light makes clear that the strategy used to rescue the Social Security system was tried only after all else had failed:

> Key players tried to draft an agreement and failed repeatedly: first in the House, next in the agencies, then in the White House, the Senate, a House-Senate conference committee, the budget committees, and finally in a national commission. None seemed capable of reaching an accord—either on the size of the coming collapse or the range of possible solutions—and the courts had no authority to respond. (1985, 3)

Such a litany of frustration is typical of constituentless, dedistributive policy problems, whose responsible solutions will have only opponents and no supporters and will impose only pain and no pleasure on large segments of the population. But these are precisely the sorts of policy problems the federal government will confront at the close of the twentieth century. Multi-billion dollar budget deficits, a huge and growing defense budget, funding for benefit programs like Medicare, coping with Soviet satellite states in the western hemisphere, all pose problems that will involve choices unlikely to generate enthusiastic support. As with Social Security, presidents or members of Congress who devise solutions to these kinds of problems will receive few votes and little support—and invite political ruin. To work openly through normal channels is to permit the interests and lobbies to eviscerate real solutions. C-SPAN (Cable Satellite Public Affairs Network) television coverage of House proceedings makes a public spectacle of policy debates, which lessens the prospects for candor and courage. Only stalemate can result.

Without years to educate and convince the public of the urgency of a problem like Social Security, and of the unavoidability of solutions that impose pain, the only apparent option is to move behind the scenes and to camouflage the costs of and responsibility for the solutions. Presidents are in the best position to undertake the educational effort needed to persuade the public to accept the truth, but the political arrangements do not motivate them to do so. Their time is too short, the political costs of bad news too great. Complicating the situation are issues that stimulate deeply antagonistic partisan passions. Social Security is just such an issue.

CPS 6   To resolve tough, no-win policy questions on which either
Congress or president can force a stalemate, it is necessary
to: (1) conduct negotiations outside normal channels, without media, interest group, or formal congressional involvement; (2) provide a cloak of secrecy and deniability for the
legislative and executive branch principals, who must ratify any agreements; (3) write the final legislation in codes
complex enough to inhibit and confuse the public and
interest groups long enough to prevent effective opposition;
and (4) force a quick, "up-or-down" congressional vote,
thus sidestepping traditional delaying maneuvers by opponents.

CPS 6 is less complicated than it appears. The following brief notes
relay the essentials of this competent process standard.

The basic dilemma posed by the Social Security funding crisis was a
conflict between the urgent need for responsible government action and
the diametrically opposed views concerning what that action should be.
To Reagan and the Republicans, the solution was to cut benefits. To
House Speaker O'Neill and the Democrats, it was a tax increase sufficient to finance benefits at existing levels. Neither side had the votes to
compel acceptance of its solution, but both had the power to stalemate.
Presidential initiatives could not pass Congress. The Democrats did not
have the votes to override a veto. To the president, Social Security was a
symbol of the welfare state he sought to dismantle. To O'Neill, it was
the backbone of the Democratic party's commitment to social justice.
Neither would lightly abandon his heartfelt principles, but both recognized that, with the fund in serious trouble, a compromise was essential.

After two years of bloody political battle, both sides were convinced
that they could not prevail through the normal channels. In 1981, the
Reagan forces attempted to reduce the benefits to those opting for early
retirement and failed. They proposed cutting basic benefits and post-
poning by three months the cost-of-living adjustments (COLAs) and
failed. Later, they tried to eliminate the minimum benefit under Social
Security and to again the postpone the COLAs, and failed. These
unsuccessful efforts enabled the Democrats to paint the administration
as unfair and to charge that the president was trying to balance the
budget on the backs of the elderly and poor. With the 1982 midterm
elections approaching, the issue would harm the Republicans unless it
was removed from the front pages. For their part, the Democrats recognized the imminence of the funding crisis, knew they would share the
blame for inaction, and had no desire to go on record, just before an

election, in support of a solution that all citizens would find unpleasant. The Democrats were thus willing to go along with the president's proposal for a bipartisan national commission, which could reduce the political heat and postpone action until after the midterm elections. The commission would not itself be the solution, but it would buy time for both sides, give the issue a bipartisan gloss, and provide camouflage for behind-the-scenes bargaining and compromise. Meanwhile, the president and the Speaker could maintain their uncompromising public postures.

When it became clear that partisan disputes would prevent the commission from resolving the issue and that the president was paying a heavy price in popular support, OMB director Stockman persuaded Reagan to allow him to approach the most pragmatic Democrats on the commission and propose secret meetings of some commission members and the White House staff. A similar strategy had been employed during deliberations on the Reagan fiscal 1982 budget without success. But those meetings showed the value of secrecy and deniability in promoting compromise. In the case of Social Security, the failure of the commission and the approaching July 1983 bankruptcy of the fund left few alternatives.

A series of secret meetings between representatives of the two principals, Reagan and O'Neill, began on January 5, 1983, and continued over a two-week period. They produced a compromise agreement that was acceptable to Congress and that rescued the Social Security system at least through the end of the decade. This forum, "a single chamber of national leadership" whose only constituents were the president and the Speaker of the House, would be the "new form of government" invented to deal with the problem (Light 1985, 143). It worked because it solved a number of problems that the normal process of legislative debate left unsolved. Because the participants in the meetings were pragmatists, not ideologues, they could move quickly to identify the issues on which bargaining and compromise were essential. Because the meetings were secret, they could bargain candidly and without posturing, safe from the danger of the morning headlines. Because the leading representatives from each camp could speak for the president and the Speaker, the support of the principals for any agreement was assured. Legislative passage was probable and a presidential veto improbable. A bipartisan presidential commission, assuming sponsorship and responsibility for the agreement, provided political protection for the president, congressional leadership, and individual members of Congress who voted for the compromise. When time came to face the voters again in 1984, all could deny personal responsibility. By then, the extinct commission could take the blame for unpopular tax increases, cost-of-living postponements, and an increased retirement age. Individual politicians could claim that they had fought to remain true to party principles but had been forced to accept the compromise to save the Social Security system from ruin.

The strategy for getting the agreement through Congress was a study in complexity, whose major components were speed, one vote on the entire compromise package, and the confusing nature of the proposed legislation. The complicated package perplexed the public, and, as a result, no massive outpouring of public opposition could be used by unfriendly interest groups to derail passage. An inattentive public found it difficult to tell whose interests were helped or harmed by legislation that provided, for example, for taxation of benefits, wherein half of all Social Security benefits were subject to the income tax, but only at upper income levels. The up-or-down vote prevented debilitating amendments, and the speed left the large interest groups who opposed the package with insufficient time to bring their considerable pressures to bear on individual members of Congress before the crucial vote.

The invention of a "new form of government" cannot be attributed to the Reagan administration alone—it was a joint invention of the executive and the Congress. It did not represent a way to impose presidential leadership, but a way to obtain a feasible solution to a problem with a deadline. One side did not leave completely triumphant because no one policy preference was adopted. The solution relied more on secrecy, guile, and public ignorance than proponents of open, democratic government and responsible citizenship are likely to feel comfortable with, but it did demonstrate that ways short of major reform could be found to make the system work.[6] In all, the invention was, as Paul Light claims, "artful work." And it does represent the state of the art for moving the national machinery on tough issues—a tactic whose broad outlines future presidents and congressional leaders will surely follow.

Conclusion

The six competent process standards are a fair sampling of what had been learned by the late eighties about how to make the presidency work. If the Reagan administration has shown that the presidency is possible again, it did so with these operational innovations as much as with the creation of a national mood of optimism.

Only the highlights of Reagan's experiences have been mentioned. In some cases, the full stories have yet to be written or understood. In other cases, they can be found in the sources cited. However, sufficient information has been presented to support the argument that competent presidential processes are potentially better grounds for here and now judgment than emotional reactions to quick political success.

A few points made earlier bear repeating. First, competent process standards should supplement other here and now grounds because they require familiarity with the state-of-the-art operation of the presidency. Gut reactions to momentum psychology, self-interest, and ideology do not. Judgment that incorporates some knowledge of the workings of the presidency is more likely to be reasonable, prudent, and responsible than judgment that does not.

Second, competent process standards are supplements, not substitutes, for grounds like leadership style, ideology, and self-interest. Competent process standards were the focus here, not because they have greater legitimacy or more fundamental importance, but because the perspective they represent tends to get the least attention in the average individual's evaluative deliberations.

Third, competent process standards are hypotheses, not commandments. Most will be modified or replaced as a result of future experience. But if presidents attend to them faithfully and consciously, citizens will come to understand more systematically and accurately how presidents can govern wisely and implement policy with lasting results. In the process, citizens can be increasingly better equipped to pass judgment in the here and now.

Notes

1. For a discussion of these hypotheses and of the relationships among preconscious and conscious grounds for judgment, see Appendix 2.
2. See Appendix 2.
3. For an effort to extract lessons from the Reagan presidency somewhat similar to the competent process standards, see Bert A. Rockman, "A Tale of Two Presidents: Carter, Reagan, and Lessons for Public Morality," *Presidency Research* 8 (Fall 1985): 3-14.
4. This controversy was still alive as the summer of 1986 approached. In a March 9, 1986, *New York Times* article entitled "New Court Sought for Benefit Cases," Robert Pear reported that the Reagan administration, which had finally succumbed in 1984 to pressure from federal judges, members of Congress, and state officials to halt its reviews of the disability rolls to weed out ineligible people, had come up with another strategy. Contending that federal district and appeals courts "award benefits to people who are not truly disabled" (p. 1), the administration revealed plans to propose a new Social Security Court, which would hear nothing but disability appeals and would take away the power of the federal district courts and most federal appeals courts to hear Social Security cases.

5. Distancing also helped Reagan stay out of trouble with his underlings. By giving those relatively close to Reagan, such as U.S. representative to the United Nations Jeane J. Kirkpatrick, the impression that decisions or actions they did not like were the work of inner-circle aides and not the president himself, the usual internal costs of such decisions (for example, unfriendly leaks, resignation, estrangement, loss of morale) were avoided.

6. Faced with a budget impasse in early 1986, an election year, congressional leaders again sought a mechanism that would allow genuine compromise without political reprisal. Several proposed a grand coalition modeled on the bipartisan commission. In a January 16, 1986, *New York Times* story entitled "Congressional Chiefs Study Plans for Coalition on Budget Proposals," Steven V. Roberts reported that "lawmakers like the 'grand coalition' concept because any budget cuts would be unpopular with affected voting groups. But if the effort was bipartisan and both parties signed on at the same time, much of the political risk could be eliminated. Lawmakers point out that the Social Security commission succeeded because it provided them with protection from partisan retaliation" (p. 6). Thus, the strategy seemed likely to be tested again, although by late spring the president was still unwilling to compromise on military spending, either publicly or privately.

CHAPTER 6

The Grounds for Choice: Presidency-Relevant Character

Who should be president? Be wary of those who presume to answer this question confidently, for despite centuries of thought and effort by theorists and statesmen concerned with identifying the qualities of political leadership, the most responsible answer that can be given is, "No one really knows." But whether experts and savants can help or not, citizens must choose presidents, and to do so requires that they answer this question repeatedly over the course of a civic lifetime. What can be said to those who wish to make knowledgeable, informed choices? My answer involves a strategy similar to that used in Chapter 5 to determine criteria to better judge presidents. Again, preconscious influences are set aside, in this case, to focus on those candidate qualifications generally acknowledged as legitimate bases for distinguishing candidates from one another and as legitimate reasons for preferring one presidential hopeful over the others. An analysis and evaluation of the traditional grounds for choice among candidates will be used to pinpoint where help is needed and improvement possible. In Chapter 5, the analysis suggested that the weak link was lack of knowledge of the sort of information most relevant to here and now judgment of presidential performance. Here, an untapped potential, not so much a weakness, exists. Citizens in general possess intuitive abilities to diagnose the personalities or characters of other human beings, but they do not have a workable method for applying these faculties to the assessment of presidential candidates. The workable method proposed here is presidency-relevant character.

The Traditional Grounds for Choice

What are the traditional grounds, the consciously acknowledged reasons, for choices among candidates for the presidency, and how are they to be distinguished from the criteria for judgment? For analytical convenience and clarity, discussion here deals only with candidates for the presidency who have not been incumbents, as will be the case in 1988. When incumbents run for reelection, the record of performance is available for evaluation. Unreflective criteria such as coin-flipping, party identification, and voting-booth impulse also were left out. With these exclusions, the traditional grounds for choice are: (1) preference for one of the policy packages offered by candidates; (2) track record or experience and reputation for competence; and (3) candidate character or personality.

Obvious parallels can be drawn between the criteria for choice and judgment.[1] Character as a basis for choice has something in common with leadership style as a ground for judgment, although character is a more inclusive concept. Candidate track record indicates the likelihood of presidential competence and results. It serves as a surrogate measure of presidential competence because it reflects the prowess displayed in the prepresidential career. And a candidate's policy positions afford clues to ideology and sympathy to the self-interest of the voter.

Policy-based choice, the preferred option of model democratic citizenship, is the most frequently discussed—by editorial writers, scholarly analysts, and attentive citizens—reason for preferring one candidate over another. Classical democratic theory, as modified by Schumpeter (1943), casts citizens into the role of comparison shoppers choosing among competing policy options. Citizens should choose candidates they prefer for reasons of their own.

This view is strongly challenged by James David Barber (1985) and others, who advise citizens to look to character first. As John P. Roche (1980, sec. 6, 2) puts it, policies "come with feet"—they are espoused by people—and citizens are better off entrusting power to a person they respect but disagree with than to one who shares their views, but whom they do not trust. That politics is about issues, Roche claims, is "the big intellectual fallacy" (1980, sec. 6, 2). Citizens do not vote for issues in elections, but for people who claim to incarnate certain political traditions, offer certain measures, and assert the ability to put them into effect. More important than what they have done or what they promise, then, is who they are. Only the virtues of character can supplement the institutional checks and balances to ensure that the use of power will neither result in tyranny nor invite disaster.

The framers of the Constitution preferred track record, as indicated by the government machinery they designed. Fearing the disruptive passions engendered by "issue arousal" campaigns and despairing of citizens' abilities to assess anything so elusive as character, they sought to restrict choice to pools of candidates with proven records of leadership because they believed reputation was the closest visible approximation of merit (Ceaser 1979, 66).

What, if anything, is wrong with the three traditional grounds for choice? In principle, not very much. Apart from their potential susceptibility to flaws when put to use, such as misdiagnosis and overemphasis, and despite the concerns just expressed, each criterion is logical and materially relevant to the evaluation of candidates. It is not unreasonable to ask what the candidate would do about national problems,[2] to find out whether the candidate has the background and experience to contend with such problems, or to determine whether the candidate is morally and temperamentally suited, as a person, to offer public leadership. All three grounds are likely to play some part in the decision-making process.

In any given election, a reflective citizen will devise a kind of simultaneous equation that ranks and weights each criterion as the immediate circumstances are judged to require. As circumstances vary, so too will the priorities and weights assigned to each criterion. Thus, for example, when a scoundrel runs against a saint, and their proposals and backgrounds seem insignificantly different, character might prevail. When two politically seasoned saints run, one of whom promises an end to the welfare state and the other a return to the New Deal, policy would be decisive, and so on. Specific choices will ultimately turn on whatever grounds separate the candidates.

But if they are free of intrinsic flaws, the criteria for choice might still be usefully distinguished from one another in two important ways. The first is *predictive validity*—the extent to which a criterion has forecasted correctly the important drift of a presidency. The second is *improvability*—the goal implicit in the familiar question, What is the best that can be done?

To demonstrate these distinctions, consideration will be given to what an effort to improve one's ability to use each criterion would actually entail and what the likely payoff would be. To get better at evaluating policy packages, for example, would require becoming fully conversant with each of the policy options presented by presidential candidates in each election. A few hardy, responsible souls will always endeavor to do this, but for most citizens it is simply impractical. In Walter Lippmann's words:

> I cannot find the time to do what is expected of me in the theory of democracy; that is, to know what is going on and to have an opinion worth expressing on every question which confronts a self-governing community. (Steel 1980, 212)

If Walter Lippmann, a man whose life was devoted to the study of politics and public policy, cannot find the time, will those whose major concerns lie elsewhere? Even if citizens could become experts, it would afford them little certainty as to the proper courses of action. Authorities themselves disagree, and a president can do little more than test the theories they espouse. Furthermore, issues come and go. A president's most important actions may involve policy issues unmentioned in the campaign. Too, the correlation between campaign promise and presidential performance is less than perfect (Fishel 1985). A choice based on campaign promises is made without assurance that as president the candidate will even try to keep them, let alone succeed. Responsible citizens will inevitably develop opinions on the broad directions that social policy ought to take, which will appropriately influence their voting choices. But the study required is too burdensome, and the results too unsure, to make a special effort to improve knowledge of candidates' policy packages.

Trying to get better at diagnosing candidate track records is also unlikely to help much. For one thing, true political novices rarely get nominated for president. The most recent was Wendell Willkie in 1940. For another, most students of the presidency agree that little relevent training is available for the presidency, apart from the presidency itself. The major lessons must be learned on the job (Neustadt 1980). History provides the most telling point—no particular kind of background or track record is uniformly associated with presidential effectiveness or success. "It has yet to be shown how much, if any, difference experience makes to the presence or absence of success in the presidency" (Rockman 1984, 210). Carter, an inexperienced outsider, was said to have failed for lack of insider Washington exposure, yet outsiders like Reagan or Eisenhower fared considerably better—in part by finding and using knowledgeable Washington insiders. One of the most experienced statesmen of his time, James Buchanan, is usually branded a dismal failure by historians—a case where experience alone was clearly not enough. Certain kinds of experience, such as directing a large staff, coping with major responsibility, making speeches, or dealing with the media, quite probably do help—if only to reduce the number of things that need to be learned and to avoid glaring mistakes. But track record has demonstrably little predictive value as a choice criterion, perhaps because the system depends on people to run it who have generally the same sorts of backgrounds. It is thus not worth the time and energy needed to get better at determining and evaluating track records. Efforts to improve choice should focus elsewhere.

Character is left, and it has difficulties of its own. For example, it is extremely difficult to read with accuracy and precision. As Alexis de Tocqueville wrote:

> Consider the manifold considerations and the prolonged study involved in forming an exact notion of the character of a single man. There, where the greatest geniuses go astray, are the masses to succeed? The people . . . are bound to make hasty judgments and seize on the most prominent characteristics. This is why charlatans of every sort so well understand the secret of pleasing them, whereas for the most part their real friends fail in this. (1969, 198)

Too, the relevance of character to performance, and by implication to the prediction of performance, is the subject of heated debate within contemporary political science (Barber 1985, 521; Rockman 1984, 175-214; Page and Petracca 1983, 83). Skeptics play down character as a factor whose impact on significant presidential behavior is often marginal and, in most cases, unmeasurable in any reliable way (Rockman 1984). Personality, some argue, "may sometimes be virtually irrelevant to behavior because individuals with varying personal characteristics will tend to behave similarly when placed in common situations," such as in the presidency (Page and Petracca 1983, 83). Furthermore, establishing the causal importance of personality factors in explaining presidential behavior, given the multiplicity of other influential forces, can be monumentally difficult (George 1974).

Still, the impact of a president's character on performance in office is undeniable, however difficult it is to measure or demonstrate with scientific precision. Would critics seriously contend, for example, that an Alexander Hamilton in George Washington's shoes would have sustained the degree of comity between Federalists and Democratic-Republicans that the first-term Washington did? Or that a Herbert Hoover would have been compelled to adopt Franklin D. Roosevelt's methods for dealing with the Great Depression or the Second World War? Or that Ronald Reagan's character and personal style had no unique effect on his political fortunes? The strict scientific controls that would permit unequivocal demonstration of the purely personal impacts of these presidents do not exist. History cannot be replayed exactly, substituting one actor for another, to show the precise difference each would make. But if this could be done, individual differences would turn out to matter greatly, and important differences would involve attributes more central to character than background experience or policy positions. My reading of history suggests that the rare moments of truly crucial presidential action have much more often depended on who the president was than on anything he had achieved in the past or promised in the campaign. Character thus has had considerably more predictive potential than either policy package or track record.

In addition, use of the character criterion might be improvable, in ways not true for policy package and track record. All citizens, whatever their level of political sophistication, are instinctive personality theorists, and tolerably good ones if they have been able to make their own lives work. People live daily with the consequences of choices they have made among other people, and unpleasant results have tended to sharpen their skills. If skill in assessing character is now largely implicit and intuitive, there can be value in an effort to make it explicit and to bring it to bear on the problem of choosing presidents. To focus improvement efforts on character is thus to play to the strength of citizens, to build upon what they do best.

The Diagnosis of Character

Character may have potentially greater predictive validity than other choice criteria, and citizens may be intuitive diagnosticians of character, but neither is of much value unless means can be found to overcome the problem identified by the framers of the Constitution, de Tocqueville, and others: how to diagnose character accurately—such that reasonable people can agree on what a candidate's character is. Equally important is how to take a character reading that is relevant to performance in the presidency, that pertains to a candidate's ability to do presidential work. The solutions to these problems must be strong enough to overcome efforts to distort citizens' access to their intuitive abilities. The media age greatly enhances these efforts, placing awesome resources at the disposal of those who would manipulate both information and emotions.

Citizens therefore require help to contend successfully with diagnosing character. One source of help is a theory of attention—guidance concerning where to look and what to look for—that can supplement intuition by orienting citizens toward useful information. The other can only be supplied by citizens themselves. It is aimed at minimizing the harmful effects of impulse and passion of the sort described by de Tocqueville and illustrated in Chapter 3. It can be labeled self-discipline, self-restraint, or right attitude. To framers like Alexander Hamilton, philosophers like de Tocqueville, editorial pundits like Walter Lippmann and H. L. Mencken, and politicians like Richard Nixon, citizens cannot be expected to cultivate conscious emotional control so that they might gain access to their own intuition and work to refine it. But to those, like Thomas Jefferson, V. O. Key, James David Barber, John P. Roche, and myself, who place greater faith in the rough intuitive wisdom of ordinary people than in institutions or experts, citizens can be asked to exercise self-discipline.

Two major diagnostic options are presently available to those who wish to improve their ability to read character. The first, trait theories, is illustrated by the everyday language citizens use to describe ideal presidents, for example, honest, competent, decisive, courageous, trustworthy, and vigorous. Adjectives such as these can be found in the majority of presidency textbooks dating from the emergence of the genre (Small 1932; Laski 1940; Hargrove 1974b; Hess 1974). The premise of trait theories is that the desirable personal qualities in potential presidents can be defined in terms of collections of traits, which combine individual skills, like persuasiveness or eloquence, with moral virtues, like integrity or honesty. The lists of qualities are typically drawn from impressions of the strengths and weaknesses of past presidents. Trait theories have the considerable advantage of employing words commonly used to intuit character in everyday life. But they suffer from two significant drawbacks. First, the accurate attribution of virtues to candidates is not usually possible. Clear, unarguable evidence about candidates' integrity or decisiveness, for example, is hard to come by, and traits can be simulated, only to disappear after the election. Second, and more importantly, the precise relevance of any virtue or collection of virtues to the fit between person and presidency is rarely addressed systematically by the listmakers and is by no means intuitively or otherwise obvious. Integrity and competence, for example, seem equally relevant to any job, as do honesty and decisiveness. They thus offer little insight into the unique personal requirements of the presidency.

The second option is Barber's pathbreaking characterology (1985). Barber defines presidential character in more comprehensive and sophisticated terms than do trait theories, and he links character to concrete hypotheses about presidential behavior—for example, active-positives are likely to get results, while active-negatives cling to failing courses of action. But the frequent controversy over how to classify particular presidents in Barber's terms suggests that he has not laid the problem of diagnostic accuracy to rest. For example:

> The success of Barber's analysis was launched by his devastatingly accurate prediction of President Nixon's behavior. But Barber was probably as far off base with Jimmy Carter (whom he called an active-positive) as he was on with Richard Nixon. (Lowi 1985, 136)

Barber, however, disagrees, claiming that "by my simple scheme [Carter's] place on the active-passive dimension stayed clear all through his presidency" (1985, 450). While admitting that the "positive-negative dimension is not as clear cut," Barber still concludes that "tentatively, pending intimate revelations yet to come, I judge the balance positive" (1985, 451).

Barber conceives of character in terms that seem to apply more directly to the presidency than do trait theories, in part because his case studies suggest how energy level and emotional outlook (the two continua whose juxtaposition creates his four character types) affect individual behavior in response to such demands as "the power situation" and the "climate of expectations." But it seems possible, and potentially useful, to go further and more explicitly into the question of what the presidency requires of character than Barber does.

An approach expressly designed to address the problems of conceiving character accurately and in a manner clearly relevant to the demands of the presidency is the approach of the organizational psychologist. When responsible for devising ways to select personnel for complex jobs like manager, foreman, air traffic controller, or teacher, the psychologist starts with a job description, phrased and intended to define where and how the job touches and uses the people who fill it. The job description is set up specifically to point only to those aspects of character that are relevant to staying on equal terms with the requirements of the job, while ruthlessly ignoring all the rest. For the job of president, the aspects of character identified in the job description become the definition of presidency-relevant character, tailored to the problem of selection.

Presidency-Relevant Character

The presidency makes three great demands on the purely personal resources of the incumbent. The president must: (1) establish and maintain a successful relationship with the American people; (2) devise ways of combining personal skills, energies, and limitations with those of other people to work toward policy goals under severe resource and time constraints; and (3) contend with the presidential experience—a constellation of psychological pressures strong enough to affect behavior in ways potentially dangerous to the president and to the nation (Buchanan 1978). These demands point, respectively, to three related but distinguishable and observable components of character: self-presentation, self-concept, and self-esteem. The following will focus on the interaction between each demand, the character component it uses, and the assessment of these character components in presidential candidates.

The Relationship Demand and Self-Presentation

The first demand, establishing a successful relationship with the American people, is perhaps the pivotal requirement of contemporary presidential leadership. A successful relationship is one in which a majority of the electorate believes in and is favorably disposed toward the president, who is then rewarded with strong public support.

This demand is not exclusively met by character, for it is also a function of public satisfaction with performance. But self-presentation does have a significant impact on how easily the president can fulfill this demand. A central point brought out in the comparison of Reagan with Carter was that each president's mode of presenting himself influenced what and how much was expected of him, as well as the evaluative conclusions reached about him and his performance by the American people.

An important implication of the character test was the power of influence available to such beguiling personas as Jackson, TR, FDR, and Kennedy because of the emotional impact they had as human beings on the mass public. Nor are such effects reserved for the charismatic alone. Low-key but popular personalities like Jefferson, Eisenhower, and Reagan enjoyed the public's support. A self-presentation that adequately addresses the subjective criteria of judgment can soften criticism, win the benefit of the doubt, result in creation of a privileged cushion, and get the president off probation. Such was the case with Reagan. A handful of presidents who were not adept at disposing others positively toward themselves and who paid a price in lost influence, antipathy, or lack of support included the two Adamses, Andrew Johnson, Hoover, Nixon, and Carter. All were talented men, but with no special knack for sparking favorable, supportive personal feelings toward themselves in large numbers of others in any enduring way. In each case a discernible impact was felt on the president's political fortunes and made his task that much more difficult.

However irrational or unreasonable it may seem, it is a striking fact that certain modes of self-presentation can dispose others to view the presenter favorably and to judge the presenter tolerantly. This, however, does not apply only to presidents. Social psychological research has also shown that people in general who are liked, for whatever reasons, experience less demanding evaluations than those who are less liked (Huston and Levinger 1978). The focus here is the presidency, however, and the implication for the selection of presidents seems clear.

The president's personal impact on the electorate affects the stringency of the expectations that must be met, the price that must be paid for mistakes, the amount of support a given level of performance is likely to generate, and the stability of public support over time that is enjoyed. With the close relationship between the level of support and the chances for effectiveness, self-presentation also affects how difficult the presidency will be for the person occupying the office. Factoring this component of character into the calculus of choice is a prudent thing to do, for it is unarguably relevant to success in the presidency. In addition, the declining support trends of the post-Vietnam, post-Watergate era and the media age place an even greater premium on the president's ability to project an appealing persona. In light of these realities, the problems posed by citizens relying too much upon their gut reactions to the leadership style or charisma of candidates or by the danger that a personally popular, cushioned president has less incentive to learn from mistakes will probably have to be addressed by means other than ignoring or playing down the value of self-presentation.

Self-Presentation as Character. That self-presentation is appropriately conceived as a component of character is suggested by the fact that it radiates initially from within, in the form of chemistry, magnetism, or vibrations. True, every person, in the words of T. S. Eliot, "puts on a face to meet the faces that we meet" and is thus acting to some extent. In addition, misrepresentation of self is expected in politics. The self presented to the electorate by a candidate is often packaged by the creation of inauthentic images. But self-presentation, as the term is used here, refers to dimensions of a human being that cannot be successfully disguised indefinitely or at all. The totality of the self that is presented by a president and that seems to matter to the electorate includes such things as personal appearance, physical stature, carriage, demeanor and deportment, the style, rhythm, and cadence of speech, the projection of calmness and self-confident ease or nervous tension, the use of emotional coloring in speech and demeanor, such as humor, sincerity, forthrightness, anger, piousness, arrogance, warmth, aloofness, determination, caring, compassion, and concern, the facility with which moods are varied to fit circumstances, and so on. Traits are communicated through television cameras and subliminally received and registered in living rooms across America. Albeit in imprecise, poorly understood ways, they unarguably contribute to emotional convictions about the suitability of candidates and presidents. They help people decide whether, for example, a candidate seems presidential, is trustworthy, is likable, is competent and up to the job, is able to provide acceptable leadership, and is deserving of respect and support.

Chemistry as a qualification for the presidency has its critics and is often viewed as part of a deplorable trend toward government by television, personality, and public relations gimmickry, which contributes to an ever-widening chasm between image and reality. The importance of character cannot be denied, however, and it affects the president's ability to strike up and maintain a successful relationship with the American people. Other factors can and do override it, such as dramatic presidential success or failure. But a president whose personality evokes instinctive, positive sentiments has a crucial resource to help close the gap between expectation and performance. Given that the bonds linking presidents and people are personal and emotional as well as contractual, self-presentation is not only an inevitable but also a legitimate test of a candidate's mettle. As a result, measuring candidate character partially in terms of self-presentation and including the conclusions drawn in the choice decision make sense.

Self-presentation is thus clearly relevant to performance in the presidency, but how can it be measured? Fortunately, the dimensions of self-presentation that matter to the electorate need not be pinpointed precisely. For purposes here, the most useful gauge of candidate self-presentation is the reactions of audiences rather than the traits that produce the reactions. Most Americans want to feel that candidates and presidents are competent and trustworthy (Kinder and Abelson 1981). In principle, an expert is not required to determine whether candidates, through their self-presentation, have evoked such convictions.

The cultural parameters that delimit the range of presidential styles of self-presentation are broad enough to accommodate and approve of such dissimilar styles as Eisenhower and Kennedy but put a wide range of other styles at a serious disadvantage. The media age has placed a greater premium on a professionally smooth platform demeanor. Great presidents like the stodgy, boring George Washington, the soprano-voiced Thomas Jefferson, or the homely Abraham Lincoln would fare less well in the modern era, with television cameras that magnify every quirk, gesture, and characteristic, right down to the color of the tongue and the alignment of the teeth. Modern candidates and presidents have suffered or benefited accordingly. Homey, plainspoken, uninspiring Harry Truman was disdained for his demeanor, particularly in contrast with the eloquent, patrician Franklin D. Roosevelt. A similar comparison was often made between the stiff, preachy television style of Lyndon Johnson and the crisp, elegant style of John Kennedy. Richard Nixon's nervousness, his tendency to perspire freely, and the jerky, phony quality of his physical gestures (which became a meal ticket for impressionists like David Fry and Rich Little) communicated insincerity. Jack Valenti argues:

> Nixon's problem was a lack of believability. Well, one might say, why, if he was unbelievable, did he have such great success at getting elected and reelected? Remember, in 1968 he won by a margin of only one half of one percent of the vote, at a time when Hubert Humphrey had come off the Chicago convention disaster ... deserted by the liberal wing of the Democratic party, struggling desperately to make up lost ground, coming from thirty points behind to lose by only a sliver. [And] in 1972, George McGovern was simply out of the mainstream of American political thought.... (1982, 110-111)

Valenti also offers a diagnosis of the self-presentation problems that beset Gerald Ford:

> I was continually surprised to find him on television seemingly incapable of speaking a complete thought without groping and searching. While the ability to utter sentences that parse is not in itself so important an asset, the outward evidence of an untroubled line of thought—emerging through the speaker's voice and apparent conviction—is crucial. The rhythm and balance of Ford's presentation was always marred by the lurchings of his speech. It is difficult to inspire, much less persuade, if the audience wants to reach into the speaker's throat with tongs to grasp the next dozen words and pull them out. I wanted so much for him to do better because I believed him to be a good president. (1982, 112)

Critics deplore the elimination of otherwise highly qualified individuals from consideration or election to the presidency because they lack the ability to evoke strong positive reactions by their words and demeanor. Implied is that this ability involves little more than Hollywood tricks, with no legitimate relevance to the serious work of the presidency. But establishing a successful personal relationship with the American people is a crucially important demand of the presidency. And the traits that govern self-presentation unquestionably influence a president's ability to meet that demand. These traits could only be removed as a qualification for office if emotion could be eliminated altogether from choice and judgment. Such traits are instinctively taken by the American people as cues to the basic competence and trustworthiness of leaders. The correspondence between such cues and deep-rooted character may not be perfect and can be misleading, but, for better or for worse, it exists.

Self-presentation is measurable in the reactions of audiences to presenters. Reactions in a candidate's prepresidential career can be used tc foretell the probable reaction of the citizenry to self-presentation should the candidate win election. As a partial test of these claims, consideration will be given to whether the reactions generated by Jimmy Carter and Ronald Reagan could have been predicted.

The Strange Case of Jimmy Carter.   Getting down to cases always exposes the imperfect fit between any conceptual scheme and reality, for situations and circumstances often change the subjective reaction to such candidate characteristics as self-presentation.

The strange case of Jimmy Carter illustrates the problems with applying a conceptual scheme and provides a setting for ironies. In some senses, Carter was clearly miscast as an aspiring president. On the other hand, his was a fresh and novel self-presentation that, during his candidacy at least, almost perfectly suited an electorate primed for a major break from traditional styles and practices.

Small of stature, with a high-pitched voice and an uneven, sometimes confusing cadence, he neither looked nor sounded presidential, as that concept is embodied in the public mind. An early biographer, James Wooten, writes that a few "irreverent wags" described Carter as "Eleanor Roosevelt's illegitimate son" because of his large, toothy smile set in a spacious mouth with "lips that seemed, like a clown's, to reach beyond their actual dimensions" (1978, 23). As a candidate, Carter spoke with more of a drawl than he would later as president:

> 'Ahmuh fahmuh and ahmuh Suthnuh,' he would say, and somehow it just didn't sound quite right within the context of an American presidential campaign, neither the words nor the voice. There were no measured tones from him, only a twangy singsong, high-pitched to some ears, almost effeminate to others. (Wooten 1978, 26)

But in other respects, the campaign presaged the awkward, discomforting style of his presidential discourse:

> In his presidential television appearances, Jimmy Carter, a quick study, masterly in his command of the facts, had a singsong delivery and a curious way of popping his eyelids at the end of a sentence. In a close-up this took on the characteristics of a tic. After a while viewers came to wait for the climax of a thought, and sure enough, the eyes popped. . . . He also had a habit of dropping his voice level at the end of a sentence, trailing off rather than emphasizing. These added up to an on-camera image that elicited a grudging ear to listen and a discontented eye to watch in living rooms all over the country. (Valenti 1982, 113)

The size, the demeanor, the voice, the characteristics, were there to see throughout Carter's prepresidential public career. As Wooten suggests, they were obviously not in the traditional mold of leadership, particularly media-transmitted leadership. They would make Carter an object of scorn and derision during the low points of his presidency. It would seem easy, then, to claim that all this could have been predicted well before he was elected.

However, during Carter's candidacy, many of these same characteristics were perceived by great numbers of Americans as sources of charm, things that made him seem like a breath of fresh air, partial explanations for his dazzling rise to prominence and political strength. Separating the traits displayed through self-presentation from the substantive content of the message to assess their independent effects is always difficult, but Carter's way of being himself was clearly a positive asset in the 1976 campaign. Most important, it charmed and beguiled his audiences:

> Personally, he was a spellbinder with some groups. His ability to weave his magic over a wide variety of people—blacks, county sheriffs, children, college students, residents of "old folks" homes—impressed reporters and political activists alike. . . . This charm was most directly related to Carter's ability to connect, seemingly on a personal and intimate basis, with many different types of people. . . . He has one truly remarkable platform gift—the ability to establish an intimacy with each member of an audience. (Glad 1980, 363-364)

Which of Carter's traits contributed to the impact he had on audiences? Although no direct testimony is available to support the idea that his physiognomy, his physical stature, or his voice were particular assets, save occasional references to his icy, bright-blue eyes, these characteristics, during the campaign, were not the hindrances that they would later become. References have been made to the positive impacts of his speechmaking, such as David Broder's comment, following a Carter speech to a crowd of black YMCA members in Milwaukee, Wisconsin, that Carter spoke "with an eloquence, a simplicity, a directness that moved listeners of both races. . . . One would have to be made of stone to be unmoved by the surge of emotion—the communion—between those black listeners and that white speaker who hopes to be their president" (Glad 1980, 364). But perhaps most important was the context, the historical moment, that made Carter's way of being uniquely, if temporarily, appropriate—even ideal. Betty Glad explains:

> Carter's anonymity at the beginning of the race, his ability to forge out of that situation an idealized self-presentation that most people bought, a complex set of values and issue stances that could be variously interpreted, his personal power manifested in his ability to weave a spell over the people as well as the elites, and the final proof of his extraordinary ability in the miracle he pulled off—these were all elements in making him the subject of so many fantasies. (1980, 365)

Had Vietnam and Watergate not soured the American people on government, had Gerald Ford not pardoned Richard Nixon, had Ford not been so wooden and uninspiring a performer, candidate Carter's idiosyncratic demeanor might have affected audiences more like President Carter's did. America's infatuation with the candidate thus seemingly had more to do with his uniqueness and his newness than anything else. He was different and, for a time, refreshing.

Evidence of Carter's style of self-presentation before 1976 and during the 1976 campaign could not have dismissed the possibility that it might have worked well in the presidency. But given how different it was from the norm, more prudent citizens might have predicted that if Carter, an anomalous personality, were to get into trouble once in office, he would be unlikely to derive any protective cushion or benefit of the doubt amidst his difficulties from the respect or love generated by his style of presenting himself alone. Newness wears off quickly, and uniqueness is prized only when things are going well. Otherwise, anxiety mounts and the urge to return to the familiar inevitably reasserts itself.

The Reagan Restoration. Reagan represented a return to the fold, but not in the sense of his policy promises or his conservative ideology, which were, of course, unprecedented departures from the status quo. Instead, he was someone who looked, acted, and sounded like a traditional president—reassuring, inspiring, and comfortable.

Could it have been predicted, from the precandidate record, that Reagan would derive a competitive edge from his style of self-presentation alone? Not with absolute certainty, perhaps, but Reagan clearly had a much better chance than Carter ever did to link himself with the traditional style displayed by successful and popular presidents. Tall, handsome, charming, and with a platform poise honed before Hollywood cameras, Reagan had a self-presentation, it could be assumed, that would not detract from his overall performance. Carter's crinkly-eyed, tooth flash was a jarring departure from a tradition into which Reagan fit naturally. It worked for Carter in the campaign, but not for long in the presidency. Why? Betty Glad suggests it was because Carter himself underwent a subtle transformation, due to an increase in the prestige and skepticism of the audiences a president must face:

> As President ... his formal addresses to Congress and to the people have shown a stiff quality. Indeed, Carter has two speaking styles. With blacks, children, the "people"—the powerless?—Carter is at the height of his emotional spontaneity and warmth. But before larger, more prestigious audiences, such as the American Bar Association and the Chicago Council on Foreign Relations, or in situations where he might

> lose, Carter is likely to hide behind facts and figures and a monotone.
> (1980, 502)

Reagan is not afflicted with nervousness or stage fright. As president, he continues to do what he always had done—read his serious lines with force and conviction, display his reassuring manner, disarm his critics "with self-deprecating little jokes and that winning smile" (Cannon 1982, 98), and charm his friends with "a folksy little waggle of his head and shoulders" (Miller 1982, 32).

Reagan's post-Hollywood and prepolitical employment was a series of speaking assignments that enabled him to display and to hone his appealing qualities not only before mass television audiences on the "General Electric Theater" (where he "fit the role of host like a lightbulb fits a socket" [Leamer 1983, 176]), but also before the National Association of Manufacturers, the American Medical Association, and numerous business and service clubs. His political message was conservative, and he had a special appeal to "the mindset of men on the make in the Eisenhower years" (Barber 1985, 477). However, he charmed nearly everybody who heard him speak. Over a period of 10 years, he proved his ability to win over virtually every sort of audience in almost every imaginable setting. His words struck some audiences as radical, but his manner was always reassuring (Cannon 1982, 98). Roderick P. Hart, an expert in speech communication, notes that Reagan is unusual among presidents in avoiding colorful, adjectival language, preferring straight, unadorned, even hackneyed speech. This works for Reagan, argues Hart, because he is a "communicator whose body, voice and smile do the necessary emotional embellishing" (1984, 221). These gifts were apparent long before Reagan's entry into politics, let alone before he began to seek the presidency. No other modern president had displayed his self-presentation talents so convincingly or so thoroughly before entering the political arena.

When Reagan made his famous TV speech for presidential candidate Barry Goldwater in 1964, he caught the attention of a group of ultraconservative California businessmen who were determined to enlist him to run for governor of California. These men had seen that Goldwater's "extremist" brand of conservatism had just not sold (Barber 1985, 481). But Reagan was a communicator who could take an unpopular doctrine and make it palatable, even appealing, to the mass public. Said millionaire oil man A. C. (Cy) Rubel: "Reagan is the man who can enunciate our principles to the people" (Cannon 1982, 103).

Self-presentation is by no means the only dimension of character that is relevant to the presidency. Candidates like Harry Truman, Richard Nixon, or Jimmy Carter can get elected without extraordinary winsomeness and can even perform well. Conversely, great communicators cannot expect to be saved from otherwise dismal performances by charm alone, and without genuine achievements may find themselves swept into the dustbin of history once the charm has faded from memory. But all by itself, self-presentation does afford an effective presenter some leeway that is simply not accorded to the less effective. In an era of fragile public support and probationary presidencies, it is imprudent to ignore any candidate's impact on the audience, for it is visible to the naked eye and it is relevant to the presidency.

The 'Use Self and Others' Demand and Self-Concept

The second of great demands made by the presidency on the personal resources of the president is that the president's skills, energies, strengths, and weaknesses be effectively integrated with those of other people to work toward goals under severe time constraints. This is the stuff of the workaday presidency, reminiscent of traditional management's POSDCORB (planning, organizing, staffing, directing, coordinating, reporting, and budgeting) (Gulick and Urwick 1937). It involves such questions as, What will the president do all day, and how will that relate to what everybody else is doing? Presidents must choose people, divide up the work, establish procedures for getting it done, and determine what part they will play in the arrangements they create. In much of the presidency literature, the unique choices made by presidents about organization are classified under the heading "the advisory system" (see, for example, Cronin and Greenberg 1969). Richard Tanner Johnson calls it "management style" (1974). Whatever it is called, what is meant is an individual president's unique ways of using self, others, and work processes to get results.

Theodore Sorensen argues that "each president must determine for himself how best to elicit and assess the advice of his advisers" (1969, 3). Sorensen could have added that each must also determine who those advisers will be and what they will do besides offer advice. The range of discretion a president has in these matters is extraordinary, which is why the choices a particular president makes are so revealing. Choices are obviously influenced in part by things other than deep-rooted character. The views of management experts played a part in the design of the Reagan system, for example. The premium placed on speed, responsiveness, and political sensitivity in the White House will push every president toward certain kinds of decision-making procedures and away from others. Public expectations of openness in government may lead a president to invite the press to cabinet meetings, and political pressure can motivate the creation of special advisory positions for women's or minority affairs. None of the choices made for these reasons would tell much about the person behind the system. But in time, particularly after the initial period of adjustment, how a leader works and what commands attention becomes apparent. The major contours of the system put in place become extraordinarily revealing of the president's "ideal" and "real" selves.

Establishing an organization is like a Rorschach test. Just as the unique interpretation of inkblots offers a glimpse of the inner world of the interpreter, so too do the choices made by an organization builder about people, procedures, and allocation of responsibility. If anything, these choices are even more revealing, because much more is at stake. A president chooses people for their expertise and for their compatability. Those appointed and hired reveal the technical demands of presidential work and how the president wants to be treated as a person—the values and the self-image the president wants confirmed and reinforced. Procedures and routines stem from a rational analysis of how most efficiently and effectively to accomplish work. They also serve to indicate presidential decisions about what makes for a comfortable working environment, what sort of help is needed from others, how hard to work, and how involved to get in which particular matters. The tasks a president handles may reflect a hard-nosed assessment of what needs doing most or theoretical principles about what a president should do personally. But they also offer a glimpse of the person who is president—what that person believes self to be good at, what that person considers the big plays to be, and what the personal dreams of achievement are.

The pattern of response to the organizational Rorschach test is management style and serves as a good indicator of presidential self-concept. The relevance of organization to choice is not that there is one best way to manage the presidency, but that: (1) some management styles and self-concepts clearly fit the presidency better than others and thus deserve more explicit consideration in choice decisions than citizens or journalists now give them; (2) management styles, like modes of self-presentation, are quite visible and, in principle, measurable in the prepresidential record; and (3) this particular measure of candidate self-concept is an extraordinarily important and promising predictor of how a candidate would operate in the presidency.

Why Management Style Matters. Management style matters because each pattern of management is associated with certain costs and benefits that surface when a given approach is used. "In other words," says Richard Tanner Johnson, "given a particular style of management we can anticipate the likely consequences of that style on the quality of decision making and its implementation" (1973, 2). Johnson illustrates his point by examining the consequences of three different styles: the formalistic, the competitive, and the collegial. The formalistic style, used by Eisenhower and Nixon, stresses an orderly decision-making process that enforces a comparatively thorough analysis of issues and options. The president sits atop a hierarchy staffed by functional specialists with clearly defined responsibilities, including careful preparation of written analyses for decision makers near the top, and with stable and restricted patterns of communication. The system guards the president's time and attention by carefully limiting the issues addressed. The president is thus free to specialize and to decide which issues require personal attention. The formalistic style yields high quality analysis and maximizes the chances for optimal decisions, but it also involves certain risks. As Johnson notes, the hierarchy that screens information may also distort it. The top person is isolated from all but special issues, and the bureaucracy below tends to overemphasize technical questions and underemphasize political pressures or public sentiments. This style is also cumbersome and may respond too slowly to crises or deadlines.

The competitive style, exemplified by FDR, places the president at the center of an informal network of advisers with overlapping and conflicting responsibilities. The president is a generalist and goes outside the advisory network to seek unconventional sources of information and intelligence to ascertain whether plans or decisions will be doable or politically feasible before they are made. The competition among advisers generates creative and innovative ideas, and the conflicts among advisers, plus the extensive outside contacts of both advisers and the president, ensure that the president will receive early warning of potential problems or difficulties. As a result, the system is extraordinarily sensitive and responsive to the external environment. The dependence of advisers on the pleasure of the president and the low level of delegation of power or responsibility to advisers enable the president to maintain the dominant position. Others have few chances to build fiefdoms or empires. This highly mobile, flexible, and ultrasensitive management style is in many respects an ideal match for the operational requirements of the presidency. The problem is that few human beings can cope with its burdens. It makes excessive demands on the time and energy of the central figure, and the competition creates a tense, unpleasant environment, requiring considerable mediation. The disorderly, ad hoc nature of intelligence gathering encourages a tendency to settle for the practicable decision rather than to strive for the optimal one. The aggressive climate fostered by instability and competition yields high staff turnover and threatens betrayal of the president's interests.

The collegial style, illustrated by Kennedy, tries to avoid the weaknesses of the other approaches while retaining their important strengths. The president maintains an informal, unpredictable pattern of intervention in the information network and establishes a formal system to ensure an orderly development of policy options. Creative, casual interaction is encouraged, but the emphasis is on teamwork, not competition, which eliminates some adverse effects. The drawbacks are fewer but remain substantial. As the hub of a many-spoked wheel, the president is involved in everything, which amounts to a superhuman workload. Additionally, sustaining an atmosphere of teamwork requires unusual interpersonal skill and attention to group processes. And the president can succeed too well, with the result that teamwork degenerates into a closed system of mutual support, groupthink, and misperception of reality.

The three management styles are ideal types, rarely if ever encountered in pure form in any administration. Too, most presidents have varied their approaches somewhat from situation to situation. Fred Greenstein argues that Johnson's classification scheme does not take adequate account of this, nor does it leave room for different advisory modes in different policy areas (1983, 162). Still, it does illustrate, if in exaggerated form, the potential consequences of varying approaches to the use of self and others. These consequences can be traced back to the character of the president, as revealed in routines established and atmosphere created. The Eisenhower style, for example, whether purely formalistic or not, was in part an expression of his preference for orderly procedures, his distaste for rough and tumble political confrontation, and his belief in his ability to manipulate people and events by indirection. "Eisenhower the man," argues Greenstein, "shaped the distinctive Eisenhower leadership style" (1982, 53). The same can be said for both FDR and Kennedy. These three presidents had what are now generally considered to have been workable approaches to managing the presidency in the context of their times. Conversely, Nixon's isolated, overspecialized brand of formalism, particularly in conjunction with the aggressive attitudes he instilled in aides, is often seen as an explanation for Watergate (Safire 1975; White 1975). Carter's overinvolved style and particularly his excessive preoccupation with detail are frequently cited as evidence of his inability to distinguish the trivial from the important and of the lack of a clear sense of direction in his presidency. Reagan's chairman-of-the-board style was interpreted by some analysts as a potentially dangerous abnegation of presidential responsibility (see, for example, Cannon 1982) but can also be viewed as an innovative hypothesis concerning how to deploy the presidency and the president.

Management style thus matters, and some styles are better matches than others with the responsibilities of the presidency. Management style is also shaped to a significant degree by the manager's sense of self, ability, and responsibility—in other words, self-concept. Are the patterns of how one uses oneself and others visible in presidential candidates? Can these patterns indicate presidency-relevant character? Could Carter's overinvolved style and Reagan's disengaged style have been predicted?

Carter as Perfectionist: Management by Example. Serious candidates for the presidency probably will have revealed their management styles long before they decided to seek the office. They will have managed a law office or a business organization, created campaign organizations for other offices sought, or operated a congressional office, a bureau, or a state government. The track record aspect of background experience is now routinely examined for evidence of the ability to handle significant leadership responsibility. It is a short but potentially very important step to probe more deeply into the same evidence for what it may show of how a person functions alone and with others to perform work.

Carter's prepresidential organization-building experience consists of managing, for 12 years following his retirement from the navy in 1953, the peanut warehouse inherited from his father and organizing and running campaign organizations. Carter made a successful bid for the Georgia Senate in 1962, was reelected in 1964, entered a race for a U.S. House seat in 1966 before shifting to an unsuccessful gubernatorial challenge, and won the election for governor in 1970 and for president in 1976. He also managed his state senate office and the governor's office. Emerging from Carter's experience is a distinct management style, a way of using self and others, which would brand the Carter presidency and be found wanting by his critics.

Carter displayed a definite cognitive style—a way he used himself to contend with challenges. According to John H. Kessel, it was "based on a mastery of detail and [on focusing] on a single problem at a time" (1984, 161). As Carter told Godfrey Sperling, Jr., of the *Christian Science Monitor,* "As I studied as a naval officer, and as I studied as a governor, and as I studied when I was getting the Carter warehouse started, I studied for the presidency" (1983, 13). During Carter's stint as an Annapolis midshipman, he was known as a diligent student. While a navy officer, he helped disassemble a damaged nuclear reactor core at

Chalk River, Canada (Glad 1980, 64) and helped repair a ship engine before it exploded (Anderson 1977), proving that he had done his homework. When he returned to Plains to assume control of his father's peanut warehouse, he enrolled in an extension course to master the latest techniques in peanut farming. As a campaigner, he was relentless, devoting 16 hours a day to the stump then returning home to make detailed records of the names, addresses, and characteristics of those he had contacted. Once elected to the Georgia Senate, he kept a campaign promise to read every piece of legislation to come before that body, took a speed-reading course to make it possible, and developed a reputation as an exceptionally knowledgeable and hardworking legislator. Once ensconced in the governor's chair, he overwhelmed opponents of his reorganization programs with his intricate knowledge of the operations of the state agencies that would be affected and involved himself in such minutiae as techniques for mowing the grass along Georgia highways and methods for engaging handicapped citizens in the typing of state documents. Following his election to the presidency, Carter read dozens of biographies and autobiographies of past presidents to better prepare himself. Long before he embarked on his campaign for the presidency, he clearly had, in James David Barber's terms, a "hydraulic" world view, a mule's appetite for work, and an engineer's faith that problems would yield to the method of breaking them into their component parts to solve them. At no point in his prepresidential career was Carter a man willing to leave the details entirely to others. His unstinting devotion of energy to the mastery of any problem he might confront, including presidential problems, was apparent early on in his career.

What do Carter's experiences imply about his sense of self? They reveal a man whose identity and self-acceptance rested on the twin pillars of being exceptionally hard working and displaying outstanding ethical and moral character. The two men who served as Carter's role models, his father, Earl, and Admiral Hyman Rickover, were both exacting taskmasters and strict disciplinarians who won the respect of others by outworking them and outshining them. Carter's prepresidential management career reflects the internalization of these precepts. It is not enough merely to be hardworking and competent. Any decent person will display these virtues. One earns the right to be a leader by working the hardest and being the best. One leads by example. Carter's theory of leadership—his beliefs about how leaders should use themselves in the enterprises they direct—is also implicit in his record. Leaders are not required to specialize in public relations or in ingratiating themselves with others, although they must do these things. Their real job is to be exemplary in every detail—to be and do the best, not settle. Every system that Carter ever established for himself, from his study routines at Annapolis to his campaign organizations to his presidential management system, was as rational and as orderly as careful research, planning, and study could make it. As Carter accumulated loyal associates along the way whose talents complemented his, he used their talents and shared his work with them, but he made certain that he knew as much or more than they did about their work. He delegated tasks, but not ultimate responsibility. This style of leadership aims to produce two important consequences. First, leaders are always in a position to assess, by virtue of their expertise, the quality of the advice they get. They cannot be misled by experts, because they know whether the experts are making sense. Second, leaders set an awe-inspiring example—for subordinates, constituents, and opponents. Leadership by example is the best way to win respect and support, far better than the easier methods of charm, patronage, or cronyism, because it legitimizes the right to lead. Leaders earn their positions of prominence the hard way, not the clever way, a fact that can inspire and uplift others and even elevate the entire political process by making the status quo seem unworthy by comparison. Leadership by example is how Jimmy Carter used himself as leader, both before and during his presidency.

His pattern for using others was similarly discernible before he established his own presidential advisory system. In the navy, Carter had shown himself able to work well with others on highly technical projects requiring precision and interdependency. As an officer, he was regarded as fair and empathetic by his subordinates, if somewhat aloof and distant. He seemed particularly to enjoy the teaching roles the navy sometimes afforded (Glad 1980, 62-63), a characteristic his national security adviser, Zbigniew Brzezinski, would notice in the president (1983, 22).

Carter states in his autobiography, *Why Not the Best?* (1975), that, during his first year back in Plains after retiring from the navy, he ran the Carter peanut operation almost singlehandedly, right down to the loading of sacks of grain onto the trucks of customers. But he did rely heavily on his wife, Rosalynn. She became the front office of the enterprise, keeping books, analyzing markets, and advising Carter on important business decisions. Carter developed a healthy respect for her considerable business acumen. They forged an effective working relationship based on mutual respect and intimacy, which would continue through the White House years. Rosalynn came to be regarded as perhaps the most influential of Carter's presidential advisers. Here was first evinced a Carter characteristic that would be noted and criticized during his presidency: his tendency to rely for help and counsel primarily on intimates of proven loyalty from his Georgia years, rather than on seasoned political professionals with national political experience. His first real organization, the peanut operation, was staffed with family. His first campaign organization, put together to seek a Georgia Senate seat in 1962, consisted of Rosalynn, sister Gloria, and two close friends, John Pope and Warren Fortson, who were attracted to Carter by his determination, integrity, and diligence. The 1966 and 1970 gubernatorial campaigns were staffed by Rosalynn, Gloria, Carter's mother, and the three Carter sons. When Carter moved to statewide races, he began to attract a corps of volunteers, including Hamilton Jordan, who was a University of Georgia senior when he joined the Carter staff, and Jody Powell, who was a young graduate student in political science at Emory University. Powell said he was attracted to Carter by his "sincerity," their common rural Georgia backgrounds, and Carter's "special qualities" as a politician (Glad 1980, 125).

As his notoriety and political success increased, Carter would add more expertise, such as pollster Gerald Rafshoon, and more heavyweight legal, political, and managerial talent, such as Charles Kirbo, Griffin Bell, and Bert Lance, to his stable of advisers and supporters. All, and especially Lance, would become close friends. Most of the people who would be his most trusted confidants in the presidency—Rosalynn, Jordan, Powell, and Lance—were connected to him by 1970, as were others, like Frank Moore, Stuart Eizenstat, Griffin Bell and Jack Watson, who would occupy key positions in Washington.

How did Carter use those closest to him as president in the years before entering the White House? And what could have been predicted of his use of them in the presidency? First, the advisers with the greatest access and influence were intimate friends with a history of proven personal loyalty: wife Rosalynn, best friend Bert Lance, and the younger but well-loved Jody Powell and Hamilton Jordan. Charles Kirbo would remain aloof from day-to-day operations, but he was highly trusted and would provide counsel on important decisions. The inner circle likely would have remained intact through 1980 but for Lance's departure from OMB. Carter as president also retained the services of a number of experienced outsiders. Two—Vice President Walter F. Mondale and foreign policy adviser Brzezinski—developed reasonably close working relationships with Carter, as had expert outsiders like Rafshoon and Eizenstat in Georgia. But neither these men nor any other outsiders would ever achieve an importance to Carter comparable to his intimates. The relationships Carter formed with those closest to him were solidified for the most part during long-shot political campaigns that resulted in improbable victories against forbidding odds. That Carter's intimates would retain exclusive preeminence in a Carter presidency could not have been certain in advance, but a safe prediction could have been made that they would be among the most influential. It is not unusual for presidents to use friends in positions of importance. It is unusual, however, for intimates to maintain the kind of monopoly on access and influence that Carter's did while he was president.

Second, the principal use Carter made of his close friends, and the most valuable contribution they made to him, was to reinforce and sustain his faith in himself and his unique approach to leadership. This was true in Georgia, and it remained true in Washington. They of course performed other very important functions—Rosalynn as first lady of Georgia and of the United States, Lance as Georgia highway director and OMB director, Powell as political advance man and press secretary, and Jordan as political analyst and White House chief of staff. They were all quick studies, highly talented people who were underrated, for the most part, by critics. But their primary purpose was to reinforce the norms that helped to shape Carter's performance as state legislator, governor, and president. One such norm was a strong commitment to Carter's identity as an unusually principled, exceptionally competent, and distinctly uncommon political leader whose right to lead was a legitimate consequence of working harder and achieving more than the others. Evidence of this commitment can be found in the memoirs of Rosalynn, Jordan, and Powell. Their perception of Carter's political identity was strengthened by the string of unlikely electoral successes that proved the experts wrong, and which also bolstered the strong self-confidence Carter was noted for throughout his career. To this norm can be traced Carter's stubborn reluctance to compromise on matters of principle or policy, discernible in his dealings with the Georgia legislature and, at the outset at least, with Congress (when he attempted to defy custom by cutting pork-barrel water projects, thereby alienating the leadership of his own party). To this norm can also be traced Carter's distaste for politics as usual and the failure of his intimates to pay traditional court to the Washington power structure.

Another norm that colored the interpersonal atmosphere around Carter before and during his presidency was that he and his inner circle perceived themselves as outsiders. They successfully battled the establishment in Georgia politics, cultivated and exploited their outsider status in the 1976 presidential campaign to good political effect, and saw no reason to abandon the outsider mentality once entrenched in the White House. Their sensitivity to slurs by the Washington cognoscenti, who sniffed at their rural southern roots, encouraged them to cling to the role of outsider. This norm did not prevent a search for advice and expertise from outside their circle, but it deepened their reliance on one another and did not allow for any significant emotional penetration of the inner sanctum by newcomers or any extensive outreach to other leaders. In both Georgia and Washington, Carter would seek the counsel of others and make himself available to those wishing to offer advice, but no one outside his immediate circle ever really got to know him. Because of the nature of their rise to power, the Carter team had grown accustomed to working outside normal channels and to being self-reliant. Although they were successful in Georgia, their approach would compound their difficulties with the media and Congress in Washington.

A third norm was intense loyalty and implicit trust. Although only Kirbo and Lance of the inner circle were comparable to Carter in age, experience, and achievement, and although Carter's relationship with Jordan and Powell struck Brzezinski and others as akin to a father-son relationship, accounts suggest that within the circle the interactions were informal, candid, and essentially equal. James Wooten, for example, described Carter's relationship with Jordan and Powell as based on an "instinctive, mutual trust." While Carter was governor, he, according to Wooten, "dealt with them, in most instances, as equals, not as substitute sons, and seldom rebuked them for their occasional nonconformity.... [They were] his fellow southwest Georgians who had worked so hard in his victorious campaigns ... [and theirs was] a friendship, deep and constant, laced with loyalty.... Strategy and tactics, as proposed by any of the three, could be questioned and argued, perhaps heatedly, but the motives were never an issue in their discussion" (1978, 317-318).

The nature of these relationships would have supported a prediction that Carter would not deal expediently with aides who got into trouble—for example, that he would not banish Jordan for rambunctious, improper behavior, such as admiring the pyramidal cleavage of the Egyptian ambassador's wife or allegedly spitting amaretto down the front of a female patron in a New York nightclub or that he would not fire Lance for his banking practices, despite the disastrous public relations consequences of failing to do so and the near-unanimous feeling of distant advisers that Lance should be removed. Indeed, Carter's instinctive, unquestioning faith in Lance had prevented even routine inquiry into Lance's ethical or political vulnerability prior to his appointment as OMB director, a costly oversight (Johnson 1980, 200-211).

The loyalty norm also ensured that as Carter had relied principally on his intimates for key advice and critical performance in his campaigns and in his governorship, he would do so in his presidency. Thus, it would be Rosalynn, not Walter Mondale, whose advice would prevail in the decision to cancel a planned energy speech and convene an ad hoc group of distinguished advisers at Camp David in July 1979 to discuss with Carter and his inner circle what had gone wrong with the administration. It would be Hamilton Jordan, not Zbigniew Brzezinski or any other foreign policy expert, who would be entrusted with the delicate secret negotiations aimed at securing the release of the American hostages from Iran. And it seems to have been Rosalynn alone who shared and supported Carter's decision to invite Menachem Begin and Anwar al-Sadat to Camp David, against the unanimous advice of the experts who perceived the move as far too risky and uncertain of success.

The people who would matter, therefore, and the ways in which they could be expected to contribute were identifiable long before Carter took the oath of office. It was by no means inevitable that Carter, those closest to him, and the roles they played would yield a presidential failure. Other factors contributed as much or more to Carter's electoral defeat in 1980. But the Carter management style in place well before 1976 had some clearly defined characteristics, which could be linked to probable consequences:

> A formalistic emphasis on high quality technical analysis, which (except during political campaigns) often deliberately played down considerations of political feasibility.

> A central figure whose sense of responsibility and need for control prevented delegation of real power to any but a handful of intimates. Work delegated outside this circle of close advisers was subject to duplication by the leader.

> A central figure who was physically accessible to outsiders and patiently solicitous of their advice, but who was emotionally open to the influence of only trusted intimates, who largely reinforced the leader's idiosyncrasies.

Some of the important contours of the Carter presidency—and of the Carter character in the presidency—might have been forecast in 1976 if the right evidence had been examined and the right questions asked.

Reagan as a Property: Management by Handlers. Ronald Reagan's prepresidential management career, which followed a moderately successful stint as a film actor, consists of six terms as president of the Screen Actors' Guild and two terms as governor of California, as well as two campaigns for the governorship and two full-scale campaigns for the Republican presidential nomination (a halfhearted 1968 presidential candidacy is not counted here). Although Carter and Reagan were both governors and acquired much of their significant prepresidential management experience in campaigns for office, the similarities end there. It would be hard to imagine more dissimilar styles for using self, others, and procedures to seek goals.

As with Carter, the Reagan pattern was apparent long before his arrival at 1600 Pennsylvania Avenue and would in its important particulars be reproduced there. Indeed, three of the four components of the Reagan organizational system—extensive delegation, collegial decision making, and leader specialization—were evident in his first campaign for governor in 1966.[3] Reagan proved himself a capable negotiator as Screen Actors' Guild president and a gifted, persuasive speaker in a stirring, nationally telecast speech on behalf of presidential candidate Barry Goldwater. He valued these carefully nurtured skills in himself but had no image of himself as a political candidate. Others, notably Los Angeles millionaire Holmes Tuttle and his conservative associates, would first press Reagan to seek the California governorship. Reagan was a political person, but not an ambitious one. He thought of himself as an ordinary citizen and was flattered by this "draft." When he entered politics, Reagan was an attractive, bright "property" who held strong convictions about conservative principles, but who was reliant upon "handlers" to draw him into politics and bankroll his candidacy, to teach him enough about California politics and issues to be a credible candidate, and to organize and manage his campaign. Reagan's job was to do what he did best: be an engaging, articulate, and persuasive spokesman for conservative political philosophy. The Friends of Ronald Reagan, 41 wealthy donors headed by Tuttle, William French Smith, and others, would supply the encouragement and the money. Many of these same people would offer similar support and advice to President-elect Reagan nearly two decades later. The Spenser-Roberts political management firm would be retained to run the campaign, and they would hire another organization to prepare briefing material for speeches. Reagan's campaign would bear out his communicative strengths and show him to be an astute diagnostician of public sentiment, often sensing public mood swings before the polls did. It would also reveal his gift for establishing rapport with the working press, who grew to like him then as they would again in the presidency. But the campaign also disclosed a vulnerability—Reagan's temper and poise were apt to be disturbed by too much work and lack of sleep. Significantly, the handlers, not Reagan, concluded this. For his part, Reagan overworked because he was scheduled to do so by others and dutifully accepted their direction.

Thus, the first campaign revealed certain core features of the

Reagan style that would persist into the governorship and the presidency: Reagan pacing himself, relying on the counsel of experts for guidance in decision making, and concentrating his energies on relating to the public.

Once installed as governor of California, Reagan depended on his kitchen cabinet of wealthy backers for help in making appointments and named his campaign manager, Philip M. Battaglia, chief of staff. For the first several months, Battaglia ran the governor's office and the governor's schedule. With Reagan's willing acquiescence, Battaglia kept him isolated from the activities and issues of governance, a fact that became apparent to reporters when Reagan confessed two and one-half months after his inauguration that he didn't know what his legislative program was (Cannon 1982, 120). When an alleged involvement in a homosexual scandal forced Battaglia to resign, Reagan was among the last to learn of the gathering storm because his aides had decided that he was "better off not knowing" of the allegations. Cannon argues that Reagan had delegated so much authority that he was left uninformed about an issue that could have destroyed him politically (1982, 134).

Following the events of Reagan's early months as governor, a system of collective staff leadership was created that worked efficiently and effectively for Reagan and set the pattern for the president's White House staff (Cannon 1982, 138). Several individuals became involved as key players: William P. Clark as chief of staff (a position later held by Edwin Meese), Michael Deaver as assistant in charge of partisan political functions, and Caspar W. Weinberger as director of finance. These men would later follow Reagan to Washington. Under the direction of Clark and Meese, Governor Reagan's cabinet gradually emerged as the principal policy-making body, and the personal staff was relegated to housekeeping functions (Biggart and Hamilton 1983, 8). Twice-weekly cabinet meetings were the forums for decisions based on one-page mini-memos that targeted the issues and the options. The discussions served to educate Reagan and to routinize the flow of information and decisions up and down the state administrative hierarchy. The chief of staff ran the meetings, and Reagan's role was to participate in the discussion and ratify the final decisions of the group. The system worked well for Reagan because it required minimal involvement by him, an inexperienced governor, in the management of the process or the analysis of the issues, yet ensured that expertise was brought to bear on decisions and follow-through was tightly controlled while he maintained broad powers of direction as a kind of chairman of the board (Biggart and Hamilton 1983, 15).

As he began to think seriously about the presidency and as the campaigns were mounted, Reagan gradually took on a larger role but retained the basic pattern of relying on capable people with expertise that he lacked. Although he would be criticized throughout his political career for overreliance on others, his approach can be viewed as reflecting a sophisticated assessment of his own strengths and weaknesses and as revealing a sense Reagan has of himself quite different from the helpless puppet his critics imagine him to be. The prepresidential evidence shows that Reagan perceived himself as a leader and a communicator whose appeal to others derived from his simple, straightforward belief in certain fundamental principles shared by most other people, which he expressed in ways they found inspiring. He was persuasive, he felt, not merely because of platform polish, but because he truly believed in what he was selling and because he communicated a sincerity that was genuine. (It is often said of Reagan that he cannot be persuasive unless he believes in what he is saying [see Cannon 1982, 375].) Nor was his optimism, another crucial source of his appeal, a contrivance. Virtually everyone who knew him before or after his entry into politics noted it as a central feature of his personality. That such simple virtues were highly unique, making him a valuable political property, was obvious to Reagan or anybody else who examined the fortunes of other political hopefuls who lacked them. Thus, Reagan by no means regarded himself as merely a front man controlled by others. Instead, as a candidate and as president, "he viewed himself as the creator of the message as well as the chief messenger" (Barrett 1984, 33). This, in Reagan's mind, is why he, and not others with more experience or greater expertise, needed to be in the top job. He could do the one thing that had to be done—win the confidence and support of the electorate. And he could do it better than anybody else on the scene. This fact made experience and expertise secondary, in his view and in the minds of those around him. To them, he was a property worth handling. For his own part, he was willing to take direction but not orders.

Reagan believed he deserved to be the leader, but his behavior also reveals his awareness that he needed certain kinds of help. He felt personally secure enough to seek and use it, and his relaxed, self-deprecating, friendly manner enabled him to attract and retain it. Laurence I. Barrett, formerly *Time* magazine's White House correspondent, says of Reagan: "He had in him less vindictiveness, guile, ego or cowardice than most men who make it in politics do" (1984, 23). Such characteristics allowed him to use others more dispassionately and pragmatically than a leader like Carter. And they freed him to trust others until he had reason not to. Because he securely believed in his principles, he did not need to surround himself with ideologues who would reinforce them. Instead, he sought pragmatic managers who could do those things he could not do for himself. Because he felt personally secure, he was able to expand beyond a tight circle of loyal intimates who had been with him from the beginning. Furthermore, he repeatedly invested virtual strangers with considerable power and authority—people like John Sears in the prepresidential days, and James Baker, George Bush, and David Stockman in the White House. This is something Carter, for example, could do only rarely. And because Reagan always kept a degree of aloofness and personal independence from even his most intimate associates, he was able to endure their departures from key positions when they no longer performed well, even though he could not personally bring himself to do the firing.

Reagan's way of using himself as leader and his concept of his own special role meant that he needed others to provide certain complementary support. Someone else had to structure and organize the decision-making system, for example, and manage its operations so that he remained free to concentrate on the rhetorical, public relations aspects of leadership. He entered into the machinery only to make character-defining, directional choices from among alternatives refined by the system. The alternatives were drawn up by his campaign managers and, particularly, his chiefs of staff—Clark and Meese in California, Baker and Regan in the White House. Others had to function as Reagan's surveillance and early-warning systems and educate him about his choices because he prefers a discussion or roundtable to the study of briefs as a mode of learning. He expects others to see to it that the right issues get considered at the right time. Thus, Reagan has needed an honest broker to ensure that he was exposed to good faith renditions of the major points of view concerning issues to be decided. The issues broker in California and Washington was Meese. The California roundtable forum was the cabinet; the Washington forum was daily meetings of Reagan and his troika—Baker, Deaver, and Meese. Reagan has also shown the need for what might be called mood management—the maintenance of a tranquil and positive atmosphere in his immediate vicinity that enables him to sustain his upbeat outlook and protects him from his own tendency to let others overschedule his work and perhaps overdraw his store of energy. In California, this function was shared by wife Nancy and various members of the staff. In Washington, Michael Deaver and Nancy emerged as the principal guardians of the Reagan tranquillity. Another Reagan characteristic, which influenced how his staff related to him, was his acute discomfort with disagreement among his advisers. When aides became hopelessly split over the position Reagan, as governor, should take on a liberalized abortion bill that reached his office for signature, Reagan, who "usually could rely on the collective leadership of aides who settled their own differences before they came to cabinet," was "plunged into a state of political indecision" and left an "overwhelming impression that he just didn't want to make a final decision of any kind" (Cannon 1982, 129). A similar incident occurred during the 1980 presidential campaign, when intense friction among the staff led to a confrontation between Deaver and campaign director John Sears. As a result, Deaver resigned. The incident left Reagan depressed and angry. While it forced him to be for the first time a "participant in his own campaign," it also taught him that it was "crucial to select aides who were suited to his personality and could operate without strain" (Cannon 1982, 306). Deaver eventually returned and Sears departed.

One additional, essentially psychological, function performed for Reagan by his staff in California and in Washington is in some respects the most important, as it relates to the preservation of Reagan's most important political and personal strength: sincerity based on belief in his own principles. This function is revealed in the following comment by Deaver, quoted in *Time* magazine (Church 1982, 15): "You should never try to make him do something he doesn't believe in, because if you do that we will fail. The greatest asset this administration has is Ronald Reagan; if he can't communicate his positions, we are in real trouble. And if he doesn't believe in it, he can't communicate it." Deaver indirectly discloses a crucial service Reagan's advisers have always performed for him—a service that has allowed Reagan to behave in politically pragmatic ways and yet remain ideologically principled in his own and the public's estimation. It is to persuade Reagan that whatever pragmatic course of action they might recommend to him at any given point is actually consistent with Reagan's larger principles and instincts. Only if he believes this can he remain sincere and bring his powers of public persuasion to bear. One Reagan cabinet member referred to the "Reagan argument"—an insistence that what looks like a policy reversal nonetheless is consonant with Reagan's basic beliefs. "If it is made adroitly enough, the President is capable of what looks to everyone else like astonishing reversals indeed" (Church 1982, 15). This particular kind of staff handling had a good deal to do with Reagan's willingness, as governor of California, to depart from conservative campaign promises when confronted with political or technical obstacles. Aided by a staff that understood his needs, Reagan would continue to speak sincerely and behave pragmatically in Washington.

Reagan's way of using self, others, and procedures is surely controversial. A careful review of available evidence leaves room for two conflicting judgments: either that his style is a reckless abnegation of power and responsibility to unelected others or that it is a workable and effective method of using the kind of talent Reagan possesses, while simultaneously compensating for his weaknesses. Whatever one concludes about that debate, two facts remain: His management system is a faithful reflection of Reagan the man, and it was evident in broad outline well before he became president.

The Presidential Experience Demand and Self-Esteem

The last of the three great demands made by the presidency on the characters of presidents is the presidential experience—four distinguishable varieties of psychologically significant pressure created by exposure to the functions of the presidency (Buchanan 1978). This is a hidden side of the presidency, rarely discussed or acknowledged except in references to the cliché that the presidency is the toughest job in the world. At issue is the ability of a particular human being to cope emotionally and physically with an unusually powerful and potentially quite distorting psychological environment. The importance of an ability to cope—to deal effectively with the stresses, frustrations, temptations, and distortions of the job—tends to become apparent only after a president fails to cope successfully. The presidency reveals the character of presidents in various ways, not the least of which is by laying bare their characteristic reactions to such pressures as the numerous, intense, and conflicting job demands (stress), the celebratory treatment accorded the symbol of the republic (deference), the lure of expedient secrecy or misrepresentation as a way to avoid embarrassment or failure (temptation), and the urge to lash out at and overpower people or institutions that seek to thwart the achievement of important presidential aims (frustration). All presidents necessarily confront these pressures in doing the work of the presidency, but not every president succumbs to them. Social psychological research and the psycho-historical investigations of James David Barber suggest that the most significant personality determinant is self-esteem.[4] The higher the level of self-esteem, the lower the chances of an adverse reaction to most kinds of psychological pressure, and vice versa (Barber 1985; Wells and Marwell 1976). But as others have argued (Reedy 1970; Buchanan 1978; Wells and Marwell 1976), few human beings can remain untouched or unmarked by pervasive psychological influences, despite the comparative advantages of high self-esteem.

The record shows that presidents have not remained untouched. Many significant presidential failures have been attributed to character-rooted response to circumstantial psychological pressure. Wilson's unyielding response to the League of Nations dispute with the Senate, which blocked U.S. membership in the league (George and George 1956), FDR's attempt to pack the Supreme Court with liberal appointees to reverse its anti-New Deal stance (Barber 1985), Lyndon Johnson's determination to cling to a failing course of action in Vietnam (Kearns 1976), and Nixon's fateful decision to cover up his involvement in Watergate, are all cases in point. Other presidents have developed physical symptoms that could have been attributed, at least in part, to the psychological stresses and burdens of office. FDR died in office of a cerebral hemorrhage, Eisenhower suffered two serious heart attacks, and both Nixon and Carter aged visibly as their terms progressed.

The presidency, however, is not the setting in which to diagnose the psychological or physical suitability of presidents, despite the clarity with which it emerges there. If trouble is to be avoided, diagnoses must take place before the election. The trait theories of presidential character have all implicitly acknowledged the psychological and physical demands of the presidency by consistently listing such virtues as honesty and integrity, flexibility, morality, emotional stability, durability, and resilience, and vigorous good health as requisites to presidential success (Small 1932; Laski 1940; Hargrove 1974b; Hess 1974). Similarly, Barber's character theory stresses high energy and positive emotional outlook as preconditions to effectiveness. And both the public and the media have always understood that the presidency is no place for the weak, fainthearted, arrogant, or power-hungry. Evidence of moral or physical disability in candidates has always captured widespread attention and has often proved fatal to candidacies. Recent examples include Republican candidate George Romney, who called his own strength of character into question by remarking that he had been brainwashed by American officials on a tour of Vietnam in 1968; Thomas Eagleton, who was forced off the Democratic ticket headed by George McGovern in 1972 because of his disclosure that he had received psychiatric treatment; Edmund Muskie, a candidate for the Democratic party nomination in 1976 who undermined his prospects by bursting into tears of frustration in response to an unfriendly newspaper comment about his wife; Barry Goldwater, whose strident conservatism and loose talk about extremism made him seem too dangerous to be president; George Wallace, a candidate who projected an angry negativity and a thinly disguised racism considered unworthy of the presidency; and John B. Connally, a man of widely recognized ability who struck most voters as too nakedly ambitious and power-hungry to trust in the White House. In each of these examples, some real or imagined personal defect disqualified the candidate from serious consideration for the presidency.

Others have overcome their negatively perceived attributes and been elected—Reagan's age, for example, or Nixon's "tricky Dick" stereotype and angry tongue-lashing of the media—but not without extensive scrutiny of their suspected weaknesses.

While failed candidacies show that the electorate has often considered the moral, temperamental, and physical suitability of candidates to be of potentially overriding importance, the diagnosis of character flaws has generally been somewhat superficial and has not been guided by any sophisticated conception of exactly what it is that characters and bodies must be able to enjoy, tolerate, and endure to function effectively in the presidency. In the conventional view, it is simply a tough job that requires a highly competent, very trustworthy person.

The concept of presidential experience attempts to specify precisely where psychological pressure rubs against character, so the kinds of individuals who are likely to be pushed off course, or left unharmed, as president can be identified. Because the pressures of the presidency—stress, deference, temptation, and frustration—are analogous to those encountered in other demanding roles and circumstances, and because people in general display characteristic patterns of reaction to pressures in the course of their lives, those reactions can be discovered and used as another index of presidency-relevant character. A candidate's reactions to experiences with stress, frustration, temptation, and deference, not responses to a self-esteem questionnaire, provide a predictive measure of suitability for office.

Again a comparison will be made between Jimmy Carter and Ronald Reagan. Even though neither showed the kinds of adverse responses Wilson, Johnson, or Nixon had to presidential pressure, Carter and Reagan reacted differently enough to illustrate how the concept of presidential experience can work. The question to be addressed is: Could the reactions of these men to the presidential experience have been predicted from what was discoverable before they were elected?

Stress. In their review of human reactions to stress, Janis and Leventhal (1968) note that for most writers the term *stress* designates a broad class of events involving interaction between extreme environmental stimuli and the adjustive capacities of the organism. Stimuli are stressful because they do or are able to induce emotional tension and interfere with normal cognitive processes. People vary in their perceptions of and reactions to stress. But by any fair measure, certain features of the presidential role must be considered stressful.

Because presidents function as mediator and crisis manager for the political system and are responsible for its most pressing problems, they will be continuously beset by external demands that qualify as extreme environmental stimuli for three reasons: (1) they are numerous to the point of overload; (2) they are intermittently intense, as with dangerous crises; and (3) they frequently conflict, forcing presidents to resolve value conflicts. Such demands will have emotional significance for presidents in general because they are held accountable for unpredictable outcomes. They are continuously and visibly at risk of failure, should any significant demand be mishandled.

The worst case responses to chronic, intense stress include such things as loss of vitality, emotional instability, physical deterioration, and decline in performance effectiveness (Torrance 1963; Coleman 1960). Not everyone suffers such consequences, and, as presidents, neither Carter nor the first-term Reagan responded in these ways. But every president does display a characteristic mode of adaptation to stress. And, as the discussion of their management styles suggests, Carter and Reagan could not be more different. The Carter stance in the face of stress was to confront it head-on; the Reagan mode was to avoid it whenever possible. Carter involved himself and took responsibility for everything; Reagan carefully delimited what he would grapple with and encouraged others to accept a much more narrow definition of his accountability.

In psychological terms, Carter's coping strategy was to prevail by endurance and mastery. The more numerous and intractable the problems he faced, the harder he worked, even moving to complicate and intensify his burdens by deliberately overloading his agenda. The more perplexing and unyielding the dilemma, the more patient and persistent he became, as evidenced by his reaction to the three most personally stressful events of his presidency: the Bert Lance affair, the midterm reassessment of his administration, and the Iranian hostage ordeal. By all accounts, he derived the strength for his approach from his religious faith and from his apparently genuine belief that to endure and to keep exploring new solutions is to triumph. Carter would occasionally attempt to shift blame for a problem onto other shoulders, such as holding the Organization of Petroleum Exporting Countries (OPEC) accountable for inflation, but, for the most part, he appeared unusually willing to acknowledge personal accountability for whatever was going wrong. And when the wishes or demands of important others conflicted, Carter was never loath to resolve the conflict himself and risk the consequences, which, in cases like the Camp David negotiations or the Iranian hostage rescue attempt, were potentially considerable.

Inevitably, Carter paid a price for his adaptive mode. Most visible were the deepening lines in his face and the graying hair. He also tended to lapse into monotonic recitations of complexities and facts when he felt anxious, to the detriment of his ability to communicate and inspire. Perhaps most significantly, he overextended his cognitive processes, which seemed to accentuate his difficulties with distinguishing the important from the trivial, the greater from the lesser priorities, so widely remarked upon by critics. If his critics are right, his effectiveness was diminished by his personal pattern of adjustment to the demands of the presidency. Carter's approach to processing demands was in place before 1976 and could have been forecast as the likely presidential pattern. In quitting the navy against Rosalynn's wishes, in doggedly pressing his challenge in the state senate election, in seeking the governorship against formidable odds, in consistently seeking opportunities to prove that he could do it all himself, Carter made it plain that as president he would never try to hide from the physical or psychological burdens of office.

Reagan, in contrast, had discovered in his first political campaign that stress, in the form of overwork, palpably diminished his effectiveness and had to be avoided. In the form of value conflicts, as when his advisers could not agree on the abortion question while he was governor of California, stress attenuated his ability to reach a decision. Both before and after his election to the presidency, Reagan's ability to be decisive and persuasive required that he perceive no significant conflict and that his energy not be depleted. The Reagan management system was designed primarily to maintain for Reagan a personal atmosphere of tranquillity and harmony without which he could not be effective. Of all the pressures of the presidency, stress, in the form of numerous, intense, and conflicting demands, represented the greatest threat to Reagan.

It has been argued that a president can delegate tasks but not ultimate accountability for their successful performance. Although the workload can be reduced and the environment tranquilized, the burdens of the presidency cannot be completely escaped. If something goes wrong, the president is held responsible, not the assistant who made the mistake. Thus only the physical and a portion of the psychological pressure can be shunted aside. The burden of responsibility remains to be dealt with, even by a president like Reagan. Reagan's management system has shielded him from long hours and from much direct contact with acrimonious debate and with value conflicts between his closest advisers. Reagan copes—politically and, arguably, psychologically— with responsibility, and especially responsibility for events and outcomes that are unpopular with those whose opinion and advice he respects, in three distinguishable stages: distancing, rationalization, and denial. The distancing component of his management system allowed him to escape the political fallout from such events as the Stockman revelations about supply-side economics and the frequent embarrassments of Secretary of the Interior James Watt. The allegations about a homosexual ring in Reagan's first administration as governor of California did not cause major political problems but did result in a reportedly severe psychological fallout. Reagan was said to have been stunned by the charges. And though he immediately demanded and got his chief of staff's resignation, Reagan withdrew even further from active participation in the affairs of the governor's office. Aides found him "more distraught than he had ever been in the first nine months of his governorship" (Cannon 1982, 135). It was said that "the Governorship went into receivership" (Cannon 1982, 134). Responsibility was deflected first by ignorance, then by withdrawal.

Reagan's penchant for rationalization has been seen most clearly when he has taken action inconsistent with his promises or rhetoric. An early example was his support of a tax bill in California, called one of the "great ironies" of his governorship by Lou Cannon because "a man who said 'taxes should hurt' and who had campaigned against the profligacy of the Brown administration had sponsored a tax increase far beyond anything the state needed to balance its books" (1982, 156). When Reagan was criticized by conservatives who claimed the tax bill "hurts most those he promised to help most," Reagan simply took it in stride, viewing his action as a practical response to realities instead of a departure from conservative principles (Cannon 1982, 157). As stated earlier, Reagan is responsive to Reagan arguments—claims that apparent inconsistencies are really in keeping with his principles. Said his once closest adviser, Michael Deaver: "The President has been accused of contradicting himself and denies it, and believes his denials. He rationalizes them in his own mind. When it comes to changing positions, he convinces himself that it has to be done in the short term, but he keeps his goals" (Gelb 1985, 24). Political rationalization, then, is apparently also psychological rationalization. For Reagan responsibility is tolerable because he really did not do anything wrong, despite what the critics or some nagging corner of his conscience might claim.

The third coping pattern, denial, has been most apparent during Reagan's presidency and, like the other mechanisms, has its roots in the prepresidential career. Denial surfaces when Reagan feels threatened by something he finds unpleasant, such as conflict among his staff ("Reagan so despised turmoil in the ranks," writes Laurence I. Barrett, "that he tended to deny, even to himself, that it existed, or that he might have to impose order" [1984, 37]). Reagan sometimes uses denial when he is called to account for some misstatement or inaccuracy uttered in a speech or press conference, or when he is confronted with facts that are inconsistent with his deeply felt preferences.

Reagan has shown the pattern of denying that he was wrong by claiming to have been misunderstood, as he did, for example, when he was asked in an interview how he could have felt justified in equating Nazi soldiers buried in a German military cemetery in Bitburg, West Germany, with Holocaust victims. (When criticized for his decision to give a speech at Bitburg, Reagan had defended himself by portraying both as victims of Nazism.) "Never would I ever suggest that those other victims were victims in the same sense as the victims of the Holocaust," he said. Yet, as Leslie H. Gelb argues, "that was in fact the suggestion he had made, seeking to justify his visit to the German cemetery" (1985, 24).

Reagan has often seemed unaware (or unable or unwilling to acknowledge) that some deeply felt conviction or interpretation of his is contradicted by facts and has blithely continued to repeat the inaccuracy. Barrett offers a description:

> There was an entirely different species of Reaganesque error ... [a] virulent variety [that] came not from a verbal glitch ... [but instead] from fundamental misunderstandings on certain subjects. And these skewed perceptions virtually always complemented his general ideology.... During the 1980 election campaign this showed up in his frequent assertions that Alaska had larger oil reserve than Saudi Arabia. "We're not an energy-poor nation," he said several times during the primaries, "we're energy-rich." Liberate the oil industry from government regulation, he said, and "we won't need OPEC oil." This at a time when the United States was still importing 40 percent of its oil and when no serious expert was predicting total energy independence for many years to come. (1984, 26)

On one level, each of Reagan's various forms of denial can be interpreted as nothing more than typical political face-saving. On another level, however, they hint at a personally meaningful pattern of self-protection. A common thread is defense—against threats to his psychological security (for example, staff dissension) or against attacks on his integrity or self-respect (for example, bristling at criticisms of his mistakes or his sometimes angry insistence on the validity of his own interpretations or the purity of his motives). Consciously or not, Reagan is defending himself against pressure he cannot or will not abide. If a pressure is not really there (for example, staff dissension), it cannot hurt him. If it is not really true (for example, an inaccurate statement), it does not discredit him.

Reagan is not a complete prisoner of his defenses. He does occasionally admit mistakes and publicly accept responsibility for them, as happened when he acknowledged that he alone was accountable for the deaths of the 241 Americans (mostly Marines) killed by a terrorist bomb at Marine headquarters in Beirut, Lebanon. But even in this unfortunate situation, whose aftermath left Lebanon in chaos, Reagan insisted that the Marines' mission had been accomplished.

One final Reagan device for contending with stress must be mentioned—his unquenchable optimism. For him it serves much the same protective purpose as does Carter's religion—a form of self-reassurance and a source of strength in the face of trials. Optimism is essentially a perceptual syndrome, a tendency to place favorable, hopeful interpretations on events and future prospects. It is therefore also a form of denial. Specifically, it denies that objectively unpredictable events will turn out unfavorably and insists instead that they will turn out well. And it disregards the testimony of objective, dispassionate observers who argue that present facts make future outcomes uncertain, labeling them as pessimistic. Optimism can also be a leadership ploy, and an effective one at that, for it is infectious, inspiring, and reassuring to others. By all accounts, Reagan is not acting when he projects a sunny, upbeat confidence. "[Voltaire's Professor] Pangloss would seem a sourpuss compared to 'Dutch' Reagan, whose sunny nature and optimistic attitude have been dominant characteristics of his personal life and political career" (Cannon 1982, 22). Although Reagan's optimism is resilient in the long run, it is somewhat fragile in the short term and can be disturbed by circumstances Reagan finds stressful. His inner circle has learned to recognize its importance to Reagan's well-being and effectiveness and has typically worked to nurture and protect it. After Reagan's 1980 campaign staff shake-up, for example, Reagan was unsettled and committed a series of blunders (such as linking Carter to the Ku Klux Klan), which left his campaign reeling and his self-confidence shaken. His gubernatorial campaign manager, Stuart Spencer, was called in to help restore calm and rebuild Reagan's confidence. His method was to keep Reagan away from reporters for a time and to coach him on how to avoid damaging statements. Within a few weeks, Reagan's optimism had reasserted itself, and the candidate was free to move around naturally again (Cannon 1982, 278).

Taken as a whole, Reagan's way of protecting himself from the disruptive and threatening intrusions of his responsibilities worked well for him. First as governor and later as president, he showed less overt physical wear and tear than most other officeholders, which is all the more remarkable in light of his advanced age. Both Reagan and Carter professed to enjoy the presidency, but Reagan was more convincing. Still, Reagan did develop colon cancer early in his second term. So did his brother Neil, however, and without having endured comparable rigors, which suggests that it might have been an inherited characteristic. On the other hand, inconclusive research evidence does suggest the possibility of a link between repressed or denied emotional tension and physical "diseases of adaptation," like cancer (Coleman 1960). The relationship between mental dispositions and physical disease is a hotly disputed question. But it is not inconceivable that Reagan's mode of adapting to stress was not totally cost-free to him and may have exacted a physical price.

From the standpoint of presidential effectiveness, neither Carter's nor Reagan's mode of coping with the stresses of office can be considered ideal. Carter's wore him down and may have warped his perspective, while Reagan's appears to have cut him off from reality and placed him too greatly at the mercy of others. Although not disabling, each carried obvious advantages and disadvantages, and each was discoverable in the prepresidential record.

Deference. A symbol is a material object representing something immaterial. As the dominant symbol of government, the president represents the values, majesty, integrity, and potency of the political system. The president is invested with primordial, atavistic meaning. Sitting in Lincoln's chair and speaking with the moral authority of Washington, Jackson, and Roosevelt, a president absorbs some of their colors. This cannot help but have a significant impact on personal and professional relationships.

Any president is treated with exaggerated respect by almost everyone encountered. From a psychological standpoint, this has one critically important consequence—the president can never be among equals, is always, in effect, denied access to true peers. Thus, the recurring exposure that results from the president's symbolic role is status inequality.

Adulation and respect are, of course, painless. Their significance for presidents stems from the fact that recurring exposure poses a subtle and long-term threat to the accuracy of a president's perceptions—of self and of conditions and events. Because perceptual accuracy is sustained in large measure by interactions with peers who offer candid, critical reactions to one's assessments and perceptions, and because presidents encounter few who are willing to be consistently and unreservedly candid, they are denied the sort of social comparison interactions that people use to test reality and maintain their adjustment to it.

No president can entirely escape these dynamics, but some have been less victimized than others. Presidents like Wilson, Johnson, and

Nixon, who showed unusual hunger for the status of high office and conveyed strong expectations for respect and deference to their subordinates, significantly intensified the "yea-saying" atmosphere around themselves, with the result that their misperceptions intensified and contributed to major missteps harmful to themselves and the nation. Wilson stubbornly refused to compromise with the Senate over the League of Nations (George and George 1956); Johnson cultivated a groupthink atmosphere that perpetuated a failing Vietnam policy (Janis 1972); and Nixon fired special Watergate prosecutor Archibald Cox, which helped to ensure eviction from the presidency (Buchanan 1978).

Neither as candidates nor as presidents did Carter or Reagan offer any evidence of dangerous susceptibility to the enticements of high status or unusual hunger for the obeisance of others. On the contrary, both appeared unusually willing to treat others as equals and encouraged such treatment toward themselves. Carter biographer Wooten took note of the informal relationship between Carter and his principal advisers Jordan and Powell and describes many instances of heated, even angry, disagreements among the three of them. Reagan was known to dislike conflict and staff dissension, but he always encouraged orderly debate and actively sought to expose himself to real, as opposed to prearranged, decision options by making an honest broker an integral part of his staff. He was accustomed from the beginning to taking rather than giving direction to the staff, hardly evidence of an insistence on worshipful loyalty. During their prepresidential careers, then, both Carter and Reagan followed the practice of encouraging disagreement and debate among advisers, insisting only that the ranks be closed once a decision was reached.

In addition, neither had any history of looking upon disagreement as disloyalty or been accused of using subtle cuing or overt intimidation to signal the expectation that their preformed perceptions be endorsed. Neither has been accused of arrogance or egotism by those who worked closely with them (although Carter sometimes gave this impression to outsiders, both as governor and as president) or been described as having treated or regarded others as lesser beings. As president, Carter was noted for his willingness to patiently endure some of the most brutally frank and hard-hitting criticism any president ever got in face-to-face sessions periodically arranged with members of Congress and others (Johnson 1980, 154-160). His de-emphasis of the royalist dimensions of presidential symbolism and his modest, soft-spoken, self-effacing public demeanor were so pronounced that he was soon criticized in the press for failing to inspire people (Johnson 1980, 151). For his part, Reagan was perhaps more inspiring, but no less approachable and unaffected, once installed in the White House. Says Lou Cannon: "He made a point of treating those closest to him the way he had always treated them. It was not a hard thing to do, for Reagan was not puffed up by the presidency. . . . He did not put on airs with his aides or his old friends or the congressmen who came to see him" (1982, 305). And Laurence I. Barrett says: "Reagan is in fact quite nice in any number of ways. He is remarkably free of arrogance. He is willing to kid himself. He is abundantly kind to all those in his service, great or humble" (1984, 43).

On the other hand, some or all of the negative characteristics neither Carter nor Reagan possessed—warning signs of susceptibility to the distortion potential of deference—were discernible in varying degrees in the prepresidential careers of Wilson, Johnson, and Nixon. Since these warning signs can lead to trouble, they are worth looking for in presidential candidates. They would not have been found in the patterns of either of the presidents considered here.

Temptation. The pressure of temptation springs from the fact that the presidency invites presidents to misrepresent themselves to their various constituencies. The temptation to misrepresent is intensified by the comparative ease with which embarrassing information can be withheld or suppressed. Furthermore, the symbolic and policy advocate functions of the office accustom presidents to acceptable patterns of misrepresentation as a matter of course.

Symbolically, presidents are expected to embody the nation's important values and inspire citizens' betterment. This responsibility encourages presidents to speak and act in ways consistent with all the noble but often mythical qualities citizens want to attribute to them. Misrepresentation ensues because presidents are human beings and possess human failings, which, if revealed, would seem inconsistent with their symbolic status. They thus routinely de-emphasize warts, present themselves as serene and decisive whether they feel that way or not, and otherwise attempt to project an idealized image.

Politically, a president is led toward misrepresentation for different reasons. The symbolic president must inspire, but the political president must sell—programs and party. As a partisan advocate, the president is bound to put forth the party's case as favorably as possible, which often means seeking complete credit for accomplishments, shifting the blame for mistakes to others, and rarely or never admitting anything that would cast the administration in an unflattering light.

As experience grows, any president becomes more familiar and more comfortable with dissemblance. Augmenting this acculturation is

the morally flexible milieu of the presidency. Seasoned political professionals and diplomats expect a savvy president to bend the truth in
search of worthy aims. A climate of tolerance is nourished and sustained
by the longstanding tradition of presidential secrecy in the interests of
national security. David Wise (1973) argues that a right-to-lie norm
pervades the presidency and the highest policy councils of government.
It is thus highly likely that most presidents will perceive the control or
distortion of at least some kinds of information as an essential and
legitimate political resource.

The danger emerges, of course, when—as inevitably happens—the
president is tempted to employ the secrecy resource in areas not infor-
mally sanctioned by custom and usage. The morality of the president's
personal behavior is judged solely by the president, who is left to
experience a variety of situational temptations in the absence of social,
interpersonal, and moral constraints that inhibit the actions of others.
In tough, complex circumstances, when disclosure would be damaging or
fatal, a president is going to be tempted to lie. When such temptation
arises, the only effective resistance available is internal, in the character,
integrity, or honesty of the president.

At least four American presidents—James K. Polk, Theodore Roosevelt, Lyndon Johnson, and Richard Nixon—have responded to situational temptation with what can be termed "big lie" strategies. Polk
misrepresented the national motive for war with Mexico to the American people, Roosevelt secretly fomented the rebellion that would create
a nation willing to cede the territory on which the United States could
build the Panama Canal, Johnson misrepresented the costs and the
nature of the war in Vietnam, and Nixon lied about his involvement in
the Watergate coverup. All four incidents created immediate or even-
tual trouble for the United States. The potential for trouble makes
temptation worth worrying about. It explains why the characteristic
response to temptation displayed by a presidential candidate bears
examination.

Both as candidates and as presidents, Carter and Reagan displayed
the normal range of political misrepresentation, but neither ever responded with a big lie. Gubernatorial candidate Carter would indulge in
an unsavory blurring of his position on racial integration to attract the
support of state leaders like Lester Maddox, whom he described as "the
embodiment of the Democratic party" (Wooten 1978, 293). Carter thus
deliberately invited a public misunderstanding of his actually very
liberal position to get elected and allegedly was later "distraught" by
the campaign he had run. Governor Reagan would acquiesce to an
attempt to cover up the supposed homosexual ring in his office but

would defend himself: "If there is a credibility gap and I'm responsible, it is because I refuse to participate in trying to destroy human beings with no factual evidence" (Cannon 1982, 137). Beyond these fairly typical political incidents, little evidence is available to suggest a weakness for ethically questionable misrepresentation in the prepresidential records of either man. Those who knew them and wrote about them prior to their involvement in presidential politics describe both as unusually straight shooters with unimpeachable moral and ethical reputations, judgments that, for the most part, were borne out by their performances in the White House. If neither president was above self-interested political misrepresentation, neither was he given to outright lying. Guile, stealth, craft, and cunning were not prominent features of either man's administration.

Frustration. As the agent charged with diagnosing the nation's ills and prescribing remedies in the form of legislative proposals, the president must advance solutions and push for their adoption. But as only one member of a constitutional system of shared powers, the president does not have a free hand. Of the four pressures, only frustration—the inevitable consequence of shared powers—has direct roots in the Constitution. The constitutional sources of frustration have been supplemented over time by the emergence of an entrenched bureaucracy, mass media, and a variety of politically powerful interest groups, all of which occasionally emerge as major obstacles to presidential initiatives.

These forces comprise the external sources of frustration, defined as an obstruction in the path between an organism and its objective (Costello and Zalkind 1963). Internally, a president's feeling of frustration stems from the discrepancy between aspirations and what can be attained after the necessary and inevitable accommodation of legitimate political opposition. This gap is the classic experience of democratic political leadership. It has been the fate of most American presidents to fall short of their important policy objectives.

What is particularly vexing and frustrating in the personal sense is that presidents are expected to find ways to prevail—to put their personal stamp on outcomes—despite all obstacles. Great presidents have been those who found ways to circumvent the opposition. The traditions of the presidency celebrate the effective use of presidential power. Presidents realize this, yet find that barriers emerge to derail even their most innocuous and well-intentioned aims. After a while, they find that opposition seems not principled and reasoned, but mindless and reflexive.

Presidents are thus forced to confront the possibility of failure in areas likely to concern them deeply and personally. Though similar in import to stress, frustration involves issues on which the president has chosen to stake public prestige. Defeat, then, is that much more painful and less tolerable than it is on issues that emerge without presidential initiative. It will hurt most on major priorities but sting on any proposal, and the feeling of frustration is likely to grow with the major and minor defeats. The behavior of recent presidents suggests that as it grows, a president's respect for such traditional democratic norms as strict adherence to constitutional processes and the legitimacy of such countervailing power centers as Congress or the media may begin to erode. This would help to explain what have been numerous acts of presidential defiance and aggression, ranging from outright usurpation of power (for example, Nixon's vast extension of impoundment powers) to open warfare with other branches of government (for example, Wilson's conflict with the Senate over the League of Nations) to illegal use of federal police agencies like the Central Intelligence Agency and the Federal Bureau of Investigation to get the goods on political opponents (allegedly practiced by Lyndon Johnson and John Kennedy) to efforts to change the face of government to create a better chance of prevailing (for example, FDR's plan to pack the Supreme Court so it could no longer overturn New Deal legislation).

The acts of defiance and aggression in response to frustration have had damaging and otherwise undesirable consequences, and this is why it can be of considerable importance to examine the characteristic patterns of coping with frustration among presidential candidates. No president has been oblivious to frustration, and virtually all have struggled to overcome it. Most, however, have confined their reactions to less provocative or legally questionable efforts to prevail, including presidents Carter and Reagan. As with other pressures, the frustration responses displayed by these men as candidates and before would not have afforded significant grounds for distinguishing between them or fearing the election of either. But again, it is instructive to ask whether that conclusion could have been reached before the fact. Given that those who seek political power are often aggressive and determined people, it is very likely that future presidential candidates will be willing to pay any price to win, as has happened so often in the past.

Interestingly, both Carter and Reagan have been labeled as unyielding and stubborn on matters of great consequence to them, but both have displayed considerable flexibility when events made it clear that further inflexibility meant defeat for themselves or damage to other, larger interests. Too, both have also remained well within the recognized limits in their efforts to triumph over the opposition encountered along the path to the White House. But within those limits, there are differences.

In his early political career, Carter displayed more of a gritty determination to succeed and a willingness to go to greater lengths to do so than Reagan did as governor of California. One revealing incident can serve to illustrate Carter's prepresidential pattern of responding to frustration. It involved his 1962 candidacy for the Georgia state senate. Numerous blatant voting irregularities, part of a plan to rig the election in favor of Carter's opponent, had taken place in Quitman County. When the first count showed that Carter lost the Democratic primary (whose victor was virtually assured election) by 139 votes, he decided to do battle. Said his biographer Betty Glad, "He was to put an extraordinary amount of effort into something others might not consider worth the investment. In maneuvers during the twenty days remaining before the general election, he showed a tenacity . . . [that was] to mark his future political career" (1980, 89). A relentless effort followed—involving appeals to the media, to the county and state Democratic committees, and to the courts—to overcome the foul play. He was ultimately allowed to claim the prize he felt was rightfully his. Carter had responded to frustration with a characteristically tireless effort to prevail against it, but without responding in kind to the illegal political practices that had thwarted him in the first place. As governor, he would behave similarly when contested. He developed a reputation among political opponents and unfriendly journalists, described here by Reg Murphy, former editor of the *Atlanta Constitution:* "If politics is the art of the possible, Jimmy Carter won't get along with anybody in Washington, because he is a mean, hard-eyed sort of fellow who tolerates nobody who opposes him. The Governor just absolutely does not take challenges from anybody" (1976, 23). He was no saint; he was not above occasionally taking the low road in his dealings with political opponents on the campaign trail or in the legislature (Glad 1980, 490). And he would abandon positions or embrace previous opponents when it aided in the pursuit of his aims, showing a tactical flexibility that has often struck critics as inconsistent with his frequent claims to moral perfection (Glad 1980, 493). But both as candidate and as president, Carter maintained a self-concept as a morally virtuous man that operated to prevent any truly unscrupulous or ruthless attack on the objects of his frustrations. As president he would turn out to be less rigid and uncompromising than people like Reg Murphy had predicted, presumably because he realized that the strategy that had worked with the Georgia legislature would not work with Congress. But despite such provocations as an unruly and disrespectful Congress or the career-threatening intransigence of the Ayatollah Khomeini during the hostage crisis, Carter did not lash out in anger or otherwise seize upon desperate measures to put his opponents to rout. As he had in 1962, he simply kept trying, seeking, tirelessly struggling to find a path around the obstacles. His response to frustration posed no threat to democratic institutions and resulted in no significant abuse of presidential power— results that could have been predicted.

Reagan's public image as a man unswervingly dedicated to conservative principles and stubbornly determined to put them into practice was created initially in his campaign for governor. It invited the expectation that he would brook no interference with his agenda and would struggle uncompromisingly to enact it into law. Thus, his conservative supporters were surprised and disappointed to discover that he was much more flexible on policy initiatives than his rhetoric would suggest—something they continued to be surprised by as late as his second term in the White House. Reagan can surely be stubborn and will occasionally refuse to compromise, but he has never shown any penchant for "going over a cliff with flags flying," as he put it. Instead, he said, "[I'm] willing to take what I can get" (Cannon 1982, 157). Evidence of Reagan's stubbornness was far less plentiful during his California years than it would be in Washington. In his first 100 days as governor, for example, Reagan announced a variety of bold strategies aimed at fulfilling campaign promises for "squeezing and cutting and trimming" the size and cost of government, only to abandon or scale down most of them as opposition mounted or he became aware of their impracticality. One typical instance involved his pledge to order a 10 percent across-the-board spending cut in every state agency, announced on his twelfth day in office. By day 60, Reagan's finance chief was informing a legislative committee that the 10 percent budget cut was a good try, but unrealistic (*Houston Chronicle* 1980, sec. 7, 1).

While predominantly a positive, friendly personality, Reagan did show flashes of both private and public anger and hostility. The public displays were infrequent enough to be jarring and worked to his advantage, as with his declaration, "I paid for this microphone," during a New Hampshire primary debate and his televised command that a disruptive heckler in the audience "shut up" (Barrett 1984, 43-44). Private utterances, not intended for broadcast, revealed a Reagan who felt peevish and angry at his opponents, even as he laced them with humor. He would, for example, occasionally vent his spleen during prep sessions for press conferences. In response to an aide's question about how he would contend with China, he snapped back that he would turn that country into a "land of laundromats." How would he respond to criticism from

Jimmy Carter? "By calling him a little schmuck." What about attacks from the New Right? "Those bastards won't ever be satisfied," said Reagan (Barrett 1984, 25). Reagan's most famous slip, made in August 1984 while testing his voice before a radio broadcast, was a similar combination of humor and hostility: "My fellow Americans, I am pleased to tell you I just signed legislation which outlaws Russia forever. The bombing begins in five minutes" (Stoessinger 1985, 292).

This last comment for a time rekindled the concern that has always troubled Reagan's critics—that his aggressive, confrontational attitude toward the Soviet Union and his penchant for tough talk and promise of swift and retaliatory action against terrorists heightened the prospects for conflict. Before his election they predicted he would be a rigid and dangerous manager of diplomatic relations with the Soviet Union and of other potentially explosive international problems. It did not turn out that way. Although the rhetoric stayed confrontational during the first and early second term, the behavior was decidedly prudent. For example, he reacted in a low-key manner to the September 1983 Soviet downing of Korean Air Lines flight 007; he had a subdued and strictly verbal retort to the October 1983 terrorist bombing of the Marine outpost in Lebanon; and he responded patiently to the June 1985 TWA hostage crisis. Actions taken beyond national borders—air strikes against Libya, the Grenada invasion, and the interdiction of the Egyptian airliner bearing Palestine Liberation Organization hijackers of the *Achille Lauro*—were carefully measured, comparatively low-risk ventures. In the foreign arena, Reagan was never hot-tempered or uncontrolled. Domestically, his response to frustration was equally restrained. After departing the White House, Michael Deaver told Hedrick Smith of the *New York Times* that Reagan's frustration with Congress would sometimes cause the president to lose sleep, but that he "could always be counted upon to come back persistently and competitively on an issue until he won a victory or until he had seen something through that he believed was right, whatever the cost, such as the visit to Bitburg. . . . 'He'll say,' Mr. Deaver recounted, 'If I don't get what I want, don't count me out. I'll figure out another way.' The thing most people have underestimated about him is his competitiveness" (Smith 1985, 14).

Reagan the president did show more stubbornness than did Reagan the governor. He clung tenaciously to his defense spending targets in the face of concerted opposition, and he adamantly refused, well into his second term, to entertain the idea of a tax increase, making it clear that he would veto any such proposal. But the prepresidential flexibility was also discernible—notably on the revenue enhancement compromise he accepted during the recession of 1982. At no point in his political career did Reagan display anything like the rigidity or desperation of such presidents as Hoover, Johnson, or Nixon in response to frustration. Rhetoric or stubbornness notwithstanding, clear limits were always drawn on how far Reagan would go or what he would do to avoid suffering a defeat. Like Carter, his way of contending with ego-threatening opposition was tenaciousness, but it posed no danger to the institutions or the values of the republic.

Conclusion

This chapter has only been able to illustrate, not demonstrate, the utility of presidency-relevant character. More space than is available here would be required to recount all the relevant evidence on each of the conclusions reached. For reasons of currency and consistency, the chapter has relied upon the examples of two presidents who, for the most part, did not disqualify themselves from consideration by virtue of their self-presentations or their responses to psychologically significant pressure. Reagan's self-presentation was demonstrably more promising at every point, but Carter's, however unusual, was potentially tolerable. Neither man's characteristic responses to the distorting rub of an intense environment guaranteed disaster, although neither's response to stress could be considered ideal. Only on the question of management style, a classic indicator of how a person copes with external demands, could serious problems be predicted for both men. Carter's would predictably bury him, while Reagan's would dangerously isolate and distance him.

Other presidents, like Wilson, Hoover, Johnson, or Nixon, have offered much more dramatic evidence of the value of asking the right questions in advance. The elections of 1912, 1928, 1964, and 1968 would have been particularly good times to ask them. For reflective citizens, they are worth asking anew each presidential election year.

Although character will never be (and should not be) the only basis for choice among candidates for the presidency, it has potentially greater predictive potential than policy promises or previous experience, the major alternative grounds for choice. A citizen's use of the character criterion is potentially improvable, in ways not true for the other grounds for choice. Since the components of presidency-relevant character—self-presentation, management style, and the patterns of response to the presidential experience—are visible and directly relevant to the demands of the presidency, it is conceivable that the reluctance of the framers to base choice on character can be adequately if not definitively overcome.

Notes

1. See Appendix 2.
2. Candidates reveal their likely policy directions in various ways, including the sorts of advisers they retain, the sorts of investors (or campaign contributors) they attract, and what they explicitly promise or propose.
3. Like Carter's 1962 campaign for the Georgia state senate, Reagan's initial campaign for governor resulted in what James David Barber terms the "first independent political success" (1985, 7), an event that tends to entrench style and that provides an accurate forecast of presidential management style.
4. Research suggests that self-esteem is a relatively stable trait that is a consequence of the lifelong process of personality development. It is thus a useful summary index of a whole host of human tendencies, and it has been correlated with a broad range of attitudinal and behavioral dispositions such as introversion and extroversion, achievement and affiliation motivations, and emotional outlook (Wells and Marwell 1976). Self-esteem can thus be expected to be associated with certain positive presidential qualities, like the tendency to seek results or to relate successfully with others—reasons Barber (1985) gives it the prominence he does in his theory of presidential character. Without denying self-esteem's status as an indicator of these positive things, I use the concept here in another way—as an indicator of probable reaction to significant psychological pressure like that found in the presidency. Research demonstrates convincingly that however it is measured, low self-esteem is associated with adverse, maladaptive responses to pressure—anxiety, neurotic behavior, increased incidence of failure, aggression, deviance, misrepresentation, and the like (Wells and Marwell 1976, 70, 72).

CHAPTER 7

Confronting the Alternative:
The Six-Year Single-Term Presidency

The cultural and psychological influences on leadership evaluation have been described and discussed, the traditional grounds for
choice and judgment have been considered, and new theories of attention have been offered, all in the conviction that the evaluative performance of citizens in improvable. Only one task remains, and that is to
confront a major option to such improvement. The power to hold
presidents accountable for their performance at the polls, where it
counts, is threatened by the perception of a considerable body of elite
opinion that this power has not been used well. One significant alternative to improving citizens' ability to choose and judge is supported
by this body of opinion—the six-year single-term presidency. Under
such an arrangement, citizens would still exercise the power of choice,
but judgment would no longer be enforceable with the ballot. Once
elected, a single-term president would not again face the judgment of
the people.

With the most popular and strongly supported president since the
mid-twentieth century presently in the White House, the clamor for the
six-year term has nearly subsided.[1] The memory of the four failed
presidencies that preceded Reagan's has dimmed, as has anxiety about
their inability to sustain a governing majority of public support. The
presidency again seems possible. The belief that an urgent need exists to
remodel the institution has, for the time being at least, subsided. The
nation's longstanding tradition of perceiving its history and its future in
the light of the most recent headlines continues.

Nevertheless, three good reasons to believe that the matter of reform has not been permanently laid to rest by the sanguine experience of the Reagan administration can be recounted. The first is the stubborn resilience of this particular reform proposal. The past is the best source of guidance available for predicting the future, and history records that the single six-year term was discussed at the Constitutional Convention, was proposed to Congress as an amendment in 1826, and has been reintroduced no fewer than 160 times since (Broder 1979a). Despite the occasional, or even frequent, periods of presidential calm, the sorts of difficulties that have prompted this proposal so many times before will probably reappear.

The second reason is the prominence and power of those who have so consistently found this reform to be an attractive possibility. Fifteen presidents (approximately 38 percent) have endorsed it, as have numerous cabinet officers, members of Congress, industrialists, and civic leaders. Although intelligent, powerful, and influential people like these have been unable to bring about a change, it is entirely possible that in just the right circumstances, such as a failed presidency or a national crisis coupled with a plausible claim that public irresponsibility was partly to blame, they will.

The third reason is more immediate. It has to do with the scarcity of presidents like Ronald Reagan, a man who enjoys a level of popularity and a kind of instinctive support that is by no means typical of recent presidents. A situation like Reagan's cannot be expected to recur as a matter of course, and yet it is the primary source of the current optimism about the state of the presidency. Should the post-Reagan institution revert to the state of its recent past, a possibility that cannot be lightly dismissed, the impetus for reform will surely return.

For all these reasons, an argument will be presented here against the six-year single-term presidency. It will be done the hard way—by considering as fairly as possible the merits of the reform and the major points offered in support of it. For only if the opposition entertains and deflects the strongest advocacy arguments can it expect to hold its own.

The Case for Reform

What do proponents perceive the problems with the presidency to be, and how would a single six-year presidential term work to solve them? Five distinct arguments have been made, four recently by individuals who have been intimately involved with the presidency. Although each argument puts a slightly different emphasis on the inadequacies of the status quo, they all agree that it inhibits the effectiveness of the institution. They also agree that the proposed reform would enhance its effectiveness.

The most fervent and frequently repeated argument stems from the belief that any president's desire for reelection has harmful consequences. The reelection campaign has grown to such length, cost, and proportions that the president starts running again as soon as the oath of office is administered. "The new cadre of election 'experts' insulates the president and has entirely too much say in determining policy.... Re-election no longer serves the function it was intended to serve; rather than making the president independent of the legislature and accountable to his constituents, it threatens to turn the executive branch into a permanent campaign headquarters...." (Robinson 1985, 172-173).

Another harmful consequence according to the "politics is bad" view is that instead of doing what is courageous or correct, from a policy standpoint, a president is obliged to do what is popular, to protect political prospects, and can even be motivated to do something illegal and foolish, like condone the Watergate break-in. Jack Valenti, an ardent spokesman for the six-year term, puts the argument as follows:

> Indeed one of the main advantages of the six-year term is the elbow room it would give a president to make hard choices in the public interest without nagging doubts as to whether his decisions would affect his re-election chances ... the freedom it gives a president to decide the tough issues without burning his re-election bridges. I am not saying that all presidents are totally swayed by the prospect of re-election to the detriment of their clear duty. But a second term is mighty inviting. In 1970 Kenneth O'Donnell, chief aide to President John F. Kennedy, wrote an article for *Life* in which he candidly unveiled this dilemma. Here is what O'Donnell had to say about a meeting with Mansfield and President Kennedy concerning Vietnam: "The President told Mansfield that he had been having serious second thoughts about Mansfield's argument and that he now agreed with the senator's thinking on the need for a complete military withdrawal from Vietnam. 'But I can't do that until 1965, after I'm re-elected,' Kennedy told Mansfield. President Kennedy felt that if he announced a total withdrawal of American military personnel from Vietnam before the 1964 election, there would be a wild conservative outcry against returning him to the presidency for a second term." Is there a possibility that if President Kennedy were serving a one-term six-year presidency, he would have withdrawn from Vietnam before we had lost thousands of American lives and spent so much of our treasure? The possibility exists, and its very presence is powerful motivation to order a six-year term now! (1973, 22)

In a pamphlet published by the Foundation for the Study of Presidential and Congressional Terms, examples from the Kennedy administration are again used in support of the proposal:

> John Kennedy talked often with his cabinet officials of the prospect that his administration's significant accomplishments would not come until the second term. This was because the major focus of the first term was on getting reelected.... Most recent Presidents have shared this inclination to wait for the leverage of a second term to deal with problems that only lend themselves to long-term solutions. One consequence of this practice, particularly in times like this when the White House is occupied by a series of Presidents who do not win reelection, is that a great deal of important work is swept into the corner and ignored. (1980, 19-20)

A corollary to increased White House preoccupation with impending presidential elections is the imposition of diverting and diminishing political chores on an already overburdened president. Sen. Mike Mansfield told the Senate on May 22, 1973, that it is "intolerable" for any president to be "compelled to devote time, energy and talents to political campaign tasks." He said a president pursuing reelection faces "a host of demands that range from attending the needs of political office-holders, office-seekers, financial backers and all the rest to riding herd on the day-to-day developments within the pedestrian partisan arena" (Foundation for the Study of Presidential and Congressional Terms 1980, 19). LBJ voiced the same concern in his memoirs, *The Vantage Point:* "The growing burdens of office exact an enormous physical toll on the man himself and place incredible demands on his time under these circumstances. The old belief that a president can carry out the responsibilities of the office and at the same time undergo the rigors of campaigning is, in my opinion, no longer valid" (1971, 344).

Any president has better and more important things to do. Energies can be used more effectively than is presently allowed. More pressing responsibilities inevitably suffer under the needless burden of perpetually running for office.

The third argument in favor of the six-year term is alone in emphasizing the length of the presidential term. Put simply, the bureaucracy argument is that presidents do not presently have enough time to allow their policies a fair chance to work. A president spends the first three years in office just establishing control over the bureaucracy. The current four-year term is actually too short to achieve the major changes and improvements that a president seeks. The funding cycles are so long that it is well into a president's third year before an impact on policy can be expected. The argument is elaborated on by the Foundation for the Study of Presidential and Congressional Terms:

> Under the present system an administration operates for only two years under its best budget calculations. Federal budgets are prepared nine months in advance so in its first year, an administration operates

on the budget of its predecessor. In its second year it operates on the budget which reflects its early aspirations. Only the budgets for the third and fourth years are prepared on the basis of solid experience. (1980, 19)

An important part of giving a president the chance to lead is providing the time to lead. Four years is just not enough time to test any president's leadership or the merits of policy proposals. So brief a tenure can also destabilize national policy by increasing the potential frequency of abrupt policy changes.

The only really new argument to emerge from the flurry of advocacy of the late 1970s, put forward by Carter, is the credibility argument. It contends that a president who has no opportunity to be reelected would automatically be more credible to voters. Because the president would have no selfish political motives, there would be no basis for the present tendency to doubt a campaigning president's integrity or sincerity.

As it is now, [Carter] said, many of his nonpolitical actions are "colored through the news media" as possible reelection ploys. "I think that if I had a six-year term, without any possibility of re-election, it would be an improvement." It would also strengthen his hand with Congress, he added. . . . "No matter what I do as president now, where I am really trying to ignore politics and stay away from any sort of campaign plans and so forth, a lot of the things I do are colored through the news media and in the minds of the American people by, Is this a campaign ploy or is it genuinely done by an incumbent president in the best interest of our country without any sort of personal advantage involved?" (Burks 1979, 3)

A president who lacks credibility cannot be effective. The cynicism bred by politics undermines credibility and needlessly diminishes the presidency in the process.

The strongest argument in support of the single six-year term can be called the "fickle support" position. It is rarely, if ever, made explicitly and straightforwardly, because to do so would require a too-obvious frontal assault on democratic accountability. But it is implicit in the commentary of proponents of the reform proposal.

The argument emerges from the basics of presidential viability and the disturbing public support trends. Proponents start, for example, with the fact that a president needs the support of at least 50 percent of the electorate to influence Congress, to keep the media and the bureaucracy at bay, to implement a foreign or an economic policy, or to get reelected. As matters now stand, public support is the enabling energy of the presidency.

Recent trends, however, raise serious doubts about any president's ability to sustain workable levels of support beyond the initial year in office. No president since Kennedy has consistently done so, nor has any president since Eisenhower completed two full terms. Presidents like Johnson, Nixon, Ford, and Carter had their problems, but it is questionable whether each deserved, on the merits of his performance, to be driven from office. Still, that is precisely what happened. Reagan finished his first term strongly and was reelected, but even the Great Communicator had public approval problems, posting the lowest support scores after two years in office of the last five presidents.[2] And it remains to be seen whether Reagan's successors will be so politically resilient. Add the fact that voter turnout in 1980 and 1984 barely exceeded the 50 percent mark, and the conclusion that public support is too fickle and unreliable a commodity to serve as the engine and the drive for the presidential system is understandable.

What, then, is the solution? Reduce the importance of public support to the viability of the presidency. How can this be accomplished? By means of the single six-year term, which would cut in half the extent of formal citizen engagement in the evaluation of presidential leadership. Fundamental changes in the origin of presidential influence would result. Citizens would still choose the president, but the fact that they would no longer have the opportunity to demonstrate their judgment formally at the polls would substantially dilute, and eventually might even eliminate, the importance of strong support in the day-to-day effectiveness of the president. Why should this be the case? Because the ebbs and flows of public support—the public opinion that preoccupies the media and the Congress—is now considered interesting and important largely because of its potential impact on the president's political fate and on the political fortunes of those in the Congress who oppose or support the administration. What the people want or expect is important only because the people now have real power—the power to remove a president or a member of Congress they do not support. This is why public support emerged as the hard currency of presidential power in the first place. Extract the sharp teeth of electoral accountability and the likelihood is that public support for presidents would decline in importance to little more than honorary status, significant only when displeasure neared rebellious levels. A president thus released from the pressures of public opinion would be free from a dependency that inhibits more than it helps. Such a president would be free to draw strength from other sources and to personally decide what is right, hampered only by the need to convince other power brokers, principally in Congress. Ironically, public support would likely increase, even as its significance diminished, because of the enhanced credibility suggested by Carter. It might thus even occasionally be used against a stubborn Congress, as it is now, but without its present potential for crippling a sitting president.

The Case Against Reform

The case against the single six-year term begins with certain concessions. The first is that the national political machinery is not perfect. It is, as numerous critics have observed, distressingly prone to deadlock, which inhibits the exercise of leadership in response to national problems. It has proven necessary to supplement the formal design with certain extra-constitutional inventions—first the cabinet, then mass public support, and most recently devices like the Gramm-Rudman balanced budget law, or the bipartisan national commission that negotiated to produce the Social Security compromise—to empower the presidency with the capacity to exercise leadership and the government to address problems. The second concession is that these inventions have themselves been imperfect. The cabinet mechanism required rare interpersonal skills to be made to work. The Gramm-Rudman law was ultimately declared unconstitutional in important particulars. Mass public support has proven to be a volatile, changeable commodity. Cultivating public support can become a distorting preoccupation for a president. Failure to secure it may cripple or destroy a presidency, as the recent past attests. And the subterfuge of the bipartisan commission raises ethical questions and, in any case, may not always work.

But the reform proposal does not deal with the most fundamental problem of the political system: intermittent deadlock. Furthermore, the reform is not needed to solve the five problems it does address. Every problem raised in support of the single six-year term can be adequately resolved through less drastic measures than the great reduction in citizen involvement in the electoral process that this reform would entail. Even if this were not the case, the consequences of such a change cannot be predicted with confidence. They could prove to be worse than the problems the reform was proposed to resolve.

The argument that politics is bad, that a president free from reelection worries would do what is right instead of what is merely popular, contains an implicit and highly debatable assumption that does not bear up under scrutiny. Assertions that Kennedy would have withdrawn from Vietnam and that Watergate would never have happened but for the reelection considerations of the presidents involved, for example, can be matched by equally persuasive counter-illustrations. If not for reelection concerns, Nixon would not have removed troops from Vietnam as rapidly or he might not have attempted an economic measure—wage and price controls—that deserved a peacetime test. To many, these Nixon policies were positive consequences of the electoral incentive. And if the incentive were so compelling, why didn't Carter take some sort of strong military action against Iran, which would have been highly popular and strongly supported, prior to the 1980 election? The point is that the reelection incentive is sometimes bad, sometimes good, and sometimes irrelevant (depending on the values of the observer and the temperament of the president) as an influence on presidential behavior. The assumption that what is popular is invariably at odds with what is right is historically inaccurate and tinged with antidemocratic elitism. It is not at all clear that removing electoral accountability would produce better presidential decisions all or even most of the time. Forcing elites to explain themselves, defend their decisions, and rally support is a useful discipline, more likely to yield quality results than isolated, unaccountable decision making. The possibility of unfriendly scrutiny, enforceable at the polls, is a powerful reason for presidents to think carefully and act prudently. Overgeneralization is always risky, but if a president is unable to build support for an unpopular course of action believed to be right, that action should be avoided or the political price for taking it should be paid.

The argument that a president and a White House perpetually engaged with election politics bear a needless burden has more intrinsic merit. It probably is the case that too great a share of executive resources and energies are devoted to partisan activities in comparison with other demands. Nevertheless, establishing and maintaining a relationship with the American people is a central presidential responsibility, not an irrelevant diversion, and the electoral process is one major mechanism for meeting this responsibility. As for that portion of presidential time and energy that must be saved for other things as campaigns proceed, measures short of eliminating the opportunity for reelection could serve the purpose. Although recent presidents have been reluctant to do so, there is no overwhelming structural or political reason why a good portion of the work of the "pedestrian partisan arena" could not be delegated to others. Nor is it impossible, when circumstances call for it, for a president to embrace a kind of permanent Rose Garden strategy, remaining sequestered in the White House and leaving even the public speechmaking duties to others. As George Reedy has argued and Ronald Reagan has demonstrated, a president can do as much or as little of any part of the job as desired, including the political part. And if the temptation to fight for their political survival is judged too great for presidents to resist, then what is to prevent legislation that limits the number of months and days that candidates for the presidency may devote to the hustings? The key point here is that it is the campaign process, not the structure of presidential accountability, that is the appropriate focus for reforms aimed at solving the needless burden problem. To contend that the only workable solution is to eliminate electoral accountability is tantamount to an argument that the only solution to a broken arm is amputation. In the context of this particular problem, the six-year single-term presidency constitutes overkill.

The bureaucracy argument, which says the president needs more time to implement policies, is, in effect, an effort to capture through a reorganization what now must be earned at the polls. For even under the Twenty-second Amendment, which limits a president to two terms in office, a president can get more time (eight years instead of the proposed six) if reelected. The premise on which the status quo is based is that the decision about whether a president needs and deserves more time should be shared by the electorate and not reserved for reformers or presidents. Too, the substance of the argument itself—that it requires years to get control of the budget and the bureaucracy—was blunted by the quick strike of the Reagan administration, which brought both to heel within the first year in office. An effective presidential strategy, it seems, is worth two or more years of lost time. Better, perhaps, to sharpen strategy than to extend the term of office. Of course there is nothing sacrosanct about a four-year term, other than the fact that the nation has grown accustomed to it. Absent some compelling reason to change, it makes little sense to do so. A compelling reason is precisely what is missing. On the larger question of the ideal length of a presidential term, it is hard to improve upon Woodrow Wilson's argument:

> A four-year term is too long for a President who is not a true spokesman of the people, who is imposed upon and does not lead. It is too short a term for a President who is doing, or attempting, a great work of reform, and who has not had time to finish it. To change the term to six years would be to increase the likelihood of its being too long, without any assurance that it would, in happy cases, be long enough. (Schlesinger 1986, 23)

Wilson's point is underscored by imagining what might have transpired if President Hoover or Carter, each having lost public confidence before the close of his initial term, had been required to serve two additional years. The nation came to the brink of collapse under Hoover's leadership during the Great Depression. And Carter, beset by the hostage crisis and runaway inflation, was branded a failure by a majority of Americans. While either man might theoretically have been able to rebound from his difficulties with additional time, both had exhausted political credibility and public tolerance and could not have been expected to govern effectively. More time would as likely have made matters worse.

The problem of presidential credibility, Carter's reason for supporting a single six-year term, is a real one. Presidents must indeed be credible if they are to be effective. But issue can be taken with the view that a president seeking reelection is necessarily the object of suspicion and mistrust. So far as can be determined, neither Eisenhower nor Reagan, as candidates for reelection, suffered any substantial loss of public confidence as a consequence of their candidacies. When problems of credibility arise, even during a campaign for reelection, they have more to do with the reputation, character, and behavior of the president than with the candidacy itself.

It is an undeniable fact that presidents seeking reelection do occasionally take actions aimed at enhancing their prospects—actions that might not exemplify the highest standards of devotion to the public interest. Manipulating, for politically inspired reasons, economic indicators in the preelection period (Tufte 1978), timing events and announcements for the purpose of maximizing their impact on elections, and leaking information to discredit opponents are cases in point. If the six-year term were in place, such actions would no longer be perceived as necessary by those in a position to engage in them. Unfortunately, however, removal of the reelection incentive would not do away with other, equally compelling incentives to engage in ethically or legally questionable behavior. Other sources of frustration—an obdurate Congress, hostile media, publicly critical opponents—would remain to goad a president susceptible to temptation into ill-advised actions. The only consistently effective solution to the credibility problem or to public suspicion and mistrust is not structural reform but presidential behavior and character that elicit respect and trust. No structural remedy can ever guarantee credibility, including a single six-year term.

Before the final, fickle support argument is considered, two consequences of the six-year term that supporters of the reform do not expect or intend must be introduced and illustrated. Both pertain to the stability and durability of the American political system. Would-be reformers cannot rule out these consequences and must deflect such worst case scenarios before the support of their critics can be expected.

The first scenario is the possibility that the six-year single-term presidency would precipitate a decline in the legitimacy accorded to the government by the governed. The reform covertly (and perhaps unintentionally) attacks both the theory and the practice of democracy—the moral and ethical basis for the right to wield power in the political system. The theory of democracy holds that for a system to be democratic, leaders must be subject to a significant amount of control by followers. The major mechanism by which such control is exerted is the electoral process. Citizens control leaders in part by choosing them in the first place, a practice the proposed reform leaves undisturbed. But a more direct and significant type of control, and one that this reform would eliminate, is the control implicit in what can be called the power of anticipated approval. Any president who seeks reelection confronts the certain knowledge that accountability is inevitable, that the record of performance will be evaluated. As a result, the president cannot help but anticipate how present actions might affect that future judgment. In most presidential minds, the desire for reelection becomes equivalent to the need to take the probable reactions of voters into careful consideration. For the most part, a president will behave in ways the electorate would be expected to approve. This is precisely how democratic control is most tangibly, consistently, and meaningfully exercised, as presidents routinely calculate how each action will be received by the electorate. Proponents of the single-term presidency wish to remove the power of anticipated approval, on the grounds that it leads presidents astray.

Eliminating this sort of accountability, the most pervasive and forceful instrument available to citizens for controlling the president, poses a threat to legitimacy. The opportunity to evaluate and judge presidential behavior could turn out to be the bedrock of legitimacy. Citizens might become unwilling to accept leadership cut loose from such moorings.

It is by no means preposterous to suggest this possibility. Mistrust of power is, after all, a deep strain in the American character. The authority of a relatively strong central executive was accepted by the framers of the Constitution only because of such counterweights as checks and balances and accountability. Presidential strength only achieved full public acceptability with the conversion of the presidency into the people's office, initially by Andrew Jackson. That acceptability emerged under conditions of reciprocal power, reflected and enforced on the public side by electoral accountability. This reciprocal relationship is a core element of American political culture and national identity. It is possible, as proponents contend, that the six-year term would stir not a hint of disaffection in an apathetic public little concerned with the subtleties of political theory and popular sovereignty. But given that deep-rooted, character-defining doctrines of national value and meaning would be tampered with, it is also possible that long-dormant, largely forgotten sentiments of mistrust and skepticism would be rekindled, to the detriment of popular support for an unaccountable executive. The stability and viability of the presidency could be disturbed in ways not contemplated by the architects of reform. The proposed reform could further alienate, estrange, and separate the American people from their government. Before undertaking even a slight risk of this sort, more compelling reasons than those advanced thus far should be required.

Another worst case scenario is suggested by the early experience of the second-term Reagan. Despite public support scores in the mid- to high sixties, Reagan was a notably less politically potent president than he was during his initial year in office. The significant difference was that by virtue of the Twenty-second Amendment, Reagan was a lame duck president.

For the second-term Reagan, public support had lost much of its empowering vitality. Critics of the six-year single-term presidency argue that a similar fate would be in store for any president under that arrangement. The fickle support position might applaud the diminished importance of public support. To be sure, Reagan was finally free to be Reagan, with no further need to cater to the whims of public passion. But so far as can be discovered, no proponent of the single-term presidency has addressed with care the question that came to preoccupy the Reagan team in 1985 and 1986: What is to replace public support as the enabling energy of the presidency? Instead, the lame duck status of a president is ignored. Proponents seem to assume that while public opinion would have no further power to lead presidents astray, it would somehow still be available to supply the necessary power and drive to fuel presidential leadership.

The Reagan experience appears to suggest otherwise. It suggests that unless public support is convertible into electoral clout for the president and those who support the president, it becomes palpably less imposing or effective as a political resource. This is an argument for repealing the Twenty-second Amendment rather than for installing a single-term presidency. Under a single six-year term, a president might well be free to draw strength from other sources, but unless some other extra-constitutional invention comparable to the cabinet or the introduction of mass public support were contrived, the possibility of a return to the paralysis of the pre-Jackson era could not be dismissed.

The fickle support argument says the real problem is not burdens, budgets, credibility, or the evils of politics. The real problem is the existence of evidence that lends credence to the conviction of presidents, cabinet officers, and members of Congress that the citizenry has not used its electoral power wisely enough to deserve it. Implied is the belief that what is popular will rarely if ever be equivalent to what is right, insofar as presidential action is concerned. The public cannot be relied upon to exercise the discipline to control momentary passions, to see past gimmickry and flimflammery, or to learn enough of the issues to wield its constitutional power responsibly.

Thus a return is made to the age-old debate between those who do and those who do not place greater faith in the rough wisdom of ordinary people than in experts or institutions. Proponents of a single six-year term clearly do not, and they have some evidence to support their position. If their proposal ever is implemented, the fickle support argument will probably be why.

Several decades ago, Walter Lippmann warned that the greatest challenge to democracy would be whether citizens could develop the will and the commitment to stay abreast of the complexity of issues whose mastery was required to judge political leadership prudently. More recently, such organizations as the Carnegie Foundation for the Advancement of Teaching and the New York Times Foundation have waged war on "civic illiteracy":

> Unless we find better ways to educate ourselves as citizens, we run the risk of drifting unwittingly into a new kind of Dark Age—a time when small cadres of specialists will control knowledge and thus control the decision making process. (Scully 1981, 1)

And Thomas Jefferson could have been responding to the fickle support argument when he penned the following:

> I know of no safe depository for the ultimate powers of society but the people themselves. And if we think them not enlightened enough to exercise their control with a wholesome discretion, the remedy is not to take it from them, but to inform their discretion. (Boyer and Hechinger 1981, 1)

This book has been one small effort to do just that.

Notes

1. Nearly, but not entirely. An editorial advocating the six-year single-term presidency appeared in the December 31, 1985, edition of the *New York Times* (p. 21). It was written by former Carter attorney general Griffin Bell, former Eisenhower attorney general Herbert Brownell, former Nixon trea-

sury secretary William E. Simon, and former Carter secretary of state Cyrus R. Vance, who together serve as national co-chairmen of the Committee for a Single Six-Year Presidential Term. Arthur Schlesinger, Jr., expressed an opposing view in an article published in the *Times* on January 10, 1986 (p. 23). The reform proposal is also given a balanced but unenthusiastic review in a new book by James L. Sundquist, *Constitutional Reform and Effective Government* (Washington, D.C.: Brookings, 1986), 122-133.

2. A United Press International story, published in the January 17, 1983, *Houston Chronicle,* reported that a Gallup poll conducted in mid-December 1982 gave Reagan lower performance marks halfway through his first term than four of his recent predecessors at their midway points. Reagan's scores were: 50 percent disapproval, 41 percent approval. The percentages approving the performance of previous presidents at the same point in their first terms were: Jimmy Carter, 51 percent; Richard Nixon, 52 percent; John Kennedy, 76 percent; Dwight Eisenhower, 69 percent. Gerald Ford and Lyndon Johnson, who entered office by succeeding presidents, could not be rated by the same two-year measure.

Sample

The discussion of contrasting visions of the presidency in Chapter 3 is based on a questionnaire survey conducted on a sample of 382 undergraduate students at the University of Texas at Austin. Questionnaires were distributed in the spring and fall semesters of 1983. The factor procedures were conducted across all 382 analyzable responses. The 204 students whose responses form the basis for the group comparisons in Chapter 3 were those who identified themselves as moderates, liberals, or conservatives in each of three policy categories—domestic, economic, and foreign policy. This reduced the sample size but increased the likelihood that ideological self-descriptions indicated genuine normative commitments, a matter of some importance to the argument presented in the text.

Structural Model

The complete set of 72 items included in the original questionnaire purports to measure evaluative attitudes toward presidential performance, which are in turn presumed to influence evaluative behavior. The items were generated from the structural model depicted in Table A-1, which also identifies sample items within each of the model's categories. The model itself derives from general familiarity with the historical record of presidential performance (Thach 1969; Small 1932; Tugwell 1960; Burns 1965; Schlesinger 1973; Rossiter 1960; Corwin 1957) and with critical scholarly and media commentary on such performance (Schellhardt 1981; Rockman 1984; Fisher 1985; Neustadt 1980; Cronin 1980). It assumes that all appraisals of presidential performance stem from one or more of three fundamental value categories, labeled effectiveness, stability, and morality (horizontal axis). The effectiveness and morality values were included because available research evidence indicates that competence and integrity, human attributes related to effectiveness and morality, are pervasive and enduring thematic grounds for the evaluation of both presidential candidates and leaders in general (Miller, Wattenberg, and Malanchuk 1982; Kinder, Fiske, and Wagner 1978; Kinder, Peters, Abelson, and Fiske 1980). The stability value was included because of the episodic but great importance of crisis management as a performance requirement of the presidency.

The vertical axis identifies the performance categories within which the model presumes that presidents are evaluated. No previous research exists in which citizens were allowed to define their own categories, but it is reasonable to expect that citizens' categories are influenced by exposure to the print and electronic media, which typically discuss presidential performance in general terms and in terms of economic, domestic, and foreign policy.

Data Analysis

The model was estimated with factor analysis. The method of factor extraction was principal factors, varimax rotation using multiple regression coefficients as initial communality estimates, and the Kaiser criterion (eigenvalues greater than one) for identification of factors.

Two factor procedures were used to test the assumptions of the model. A first order analysis tested for the number and within-cell contents of evaluated categories. (Table A-1 predicts 12 categories but due to space limitations does not reproduce the entire predicted within-category item content.) A second order (higher order) factor analysis was computed across the first order factors that emerged from the initial procedure to test the assumption that three orthogonal value dimensions—effectiveness, stability, and morality—underlie and organize one general category and three specific policy categories of evaluation each.

Results

The initial factor procedure disconfirmed the categorical predictions of the model. Nine rather than the predicted 12 categories of evaluation emerged, and individual items frequently loaded on unexpected rather than predicted factors. The nine factors and the items that survived when weak and double-loading items were removed are identified in Tables A-2 through A-10. (Items were eliminated to maximize each factor's simple structure and thus its substantive interpretability.) Each of these tables also contains item factor loadings, communality estimates, and estimates of internal consistency (Cronbach's alpha). The estimates of internal consistency are included as an index of the reliability of the item-clusters (factors) as scales of measurement. The controlled (partial) and uncontrolled (zero order) Pearson correlations among the factors are included in Table A-11. Comparison of the within-factor internal consistency estimates with the between-factor correlation coefficients shows that, in all cases, the magnitudes of the former exceed those of the latter. Each factor thus measures something different from the others. No evidence of construct validity is available, but face validity is apparent from examination of the items. There is no reason to suspect that these factors measure anything other than what their item content implies they measure.

The results of the higher order factor analysis of the factors in Tables A-2 through A-10 are reported in Table A-12, which depicts an orthogonally rotated final factor solution. As is apparent, they disconfirm the value-dimension predictions, showing the nine factors to be organized by two and not the expected three higher order dimensions, with stability washing out. Examination of the loading patterns suggests that the surviving dimensions are quite distinct from one another (a separate oblique rotation, not depicted here, revealed a strong negative Pearson correlation, −0.38, between the two factor patterns) and are similar to the competence and trust themes found in the literature. The two dimensions are labeled moral effectiveness and political effectiveness in Table A-12. Each of these second order dimensions organizes four first order factor scales, with only domestic policy agreement failing to load significantly on either dimension. Its items, which, in requiring the president to serve the values of the respondent, emphasize self-interest, argue for its interpretation as a separate value dimension (see Table A-9).

That the model was disconfirmed in its structural particulars and that the questionnaire items were rearranged by virtue of loading on unexpected factors are the basis for the claim made in the text—that it was the respondents, and not the researcher, who selected and defined the categories of evaluation. A more thorough analysis and discussion of these data are available in Buchanan 1984. A refined and extended version of the approach taken here can be found in Buchanan and Sidanius 1986.

Table A-1 Structural Model of Evaluative Attitudes Toward Presidential Performance

	Effectiveness	Stability	Morality
	I judge a president's competence by the extent to which:		
General evaluative attitudes	his programs actually solve the most important problems.	his solutions to crisis preserve the nation's safety.	his policy initiatives are constitutional and respect the rights of citizens.
	he persuades the country to follow his leadership.	his actions calm rather than inflame the people.	he shows concern for all people, not just his political supporters and friends.
Economic policy	his economic policies actually reduce inflation and unemployment.	he keeps order at home during severe recessions and depressions.	his economic policies do not favor one group at the expense of others.
Domestic policy	his domestic policy proposals actually solve the problems they are intended to solve.	he finds ways to reduce conflict among domestic special interest groups.	he respects constitutional and legal limitations on his domestic powers.
Foreign policy	he influences most world events to the advantage of the United States.	he reduces tensions between the United States and the Soviet Union.	he is a strong spokesman for human rights in the world.

Table A-2   Political Leadership

	Loading	Communality
He persuades the country to follow his leadership.	.65	.530
He takes charge of the government.	.63	.432
He persuades Congress to pass his programs.	.58	.355
He projects an image of competence.	.46	.304
	Cronbach's alpha = .69	

Table A-3   Economic Flexibility and Fairness

	Loading	Communality
He adjusts his policies to changing economic conditions.	.62	.391
His first priority is to protect the nation's economy even if he has to oppose big business.	.59	.351
He stands up to powerful economic interests to help people who have less.	.55	.314
His policies follow the best economic advice available.	.48	.326
He listens to advice from economic experts with different viewpoints.	.46	.309
	Cronbach's alpha = .64	

Table A-4   Crisis Management

	Loading	Communality
He puts the country's security and well-being above his own political interests.	.57	.347
His solutions to crises preserve the nation's safety.	.55	.346
He heads off conflict before it becomes dangerous.	.52	.335
In making decisions, he considers alternatives carefully and does not take unnecessary risks.	.47	.342
	Cronbach's alpha = .65	

Table A-5 Foreign Policy Potency

	Loading	Communality
He influences most world events to the advantage of the United States.	.67	.476
He maintains respect for America's power in the world.	.66	.447
He does his best to protect American interests, even if he cannot always succeed.	.56	.318
He dominates world affairs.	.53	.284
He wins legislative approval for important foreign policy proposals.	.47	.228
	Cronbach's alpha = .66	

Table A-6 General Policy Results

	Loading	Communality
His economic policies actually reduce inflation and unemployment.	.78	.652
The economic indicators like inflation and unemployment improve while he is in office.	.57	.377
His domestic policy proposals actually solve the problems they are intended to solve.	.53	.293
His programs actually solve the most important problems.	.49	.257
	Cronbach's alpha = .698	

Table A-7 Economic Policy Consistency

	Loading	Communality
He explains his economic policies clearly and sticks to them.	.74	.612
He keeps the promises about economic policy that he made during the campaign.	.72	.579
He coordinates the work of his advisers so that his economic policy is consistent.	.48	.381
He chooses a small number of domestic policy goals and sticks to them.	.43	.278
	Cronbach's alpha = .71	

Table A-8 World Peace

	Loading	Communality
He reduces tensions between the United States and the Soviet Union.	.69	.485
He avoids having to use the military.	.63	.410
He is a spokesman for human rights in the world.	.58	.337
	Cronbach's alpha = .66	

Table A-9 Domestic Policy Agreement

	Loading	Communality
I agree with his proposals for solving domestic problems.	.77	.629
His domestic policies promote the values that I think are most important.	.66	.469
His domestic policies help me and the groups with which I identify.	.47	.288
	Cronbach's alpha = .659	

Table A-10 General Policy Quality

	Loading	Communality
He has a clear, well thought out approach to solving the nation's domestic problems.	.71	.615
He appoints domestic advisers who know what they are doing.	.59	.493
He has a well-developed, long-term foreign policy design.	.48	.312
	Cronbach's alpha = .659	

Table A-11 Interfactor Pearson Correlations

	General policy results	World peace	Political leadership	Foreign policy potency	Crisis management	General policy quality	Economic flexibility and fairness	Economic policy consistency	Domestic policy agreement
General policy results	1.00	.28 (.13)†	.12 (−.06)	.22 (.11)	.34 (.16)*	.28 (.04)	.40 (.20)*	.22 (.00)	.17 (.08)
World Peace		1.00	.02 (−.08)	−.05 (−.14)	.15 (−.03)	.31 (.18)*	.38 (.28)	.09 (−.05)	.27 (.26)*
Political leadership			1.00	.39 (.24)*	.28 (.07)	.31 (.18)*	.27 (.08)	.32 (.10)	.15 (.09)
Foreign policy potency				1.00	.34 (.18)*	.22 (.01)	.23 (−.03)	.45 (.31)*	.15 (.07)
Crisis management					1.00	.38 (.18)*	.44 (.22)*	.30 (.02)	.10 (−.02)
General policy quality						1.00	.46 (.21)*	.28 (.04)	.17 (.04)
Economic flexibility and fairness							1.00	.43 (.29)*	.11 (−.11)
Economic policy consistency								1.00	.17 (.09)
Domestic policy agreement									1.00

† Coefficients in parentheses are partial correlations controlling for the remaining seven factors.
* Indicates significance at p < .001, partial correlations only.

Table A-12   Higher Order Analysis of Nine First Order Factors

	Communality	H Factor 1: Moral Effectiveness	H Factor 2: Political Effectiveness
World peace	.48605	*.68337*	−.13603
Economic flexibility and fairness	.54319	*.64118*	.36342
General policy quality	.37608	*.51959*	.32575
General policy results	.27213	*.46672*	.23303
Foreign policy potency	.51187	.04258	*.71418*
Economic policy consistency	.38734	.24833	*.57068*
Political leadership	.29701	.13662	*.52758*
Crisis management	.35105	.37940	*.45509*
Domestic policy agreement	.08610	.26756	.12047
Percent of Variance		76.2	23.8

APPENDIX 2

Four different clusters of evaluative criteria are presented in this book: the character, power, and success tests in Chapter 2, the three impressions that comprise the short-term success test in Chapter 4, the five traditional grounds for judgment (plus competent presidential processes) in Chapter 5, and the three traditional grounds for choice (plus presidency-relevant character) in Chapter 6. Each cluster is labeled and defined in keeping with the objectives of the chapter in which it appears. Approaching the analysis of evaluative criteria from a variety of perspectives and using different labels and emphases for each are useful for explicating the dimensions of what is in fact a quite complex and subtle collection of issues. But the risk of confusion is increased, and questions naturally arise concerning the relationships between the various evaluative concepts. Brief mention of these relationships is frequently made in the text. Still, it will be useful to include a short, centralized discussion of the connections between these evaluative dispositions for convenient reference (see Figure B-1).

The theory presented in Chapter 2 assumes that all evaluative dispositions emerge initially from culturally designated "great" presidents whose consensually acknowledged success is implicitly presumed to be a function of the interaction between certain kinds of personal attributes (the character test) and certain ways of using presidential power (the power test). Cultural influences are unconsciously implanted and help to explain the sorts of impressions candidates and presidents must usually create to be regarded favorably as well as the kinds of cues that must be evident to support such impressions. The impressions presidents seek to make and sustain are defined and their operations illustrated in Chapter 4. A president who creates the impression of standing for something (and is thus assertive, in keeping with the power test) and of knowing what to do (thus suggesting the ability to achieve success) will win brand-name status and a privileged cushion of support, particularly if others are disposed toward liking or respecting the president as a person (in keeping with certain dimensions of the character

Appendix 2

Figure B-1 Relationships Among Evaluative Concepts

	Cultural Origins (Chapter 2)	Short-Term Success Test (Chapter 4)	Traditional Grounds for Judgment (Chapter 5)	Traditional Grounds for Choice (Chapter 6)
Personal Characteristics Track	Character test	Creating a privileged cushion	Leadership style	Character
Assertiveness Track	Power test	Standing for something	Ideology and self-interest	Policy package
Results Track	Success test	Knowing what to do	Short-term results and lasting results	Track record

Preconscious   Conscious

test, such as warmth, charm, or inspirational magic).

During actual use, all the evaluative criteria of Chapters 2 and 4 discussed thus far tend to operate below the level of conscious awareness for most citizens (see the discussion of schema theory in Chapter 3), which is why they are labeled preconscious influences. They are, however, related to the traditional grounds for choice and judgment—the grounds that are consciously and explicitly discussed as rationales for evaluative behavior in informed political discourse. Thus, both leadership style (Chapter 5) and character (as defined in Chapter 6) can be linked with the instinctive public responses to the personalities of specific presidents described in Chapter 4 and character test of Chapter 2. Albeit in different ways, they all deal with personal attributes of presidents. There is in this sense a personal characteristics track that cuts across all four categories of evaluative concepts. And all four categories, rather than simply one master concept, are needed so that (1) where notions of leadership character come from and (2) how they work in practice, as distinct from how they are rationalized as legitimate grounds for (3) judgment, on one hand, and (4) choice, on the other, can be separately identified and discussed.

Similarly, although somewhat less obviously, an assertiveness track links the power test with standing for something as well as with what a candidate asserts will be done about problems (policy package). Subjective assessments of how a president's stances or actions, which amount to probable or actual uses of power, affect one's self-interest or square with one's ideology can also be classified under the assertiveness track. The ideology and self-interest criteria can be applied to the evaluation of presidential results as well, of course. But the results track is reserved for criteria that emphasize skill at achieving ends of broader social relevance than is implied by particular ideologies or self-interests. This classification rule is admittedly somewhat arbitrary but has the advantage of being consistent with how the concepts were defined and used in the text.

The preconscious assertiveness criteria (the power test and standing for something) reflect the culture's implicit conviction that assertiveness and potency are desirable presidential attributes in their own right, quite apart from the particular ends they serve. It is assumed that the ends will be ethical and will command broad support, but, at this preconsciousness level, the main emphasis is upon vigorous pursuit of ends that are clearly defined (standing for something) and not the substance of the particular ends themselves. The culture wants and expects presidents not to shrink from the use of power. It is frequently said that the worst thing a president can do is seem weak or indecisive (Edelman 1964, 78). The remarks of the anonymous citizen quoted in Chapter 4 reflect the not uncommon attitude that vigorous assertiveness in any direction, agreed to or not, is preferable to inaction.

The consciously rationalized assertiveness criteria (ideology and self-interest, policy package) give explicit evaluative weight to the direction of presidential assertiveness. By these tests, power should serve particular interests and ends. But whether the basis for judgment is assertiveness for its own sake or assertiveness in a particular policy direction, the evaluated dimension remains the extent to which executive energy, vigor, and determination are displayed and brought to bear in support of clearly communicated presidential priorities.

Finally, the results track implies plausible connections between the success test, the impression that a president is competent, the belief that track record as a choice criterion is a good predictor of results a candidate would get if elected, and the short- and long-term results criteria—outcomes attributed to presidents that may or may not stand the test of time. The thread that links these categories together is the real or apparent capacity of a candidate or a president to bring about important, lasting consequences that contribute to the general good, the ultimate raison d'être of the presidency.

REFERENCES

Aberbach, Joel D., and Burt A. Rockman. 1976. "Clashing Beliefs Within the Executive Branch: The Nixon Administration Bureaucracy." *American Political Science Review* 70: 456-468.

Anderson, Jack. 1977. "What is Jimmy Carter Really Like?" *Parade,* November 13, 9-11.

Argyris, Chris, and Donald A. Schon. 1974. *Theory in Practice: Increasing Professional Effectiveness.* San Francisco: Jossey-Bass.

Asher, Herbert B. 1983. "Voting Behavior Research in the 1980s: An Examination of Some Old and New Problem Areas." In *Political Science: The State of the Discipline,* ed. Ada Finifter. Washington, D.C.: American Political Science Association.

_____. 1984. *Presidential Elections and American Politics.* 3d ed. Homewood, Ill.: Dorsey Press.

Bailey, Thomas A. 1966. *Presidential Greatness.* New York: Appleton-Century-Crofts.

Barber, James David. 1980. *The Pulse of Politics: Electing Presidents in the Media Age.* New York: W. W. Norton.

_____. 1985. *The Presidential Character.* 3d ed. Englewood Cliffs, N.J.: Prentice-Hall.

Barger, Harold M. 1984. *The Impossible Presidency.* Glenview, Ill.: Scott, Foresman.

Barrett, Laurence I. 1984. *Gambling with History: Reagan in the White House.* New York: Penguin Books.

Beatty, Jack. 1982. "The President's Mind." *New Republic,* April 7, 12-13.

Berman, Larry. 1982. *Planning a Tragedy: The Americanization of the War in Vietnam.* New York: W. W. Norton.

Biggart, Nicole W., and Gary G. Hamilton. 1983. "The Policy Effects of Management Style: A Comparison of Governors Ronald Reagan and Jerry Brown." Paper delivered at the annual meeting of the American Political Science Association, August 31-September 2, Washington, D.C.

Boller, Paul F. 1981. *Presidential Anecdotes.* New York: Oxford University Press.

Bonafede, Dom. 1985. "Presidential Scholars Expect History to Treat the Reagan Presidency Kindly." *National Journal,* April 6, 743-747.

_____. 1986. "Believability." *National Journal,* February 22, 480.

Borden, Morton, ed. 1971. *America's Eleven Greatest Presidents.* 2d ed. Chicago: Rand McNally.

References

Boyer, Ernest L., and Fred M. Hechinger. 1981. "Advancing Civic Learning." In *Higher Learning in the National Interest,* ed. Ernest L. Boyer and Fred M. Hechinger. Washington, D.C.: Carnegie Foundation for the Advancement of Teaching.

Brauer, Carl. 1983. "He Raised Expectations of the Presidency." *U.S. News and World Report,* November 21, 53-54.

Braun, Saul. 1968. "Andrew Jackson." In *American Heritage Pictorial History of the Presidents of the United States,* ed. Kenneth W. Leish, vol. 1, 207-208. New York: Simon and Schuster.

Broder, David. 1979a. "A Frail Amendment." *Washington Post,* February 11, L11.

———. 1979b. "Carter's Second Chance." *Washington Post,* December 2, D7.

———. 1982. "Reagan a Stubborn and Principled Character." *Houston Chronicle,* January 29, sec. 1, 20.

———. 1984. Reagan Right to Run for Re-Election." *Houston Chronicle,* January 3, 6.

Brody, Richard, and Benjamin Page. 1975. "The Impact of Events on Presidential Popularity: The Johnson and Nixon Administrations." In *Perspectives on the Presidency,* ed. Aaron Wildavsky. Boston: Little, Brown.

Bruner, Jerome S. 1963. "The 'New Look' in Perception." In *Psychology in Administration,* ed. Timothy W. Costello and Sheldon S. Zalkind. Englewood Cliffs, N.J.: Prentice-Hall.

Brzezinski, Zbigniew. 1983. *Power and Principle: Memoirs of the National Security Adviser, 1977-1981.* New York: Farrar, Straus, and Giroux.

Buchanan, Bruce. 1978. *The Presidential Experience.* Englewood Cliffs, N.J.: Prentice-Hall.

———. 1984. "Contrasting Visions of the Presidency." Paper delivered at the annual meeting of the American Political Science Association, August 30-September 3, Washington, D.C.

Buchanan, Bruce, and Jim Sidanius. 1986. "A Structural Model of Evaluative Attitudes Toward Presidential Performance." Working paper, Department of Government, University of Texas at Austin.

Burks, Edward C. 1979. "Carter: Limit President to Single Six-Year Term." *Houston Chronicle,* April 29, 3.

Burns, James MacGregor. 1963. *The Deadlock of Democracy.* Englewood Cliffs, N.J.: Prentice-Hall.

———. 1965. *Presidential Government.* Boston: Houghton Mifflin.

———. 1978. *Leadership.* New York: Harper and Row.

———. 1984. *The Power to Lead.* New York: Simon and Schuster.

Califano, Joseph A. 1981. *Governing America: An Insider's Report from the White House and Cabinet.* New York: Simon and Schuster.

Campbell, Angus, Phillip E. Converse, Warren E. Miller, and Donald E. Stokes. 1960. *The American Voter.* New York: John Wiley and Sons.

Cannon, Lou. 1982. *Reagan.* New York: G. P. Putnam's Sons.

Cantril, Hadley. 1963. "Perception and Interpersonal Relations." In *Psychology in Administration,* ed. Timothy W. Costello and Sheldon S. Zalkind. Englewood Cliffs, N.J.: Prentice-Hall.

Carter, Jimmy. 1975. *Why Not the Best?* Nashville, Tenn.: Broadman Press.

———. 1982. *Keeping Faith.* New York: Bantam.

———. 1984. "Current Quotes." *U.S. News and World Report,* March 19, 12.

Ceaser, James W. 1979. *Presidential Selection: Theory and Development.* Princeton, N.J.: Princeton University Press.

Church, George J. 1982. "How Reagan Decides." *Time,* December 13, 12-17.

Clarke, M. S., and Susan T. Fiske, eds. 1982. *Affect and Cognition.* Hillsdale, N.J.: Lawrence Erlbaum Associates.

Clymer, Adam. 1985. "Camp David at Top in U.S. Policy Poll." *New York Times,* April 1, 6.

Cohen, Richard E. 1984. "Many Democrats, Some Republicans Sing the Blues About Presidential Prospects." *National Journal,* March 10, 469.

Cole, Richard L., and David A. Caputo. 1979. "Presidential Control of the Senior Civil Service: Assessing the Strategies of the Nixon Years." *American Political Science Review* 73: 399-413.

Coleman, James C. 1960. *Personality Dynamics and Effective Behavior.* Chicago: Scott, Foresman.

Collier, Peter, and David Horowitz. 1985. *The Kennedys: An American Drama.* New York: Warner Books.

Converse, Phillip E. 1975. "Public Opinion and Voting Behavior." In *Handbook of Political Science,* ed. Fred I. Greenstein and Nelson W. Polsby, vol. 4. Boston: Addison-Wesley.

Corwin, Edward S. 1957. *The President: Office and Powers 1787-1957.* New York: New York University Press.

Costello, Timothy W., and Sheldon S. Zalkind, eds. 1963. *Psychology in Administration: A Research Orientation.* Englewood Cliffs, N.J.: Prentice-Hall.

Cronin, Thomas E. 1980. *The State of the Presidency.* 2d ed. Boston: Little, Brown.

Cronin, Thomas E., and Sanford D. Greenberg, eds. 1969. *The Presidential Advisory System.* New York: Harper and Row.

Cunliffe, Marcus. 1968. "A Defective Institution?" *Commentary,* February, 28.

Dahl, Robert A. 1956. *A Preface to Democratic Theory.* Chicago: University of Chicago Press.

De Tocqueville, Alexis. 1969. *Democracy in America.* Trans. George Lawrence; ed. J. P. Mayer. New York: Doubleday.

Donovan, Hedley. 1982. "Job Specs for the Oval Office." *Time,* December 13, 20-29.

Downs, Anthony. 1957. *An Economic Theory of Democracy.* New York: Harper.

Edelman, Murray. 1964. *The Symbolic Uses of Politics.* Urbana: University of Illinois Press.

Edwards, George C. III. 1980. *Presidential Influence in Congress.* San Francisco: W. H. Freeman.

———. 1983. *The Public Presidency.* New York: St. Martin's Press.

Evans, Rowland, Jr., and Robert D. Novak. 1971. *Nixon in the White House: The Frustration of Power.* New York: Random House.

Fairlie, Henry. 1982. "A Man Like Us—A Hero." *Houston Chronicle,* February 22, sec. 3, 1.

Fallows, James. 1979. "The Passionless Presidency: The Trouble with Jimmy Carter's Administration." *Atlantic,* May, 33-48.

Fiorina, Morris P. 1981. *Retrospective Voting in American National Elections.* New Haven, Conn.: Yale University Press.

Fishel, Jeff. 1985. *Presidents and Promises: From Campaign Pledge to Presidential Performance.* Washington, D.C.: CQ Press.

References

Fisher, Louis. 1985. *Constitutional Conflicts Between Congress and the President.* Princeton, N.J.: Princeton University Press.

Fiske, Susan T. 1980. "Attention and Weight in Person Perception: The Impact of Negative and Extreme Behavior." *Journal of Personality and Social Psychology* 38: 889-908.

Foundation for the Study of Presidential and Congressional Terms. 1980. *Presidential and Congressional Term Limitation: The Issue That Stays Alive.* Washington, D.C.: Foundation for the Study of Presidential and Congressional Terms, a National Heritage Foundation.

Gelb, Leslie H. 1985. "The Mind of the President." *New York Times Magazine,* October 6, 21.

George, Alexander L. 1974. "Assessing Presidential Character." *World Politics* 26: 234-282.

George, Alexander L., and Juliette L. George. 1956. *Woodrow Wilson and Colonel House: A Personality Study.* New York: Dover Publications.

Glad, Betty. 1980. *Jimmy Carter: In Search of the Great White House.* New York: W. W. Norton.

Goldman, Peter. 1983. "Kennedy Remembered. After 20 Years, A Man Lost in His Legend." *Newsweek.* November 28, 62.

Goldschmidt, Walter. 1959. *Man's Way: A Preface to the Understanding of Human Society.* New York: Holt, Rinehart, and Winston.

Goleman, Daniel. 1985. *Vital Lies, Simple Truths: The Psychology of Self-Deception.* New York: Simon and Schuster.

Greenstein, Fred. 1974. "What the President Means to Americans." In *Choosing the President,* ed. James D. Barber. Englewood Cliffs, N.J.: Prentice-Hall.

———. 1982. *The Hidden Hand Presidency: Eisenhower as Leader.* New York: Basic Books.

———. 1983. *The Reagan Presidency: An Early Assessment.* Baltimore: Johns Hopkins University Press.

Greider, William. 1981. "The Education of David Stockman." *Atlantic Monthly,* December, 27-54.

Grossman, Michael B., and Martha J. Kumar. 1981. *Portraying the President: The White House and the News Media.* Baltimore: Johns Hopkins University Press.

Gulick, Luther, and Lyndall F. Urwick, eds. 1937. *Papers on the Science of Administration.* New York: Institute of Public Administration.

Haider, Donald H. 1982. "Presidents as Budget Policymakers." In *Rethinking the Presidency,* ed. Thomas E. Cronin. Boston: Little, Brown.

Halberstam, David. 1972. *The Best and the Brightest.* New York: Random House.

Hardin, Charles. 1974. *Presidential Power and Accountability.* Chicago: University of Chicago Press.

Hargrove, Erwin C. 1974a. *The Power of the Modern Presidency.* New York: Alfred A. Knopf.

———. 1974b. "What Manner of Man? The Crisis of the Contemporary Presidency." In *Choosing the President,* ed. James D. Barber, 7-33. Englewood Cliffs, N.J.: Prentice-Hall.

Hargrove, Erwin C., and Michael Nelson. 1984. *Presidents, Politics, and Policy.* New York: Alfred A. Knopf.

Harris, Louis. 1980. "Poll Finds Carter's Job Rating at an All-Time Low." *Washington Post,* July 30, A12.

Hart, Roderick P. 1984. *Verbal Style and the Presidency.* New York: Academic Press.

Heclo, Hugh. 1977. *A Government of Strangers: Executive Politics in Washington.* Washington, D.C.: Brookings.

Heclo, Hugh, and Rudolph G. Penner. 1983. "Fiscal and Political Strategy in the Reagan Administration." In *Reagan Presidency: An Early Assessment,* ed. Fred I. Greenstein. Baltimore: Johns Hopkins University Press.

Heineman, Ben W., Jr., and Curtis A. Hessler. 1980. *Memorandum for the President: A Strategic Approach to Domestic Affairs in the 1980s.* New York: Random House.

Hess, Stephen. 1974. *The Presidential Campaign.* Washington, D.C.: Brookings.

———. 1976. *Organizing the Presidency.* Washington, D.C.: Brookings.

Hill, Kim Q., and John Patrick Plumlee. 1982. "Presidential Success in Budgetary Policymaking." *Presidential Studies Quarterly* 12: 174-185.

Hodgson, Godfrey. 1980. *All Things to All Men.* New York: Simon and Schuster.

Hoekstra, Douglas J. 1981. "The 'Textbook' Presidency Revisited." Paper delivered at the annual meeting of the Midwest Political Science Association, April 16-19, Cincinnati, Ohio.

Houston Chronicle. 1980. "Reagan Record as Governor: Bold Strategies Soon Abandoned." *Houston Chronicle,* November 28, sec. 7, 1.

Hughes, Emmet John. 1972. *The Living Presidency.* New York: Coward, McCann, and Geoghegan.

Huston, Ted L., and George Levinger. 1978. "Interpersonal Attraction and Relationship." In *Annual Review of Psychology,* ed. Mark R. Rosenzweig and Lyman W. Porter, vol. 29, 115-156.

Iyengar, Shanto, Mark D. Peters, and Donald R. Kinder. 1982. "Experimental Demonstrations of the 'Not So Minimal' Consequences of Television News Programs." *American Political Science Review* 76: 848-858.

Izard, Carroll E. 1977. *Human Emotions.* New York: Plenum Press.

Jacobs, David. 1968. "Andrew Johnson." In *American Heritage Pictorial History of the Presidents of the United States,* ed. Kenneth W. Leish, vol. 1. New York: Simon and Schuster.

James, William. 1974. *Pragmatism.* New York: New American Library.

———. 1983. *The Principles of Psychology.* Cambridge, Mass.: Harvard University Press.

Janis, Irving L. 1972. *Victims of Groupthink.* Boston: Houghton Mifflin.

Janis, Irving L., and Harold Leventhal. 1968. "Human Reactions to Stress." In *Handbook of Personality Theory and Research,* ed. Edgar F. Gorgatta and William W. Lambert, 1041-1085. Chicago: Rand McNally.

Johnson, Haynes. 1980. *In the Absence of Power.* New York: Viking Press.

Johnson, Lyndon B. 1971. *The Vantage Point.* New York: Holt, Rinehart, and Winston.

Johnson, Richard Tanner. 1973. "Management Styles of Three U.S. Presidents." *Stanford Alumni Bulletin,* Fall, 2-35.

———. 1974. *Managing the White House.* New York: Harper and Row.

Jones, Edward E., and Richard Nisbett. 1971. "The Actor and the Observer: Divergent Perceptions of the Causes of Behavior." In *Attribution: Perceiv-*

ing the Causes of Behavior, ed. Edward E. Jones, et al., 79-94. Morristown, N.J.: General Learning Press.

Kaplan, Abraham. 1964. *The Conduct of Inquiry.* San Francisco: Chandler.

Kattenburg, Paul. 1980. *The Vietnam Trauma in American Foreign Policy, 1945-75.* New Brunswick, N.J.: Transaction Books.

Katz, Daniel. 1963. "The Functional Approach to the Study of Attitudes." In *Psychology in Administration,* ed. Timothy W. Costello and Sheldon S. Zalkind. Englewood Cliffs, N.J.: Prentice-Hall.

———. 1973. "Patterns of Leadership." In *Handbook of Political Psychology,* ed. Jeanne N. Knutson. San Francisco: Jossey-Bass.

Kearns, Doris. 1976. *Lyndon Johnson and the American Dream.* New York: Harper and Row.

Kelley, Harold H. 1973. "The Process of Causal Attribution." *American Psychologist* 28: 107-128.

Kernell, Samuel. 1978. "Explaining Presidential Popularity." *American Political Science Review* 72: 506-523.

———. 1986. *Going Public: New Strategies of Presidential Leadership.* Washington, D.C.: CQ Press.

Kessel, John H. 1975. *The Domestic Presidency.* Scituate, Mass.: Duxbury Press.

———. 1984. *Presidential Parties.* Homewood, Ill.: Dorsey Press.

Kilborn, Peter T. 1984. "Reagan Economic Record Called Good but Mixed." *New York Times,* October 24, 13.

Kinder, Donald R. 1981. "Presidents, Prosperity, and Public Opinion." *Public Opinion Quarterly* 45: 1-21.

———. 1982. "Enough Already About Ideology: The Many Bases of American Public Opinion." Paper delivered at the annual meeting of the American Political Science Association, August 30-September 2, Denver.

Kinder, Donald R., and Robert P. Abelson. 1981. "Appraising Presidential Candidates: Personality and Affect in the 1980 Campaign." Paper delivered at the annual meeting of the American Political Science Association, August 30-September 2, New York.

Kinder, Donald R., and Susan T. Fiske. 1986. "Presidents in the Public Mind." In *Political Psychology: Contemporary Problems and Issues,* ed. Margaret G. Herman, 193-218. San Francisco: Jossey-Bass.

Kinder, Donald R., Susan T. Fiske, and Randolph G. Wagner. 1978. "Presidents in the Public Mind." Paper delivered at the Mass Response to Political Leadership Conference, sponsored by the Center for Political Studies, University of Michigan, May 22-23, New Haven, Conn.

Kinder, Donald R., Mark D. Peters, Robert P. Abelson, and Susan T. Fiske. 1980. "Presidential Prototypes." *Political Behavior* 2: 315-337.

Kirschten, Dick. 1984. "Communications Reshuffling Intended to Help Reagan Do What He Does Best." *National Journal,* January 28, 153-157.

Kissinger, Henry. 1979. *White House Years.* Boston: Little, Brown.

Kramer, Gerald H. 1983. "The Ecological Fallacy Revisited: Aggregate- Versus Individual-Level Findings on Economics and Elections and Sociotropic Voting." *American Political Science Review* 77: 92-111.

Laski, Harold J. 1940. *The American Presidency: An Interpretation.* New York: Grosset and Dunlap.

Lazarus, Edward H. 1982. "Public Perceptions of Ideal Political Personalities."

Paper delivered at the annual meeting of the American Political Science Association, August 30-September 2, Denver.

Leamer, Lawrence. 1983. *Make Believe: The Story of Nancy and Ronald Reagan.* New York: Harper and Row.

Leuchtenburg, William E. 1983. *In the Shadow of FDR.* Rev. ed. Ithaca, N.Y.: Cornell University Press.

Lewis, Anthony. 1981. "There'll Be Rewards in History for Carter." *Houston Chronicle,* January 13, sec. 1, 12.

——. 1982. "Why the Kid Gloves for Reagan's Presidency?" *Houston Chronicle,* February 24, sec. 3, 10.

Light, Paul C. 1982. *The President's Agenda: Domestic Policy Choice from Kennedy to Carter (with Notes on Ronald Reagan).* Baltimore: Johns Hopkins University Press.

——. 1985. *Artful Work: The Politics of Social Security Reform.* New York: Random House.

Lowi, Theodore J. 1985. *The Personal President: Power Invested, Promise Unfulfilled.* Ithaca, N.Y.: Cornell University Press.

Lowitt, Richard. 1971. "Theodore Roosevelt." In *America's Eleven Greatest Presidents.* 2d ed., ed. Morton Bordon. Chicago: Rand-McNally.

Mackenzie, G. Calvin. 1981. "Cabinet and Subcabinet Personnel Selection in Reagan's First Year: New Variations on Some Not-So-Old Themes." Paper delivered at the annual meeting of the American Political Science Association, September 2-5, New York.

Martin, Ralph G. 1983. *A Hero for Our Time: An Intimate Story of the Kennedy Years.* New York: MacMillan.

Miller, Arthur H., and Martin P. Wattenberg. 1985. "Throwing the Rascals Out: Policy and Performance Evaluations of Presidential Candidates, 1952-1980." *American Political Science Review* 79: 359-372.

Miller, Arthur H., Martin P. Wattenberg, and Oksana Malanchuk. 1982. "Cognitive Representations of Political Candidates." Paper delivered at the annual meeting of the American Political Science Association, August 30-September 2, Denver.

Miller, Mark C. 1982. "Virtu, Inc." *The New Republic,* April 7, 32.

Miroff, Bruce. 1976. *Pragmatic Illusions: The Presidential Politics of John F. Kennedy.* New York: McKay.

Morrow, Lance. 1983. "JFK. After 20 Years, the Question: How Good a President?" *Time,* November 14, 60.

Mowery, David C., Mark S. Kamlet, and John P. Crecine. 1980. "Presidential Management of Budgetary and Fiscal Policymaking." *Political Science Quarterly* 95: 395-426.

Mueller, John E. 1970. "Presidential Popularity from Truman to Johnson." *American Political Science Review* 64: 18-34.

——. 1973. *War, Presidents, and Public Opinion.* New York: John Wiley and Sons.

Murphy, Reg. 1976. "Carter Up Close." *Newsweek,* July 19, 23.

Nathan, Richard P. 1983. *The Administrative Presidency.* New York: John Wiley and Sons.

National Academy of Public Administration. 1985. *Leadership in Jeopardy: The Fraying of the Presidential Appointments System.* Washington, D.C.: National Academy of Public Administration.

References

Nelson, Michael, ed. 1984. *The Presidency and the Political System.* Washington, D.C.: CQ Press.

Neustadt, Richard. 1980. *Presidential Power.* New York: John Wiley and Sons.

New York Times. 1980. "What Jimmy Carter Has Learned." *New York Times,* November 2, 22E.

Nisbett, Richard, and Lee Ross. 1980. *Human Inference: Strategies and Shortcomings in Social Judgement.* Englewood Cliffs, N.J.: Prentice-Hall.

Nixon, Richard M. 1978. *RN: The Memoirs of Richard Nixon.* New York: Grosset and Dunlap.

———. 1980a. "Needed: Clarity of Purpose." *Time,* November 10, 35.

———. 1980b. *The Real War.* London: Sidgwick and Jackson.

———. 1982. *Leaders.* New York: Warner.

———. 1983. *Real Peace.* Boston: Little, Brown.

———. 1985. *No More Vietnams.* New York: Arbor House.

Oates, Stephen B. 1977. *With Malice Toward None: The Life of Abraham Lincoln.* New York: Harper and Row.

Ostrom, Charles W., and Dennis M. Simon. 1985. "Promise and Performance: A Dynamic Model of Presidential Popularity." *American Political Science Review* 79: 334-358.

Page, Benjamin I., and Richard A. Brody. 1972. "Policy Voting and the Electoral Process: The Vietnam War Issues." *American Political Science Review* 66: 979-995.

Page, Benjamin I., and Mark P. Petracca. 1983. *The American Presidency.* New York: McGraw-Hill.

Palmer, John L., and Isabel V. Sawhill. 1984. *The Reagan Record: An Assessment of America's Changing Domestic Priorities.* Cambridge, Mass.: Ballinger Publishing.

Pear, Robert. 1985. "U.S. Will Resume Reviews of Rolls for Disability Aid." *New York Times,* December 6, 1.

Pfiffner, James P. 1982. "The Carter-Reagan Transition: Hitting the Ground Running." Paper delivered at the annual meeting of the American Political Science Association, August 30-September 2, Denver.

Pious, Richard. 1979. *The American Presidency.* New York: Basic Books.

Polsby, Nelson. 1977. "Against Presidential Greatness." *Commentary,* January, 63.

———. 1984. *Political Innovation in America: The Politics of Policy Initiation.* New Haven, Conn.: Yale University Press.

Pringle, Henry F. 1931. *Theodore Roosevelt: A Biography.* New York: Harcourt, Brace, and World.

Quirk, Paul J. 1984. "Presidential Competence." In *The Presidency and the Political System,* ed. Michael Nelson. Washington, D.C.: CQ Press.

Randall, Ronald. 1979. "Presidential Power Versus Bureaucratic Intransigence: The Influence of the Nixon Administration on Welfare Policy." *American Political Science Review* 73: 795-810.

Reedy, George E. 1970. *The Twilight of the Presidency.* New York: World.

Ricci, David M. 1985. *The Tragedy of Political Science.* New Haven, Conn.: Yale University Press.

Riker, William H. 1982. *Liberalism Against Populism: A Confrontation Between the Theory of Democracy and the Theory of Social Choice.* San Francisco: W. H. Freeman.

Riker, William H., and Peter C. Ordeshook. 1968. "A Theory of the Calculus of Voting." *American Political Science Review* 63: 25-43.

Robinson, Donald L., ed. 1985. *Reforming American Government: The Bicentennial Papers of the Committee on the Constitutional System.* Boulder, Colo.: Westview Press.

Roche, John P. 1980. "Focus On Candidates, Not Issues." *Houston Chronicle,* April 26, sec. 6, 2.

Rockman, Bert A. 1984. *The Leadership Question: The Presidency and the American System.* New York: Praeger.

Rohr, John A. 1984. "Civil Servants and Second Class Citizens." *Public Administration Review* 44: 135-140.

Ross, Lee. 1977. "The Intuitive Psychologist and His Shortcomings." In *Advances in Experimental Social Psychology,* ed. Leonard Berkowitz, vol. 10, 174-220. New York: Academic Press.

Rossiter, Clinton. 1960. *The American Presidency.* 2d ed. New York: Harcourt, Brace.

Rourke, Francis E. 1981. "Grappling with the Bureaucracy." In *Politics and the Oval Office,* ed. Arnold J. Meltsner. San Francisco: Institute for Contemporary Studies.

Rumelhart, David. 1978. *Schemata: Building Blocks of Cognition.* San Diego, Calif.: Center for Human Information Processing, University of California at San Diego.

Safire, William. 1975. *Before the Fall.* New York: Doubleday.

———. 1981. "Reagan Shirking His Symbolic Role." *Houston Chronicle,* September 22, B6.

———. 1984. "Lebanon is Reagan's Bay of Pigs." *Houston Chronicle,* February 28, 6.

Samuelson, Robert J. 1982. "Phantom Philosophy." *National Journal,* December 11, 2122.

Schellhardt, Timothy D. 1981. "Do We Expect Too Much?" *Wall Street Journal,* July 10, E1.

Schlesinger, Arthur M., Jr. 1964. *The Age of Jackson.* New York: Mentor.

———. 1973. *The Imperial Presidency.* Boston: Houghton Mifflin.

———. 1986. "Against a One-Term, Six-Year President." *New York Times,* January 10, 23.

Schumpeter, Joseph A. 1943. *Capitalism, Socialism, and Democracy.* London: Allen and Unwin.

Scott, William A. 1969. "Structure of Natural Cognitions." *Journal of Personality and Social Psychology* 12: 261-278.

Scully, Malcolm G. 1981. "Colleges Urged to Combat Civic Illiteracy." *Chronicle of Higher Education,* November 25, 1.

Sheatsley, Paul B., and Jacob J. Feldman. 1964. "The Assassination of President Kennedy: A Preliminary Report on Public Reactions and Behavior." *Public Opinion Quarterly* 28: 189-215.

Sherwood, Robert E. 1948. *Roosevelt and Hopkins: An Intimate History.* New York: Harper and Brothers.

Shogan, Robert. 1982. *None of the Above: Why Presidents Fail and What Can Be Done About It.* New York: New American Library.

Shweder, Robert A., and Robert A. Levine, eds. 1985. *Culture Theory Essays on*

Mind, Self, and Emotion. Cambridge, England: Cambridge University Press.

Sidey, Hugh. 1983. "Above All, the Man Had Character." *Time,* February 21, 24-25.

Simon, Herbert A. 1985. "Human Nature in Politics: The Dialogue of Psychology with Political Science." *American Political Science Review* 79: 293-304.

Skowronek, Stephen. 1984. "Presidential Leadership in Political Time." In *The Presidency and the Political System,* ed. Michael Nelson, 87-132. Washington, D.C.: CQ Press.

Small, Norman J. 1932. "Some Presidential Interpretations of the Presidential Role." In *Historical and Political Science.* Johns Hopkins University Studies, vol. 50, 93-300. Baltimore: Johns Hopkins University Press.

Smith, Hedrick. 1984. "Reagan's Effort to Change the Course of Government." *New York Times,* October 23, 18.

———. 1985. "Deaver Looks Back After a Month Away." *New York Times,* June 13, 14.

Smoller, Fredric T. 1986. "The Six O'Clock Presidency: Patterns of Network News Coverage of the President." *Presidential Studies Quarterly* 16: 31-49.

Smoller, Fredric T., and Keith Moore-Fitzgerald. 1981. "The Presidency and the People Focus Group." April 15. Tape recording, Department of Political Science, Indiana University, Bloomington.

Sorensen, Theodore C. 1969. "Presidential Advisors." In *The Presidential Advisory System,* ed. Thomas E. Cronin and Sanford D. Greenberg. New York: Harper and Row.

———. 1984. *A Different Kind of Presidency: A Proposal for Breaking the Political Deadlock.* New York: Harper and Row.

Spanier, John, and Eric M. Uslaner. 1974. *How American Foreign Policy is Made.* New York: Praeger.

Sperlich, Peter W. 1964. "Bargaining and Overload: An Essay on Presidential Power." In *The Presidency,* ed. Aaron Wildavsky. Boston: Little, Brown.

Sperling, Godfrey, Jr. 1983. "As Jimmy Carter Sees It." *Christian Science Monitor,* August 4, 12-13.

Starr, Mark, and Diane Weathers. 1985. "The Real Reagan Revolution." *Newsweek,* June 3, 25-26.

Steel, Ronald. 1980. *Walter Lippmann and the American Century.* Boston: Little, Brown.

Stein, Herbert. 1984. *Presidential Economics: The Making of Economic Policy from Roosevelt to Reagan and Beyond.* New York: Simon and Schuster.

Stimson, James. 1976. "Public Support for American Presidents." *Public Opinion Quarterly* 40: 1-21.

Stockman, David A. 1986. *The Triumph of Politics: Why the Reagan Revolution Failed.* New York: Harper and Row.

Stoessinger, John G. 1985. *Crusaders and Pragmatists: Movers of Modern American Foreign Policy.* 2d ed. New York: W. W. Norton.

Strout, Richard L. 1982. "FDR Centennial: A Look Back at His Presidency." *Christian Science Monitor,* January 26, 12-13.

Sullivan, Wilson, 1968a. "George Washington." In *American Heritage Pictorial History of the Presidents of the United States,* ed. Kenneth W. Leish, vol. 1. New York: Simon and Schuster.

_____. 1968b. "Franklin Delano Roosevelt." In *American Heritage Pictorial History of the Presidents of the United States,* ed. Kenneth W. Leish, vol. 2. New York: Simon and Schuster.

Sundquist, James L. 1981. *The Decline and Resurgence of Congress.* Washington, D.C.: Brookings.

Taylor, Shelley E., and Jennifer Crocker. 1981. "Schematic Bases of Social Information Processing." In *Social Cognition,* eds. E. T. Higgens, C. A. Heiman, and M. P. Zanna, 89-134. Hillsdale, N.J.: Lawrence Eribaum Associates.

Thach, Charles C. 1969. *The Creation of the Presidency: 1775-1789.* Baltimore: Johns Hopkins University Press.

Tomkins, Silvan S. 1962. *Affect, Imagery, Consciousness.* Vol. 1, *The Positive Affects.* New York: Springer.

Torrance, Edward P. 1963. "The Behavior of Small Groups Under the Stress of Survival." In *Psychology in Administration: A Research Orientation,* ed. Timothy W. Costello and Sheldon S. Zalkind, 128-129. Englewood Cliffs, N.J.: Prentice-Hall.

Tufte, Edward. 1978. *Political Control of the Economy.* Princeton, N.J.: Princeton University Press.

Tugwell, Rexford G. 1960. *The Enlargement of the Presidency.* Garden City, N.Y.: Doubleday.

Tullock, Gordon. 1967. *Towards a Mathematics of Politics.* Ann Arbor: University of Michigan Press.

Tversky, Amos. 1977. "Features of Similarity." *Psychological Review* 84: 327-352.

Valenti, Jack. 1973. "The Case for a Six-Year Term." *Washington Post,* June 18, 22.

_____. 1982. *Speak Up with Confidence: How to Prepare, Learn, and Deliver Effective Speeches.* New York: William Morrow.

Wayne, Stephen J. 1982. "Great Expectations: What People Want from Presidents." In *Rethinking the Presidency,* ed. Thomas E. Cronin, 185-199. Boston: Little, Brown.

Weisman, Steven R. 1984. "The President and the Press: The Art of Controlled Access." *New York Times Magazine,* October 14, 34.

Wells, L. E., and G. Marwell. 1976. *Self-Esteem: Its Conceptualization and Measurement.* Beverly Hills, Calif.: Sage Library of Social Research.

White, Theodore. 1975. *Breach of Faith.* New York: Atheneum.

Wicker, Tom. 1981. "Carter Was Bold but Not Political." *Houston Chronicle,* January 19, 18.

Wildavsky, Aaron. 1979. *The Politics of the Budgetary Process.* 2d ed. Boston: Little, Brown.

Willner, Ann R. 1984. *The Spellbinders: Charismatic Political Leadership.* New Haven, Conn.: Yale University Press.

Wills, Garry. 1982. *The Kennedy Imprisonment: A Meditation on Power.* New York: Pocket Books.

Wise, David. 1973. *The Politics of Lying: Government Deception, Secrecy, and Power.* New York: Vintage.

Wooten, James. 1978. *Dasher: The Roots and the Rising of Jimmy Carter.* New York: Summit Books.

References

Yoder, Edwin M., Jr. 1984. "Real Issue Must Be Responsibility." *Houston Chronicle*, February 23, 22.

Young, James S. 1966. *The Washington Community: 1800-1828*. New York: Columbia University Press.

Zajonc, Robert B. 1980. "Feeling and Thinking: Preferences Need No Inferences." *American Psychologist* 39: 151-175.

Zukin, Cliff, and J. Robert Carter, Jr. 1982. "The Measurement of Presidential Popularity: Old Wisdoms and New Concerns." In *The President and the Public,* ed. Doris A. Graber. Philadelphia: Institute for the Study of Human Issues.

INDEX

Index